The **BOBBY JONES** Story
The Authorized Biography

O. B. Keeler

TRIUMPH
B O O K S
CHICAGO

Library of Congress Cataloging-in-Publication Data

Keeler, O. B. 1882–1950
    The Bobby Jones story / O.B. Keeler.
        p. cm.
    Includes index.
    "Much of the material in this book first appeared in the *Atlanta Journal*"—
Acknowledgments.
    ISBN 1-57243-547-X (hc)
        1. Jones, Bobby, 1902–1971. 2. Golfers—United States—Biography.
    I. *Atlanta Journal.* II. Title.

    GV964.J6 K39 2003
    796.352'092—dc21
    [B]
                                                        2002072144

This book is available in quantity at special discounts for your group or organiza-
tion. For further information, contact:
Triumph Books
601 South LaSalle Street
Suite 500
Chicago, Illinois 60605
(312) 939-3330
Fax (312) 663-3557

Printed in the United States of America
ISBN 1-57243-547-X
Interior design by Eileen Wagner, Wagner/Donovan Design
Pencil drawings copyright © 2002 by Edward Kasper

Contents

Foreword by Bobby Jones .vii

Foreword by Jack Nicklaus ix

Preface to the 1953 Edition xix

Acknowledgments xxv

Introduction by Grantland Rice xxvii

Chapter 1: Little Bob 1

Chapter 2: The First Tournament 4

Chapter 3: The Big Show 9

Chapter 4: Seven Lean Years 13

Chapter 5: The Runner-Up Year 17

Chapter 6: The First Big Disappointment 22

Chapter 7: The First Open 25

Chapter 8: Inverness 30

Chapter 9: There Is a Destiny 36

Chapter 10: Far Afield 41

Chapter 11: Home Again—and to the Battlefront 45

Chapter 12: Old Glory and the Union Jack 49

Chapter 13: The Last of the Lean Years 54

Chapter 14: A Miracle Round—Not Bobby's 60

Chapter 15: The Long Lane Turns 67

Chapter 16: Champion 73

Chapter 17: Flossmoor .78

Chapter 18: Oakland Hills—Dethroned 83

Chapter 19: A Wedding .86

Chapter 20: The First Amateur Championship 90

Chapter 21: Alexa Stirling 96

Chapter 22: A Marathon 100

Chapter 23: More Glory for Old East Lake 106

Chapter 24: Way Down South in Dixie 111

Chapter 25: The Tide Sets In 115

Chapter 26: Invasion 122

Chapter 27: First American to
            Win the British Amateur 128

Chapter 28: Back to the Home of Golf 134

Chapter 29: T. Stewart .140

Chapter 30: The Finest Round of Golf 145

Chapter 31: Return Victorious 150

Chapter 32: The Battle of Baltusrol 157

Chapter 33: An Interview with Bobby 160

Chapter 34: The Black Scot 167

Chapter 35: The Second British Open 171

Chapter 36: The Silent Scot 176

Chapter 37: The Cup Runneth Over 179

Chapter 38: Olympia Fields 185

Chapter 39: After Brae Burn—A Look
at the Records 189

Chapter 40: The Greatest Thrill 194

Chapter 41: An Unexpected Record 198

Chapter 42: A Charming Guest 205

Chapter 43: The Big Year Opens 209

Chapter 44: Men Call It Fate 215

Chapter 45: The Double 222

Chapter 46: The D'Artagnan of Golf 229

Chapter 47: The Impregnable Quadrilateral 235

Chapter 48: The End of the Trail 241

Afterword by Dr. Bobby Jones IV 247

Chronology 251

Index 255

Foreword

O. B. Keeler and I enjoyed a very real partnership for the better part of 20 years. We traveled thousands of miles together, we lived our golf tournaments together, we wrote a book, did a radio series, and two motion pictures series, all in the closest and most harmonious collaboration. I doubt if ever such a relationship existed between performer and reporter in sport or elsewhere.

The ebb and flow of a player's confidence is one of the strange phenomena of competitive golf. I have discussed this angle with all the great players of my own and later eras and none deny or can explain the periods of uncertainty that occasionally come in the midst of the most complete assurance.

In the first qualifying round for the Amateur Championship at Minikahda in 1927, I posted a 75. I never wanted to win qualifying medals—a sort of superstition I suppose—and I had tried to coast along and do a modest, comfortable score. But I had slipped a stroke here and there and perhaps had been lucky to score 75. Suddenly I began to see that another slack round with a stroke or two more gone might leave me out of the tournament.

So I set out to find Keeler.

"O.B.," I said, "the only way for me to get out of this thing is to go out this afternoon and try to win the medal and I need you to walk with me for a few holes until I get calmed down."

I wanted just the satisfaction of having an understanding soul with me to get over that feeling of aloneness that comes when your confidence is gone. It worked like a charm. I let O.B. go after the fifth hole, finished the round in 67 for a course record and the medal, and went on to win the championship.

This is just one of the things I owe to Keeler. The bigger thing is something no one knows better than the boys who were writing sports in those days. To gain any sort of fame, it isn't enough to do the job. There must be someone to spread the news. If fame can be said to attach to one because of his proficiency in the inconsequential performance of striking a golf ball, what measure of it I have enjoyed has been due in large part to Keeler and his gifted typewriter.

I am asked now to say that I am willing to leave the record of my golfing activities to the words this man has written. Why in Heaven's name shouldn't I be? He never once gave me anything but the best of any argument.

—Bobby Jones

Foreword

Editor's note: This Foreword is reprinted from The Greatest Game of All: My Life in Golf, *Simon and Schuster, New York, 1969, with the permission of Jack Nicklaus and Herbert Warren Wind.*

□

My first golf hero was Bob Jones, and this, of course, was a very fortunate thing. I became aware of Jones in 1950 when I started golf at the age of 10, for my father was a member of the Scioto Country Club in Columbus, Ohio, our hometown, and it was there that Jones had won the 1926 United States Open. It was a wonderful victory in many ways. First, Bobby—he was in his mid twenties then, and he was known to everyone as Bobby—made a fine driving finish over the last nine holes to pick up five shots on the leader, Joe Turnesa, and edge him out by one. On top of this, earlier that season Jones had won the British Open at Lytham & St. Anne's, and with his victory at Scioto he made golf history by becoming the first man to carry off the two big national championships in the same year.

In any event, Scioto never forgot Bobby Jones. When I became a member of the club a full 24 years had elapsed since Jones' victory, but a photograph of him still hung in a prominent position in the locker room, and another in the pro shop. The latter showed him at the finish of his follow-through on a drive. (I think it must be the photo General Eisenhower used as a model for his famous painting of Jones that is on display in Golf House, the United States Golf Association's headquarters in New York City.) In addition to this, many of the older members of Scioto, who had been deeply impressed by both Jones' golf and his personal charm, were always talking about him. The most devoted of these Jones-men was Stanley Crooks, a very capable golfer, by the way, who won the club championship several times. He was a good friend of Jones' and corresponded with him, and, if anything, the passing years had sharpened his memory of Bobby's performance back in 1926. He knew every one of the 293 shots Jones had hit.

When I first showed some promise in golf, Mr. Crooks began to tell me more and more about Jones—where he liked to place his drive on this hole and how he tried to play that hole; how he had missed his par on each of the four rounds on the relatively easy 145-yard ninth; how Bobby thought one of the best holes on the course was the eighth, a long par 5, where a virtual wheat field bordered the right side of the fairway off the tee and where, in second shot range, a stream crossed the fairway and then curled to the left around the back of the green; and above all, how Bobby, needing a birdie to win on the last hole, a 480-yard par 5 that Turnesa had birdied just previously, laced out a drive that was fully 300 yards long, followed it with a 4-iron 15 feet past the pin, and got down in two safe putts. In 1950, I should bring out, Scioto had changed very little from the course Jones had tackled, and knowing how he had played it was a spur to me. It is a definite advantage for a young golfer, I believe, to grow up on a championship course, and there is something of additional value to be gained from knowing how a champion played the different holes. It gives you something concrete to measure your progress against.

Along with Stanley Crooks, there were two men at Scioto who never stopped talking about Jones. One was Jack Grout, a tall, scholarly looking Oklahoman who became the pro at Scioto the same year I took up the game. Jack was a tireless student of the golf swing. While he kept very much abreast of the times and was fascinated by the mechanics of Nelson's swing and Snead's and Hogan's, there were several respects in which he felt Jones' technique had never been improved on, and he made this very clear to his pupils. The other notorious Jones enthusiast was my father. The year the Open was held at Scioto, he was a boy of 13. He had played a little golf on the public courses, and for him, as for so many other Americans, there was no one like Bobby Jones. Through the kindness of the pharmacist he worked for after school hours, Dad got tickets for the Open, and he stayed on Jones' heels all four rounds. Watching his hero in action was the greatest experience of his young life, and it remained evergreen in his mind. I imagine his identification with Jones became all the stronger because of an offbeat incident that took place at Scioto when the Ryder Cup match was played there in 1931. Jones, who had come up from Atlanta for the event, was 29 at the time. There couldn't have been too much resemblance, really, between him and my dad, then just 18. However, my dad had the same chunky build as Jones, he parted his hair down the middle like Jones, and on this particular day he happened to be wearing knickers like Jones—and darned if the attendant at the front door of the clubhouse didn't sing out, "Yes sir, Mister Jones," when my dad approached and fling the door open for him with a flourish. Dad's ticket didn't include clubhouse privileges, and he had just been edging up to take a squint inside. With the entrance suddenly opened, he tossed the attendant a friendly smile, the way he thought Jones would have, and sauntered around the clubhouse for an hour, taking it all in.

For all these reasons, when I started playing golf I knew more about Robert T. Jones Jr. than I did about any of the current champions. Later that year I learned a good deal about Ben Hogan, of course.

This was the season, 1950, that Ben returned to golf after his near-fatal accident 16 months earlier and then proceeded to astound the sports world by winning the U.S. Open at Merion. I also knew a little about Jimmy Demaret—very little; I knew he wore bright clothes and might stride onto the first tee any day wearing one blue shoe and one green shoe. Beyond this, the other "name golfers" were just a blur to me. That summer, however, I got a firsthand look at many of them, for Scioto was host to another championship, the 1950 P.G.A. (That was the year Chandler Harper beat Henry Williams Jr. in the final.) By this time my dad was a member of the club, so there was no problem about the front door, but the locker room was off limits except for the players. However, Skip Alexander, one of the top touring pros, saw me with my autograph book at the door and put his arm around my shoulder and led me into the locker room. With Skip's help, I got the autographs of nearly all the players. Outside of how pleasant and considerate Skip was, little else sticks in my mind. I remember watching Lloyd Mangrum playing cards, a tall drink in one hand and a cigarette dangling from his lips beneath his moustache. It was a picture that would make an impression on any 10-year-old boy—there he was, the complete riverboat gambler come to life. I also remember catching a glimpse of Sam Snead. Sam must not have had a very good day. He was scowling and silent, and he was in and out of the locker room in 30 seconds.

Soon after that P.G.A. Championship, my friend Skip Alexander almost lost his life in an airplane crash. Although he made a phenomenal recovery from his injuries, he never regained full use of his hands and fingers, and his career as a tournament golfer was over. Skip stayed in the game, though. Today he is the pro at the Lakewood Country Club in St. Petersburg, Florida, and I get to see him when he comes over to the Palm Beach area for a tournament or a pro-am. Skip usually stays with my neighbor at Lost Tree Village, Cary Middlecoff.

I did not meet Bob Jones until five years later, in 1955, when I qualified for the United States Amateur Championship for the first time. It took place that year at the James River course of the Country Club of Virginia, in Richmond. Since 1955 marked the 25th anniversary of Jones' last appearance in that championship—his victory in the 1930 Amateur, at Merion, was the fourth and final trick in his incredible Grand Slam—the U.S.G.A. had asked him to come up from Atlanta and speak at the players' dinner. He undoubtedly would have honored this request anyway, but I have a feeling that the fact that this was one of the rare occasions when a national championship was being held in the South contributed to Jones' decision to attend. The day before the start of the tournament, when the field was getting in its final warm-up rounds, Jones parked his golf cart behind the last green to take in some of the play on that hole, a 460-yard par 4 over breaking, hilly ground. It so happened that I hit the eighteenth green that afternoon with two good woods and, furthermore, that during the time that Jones was watching, no other player had got home in two. He asked a newspaper-man with him who I was, and on learning that I was only 15 years old, he said he would like to talk with me. My father and I went over together. This session with Jones was a tremendous thrill for me, but I am sure it meant twice as much to my dad. Our chat lasted about 20 minutes— a good deal of it was about Scioto, naturally—and then Jones turned to me and said, "Young man, I've heard that you're a fine golfer. I'm com- ing out to watch you play a few holes tomorrow."

My first-round opponent was Bob Gardner, a Californian who had moved to the New York area, a well-grounded golfer who was subse- quently a teammate of mine in the 1960 Eisenhower Trophy and the 1961 Walker Cup matches. We had quite a battle that day in Richmond. At the end of the first nine we were even, and then I went 1 up by birdieing the tenth. As we walked to the eleventh, there was Bob Jones sitting in his golf cart on the edge of the tee. I wanted to play my very best in front of him, and I thought I might, for I'd been hitting the ball straight and crisp that morning.

Well, it didn't work out quite that way. I missed my par on the eleventh, a 412-yard par 4, when I took three from just off the green. I lost that hole to Gardner's par. On the twelfth, a par 4, 423 yards long, uphill most of the way, I was even more brilliant—I took a double bogey: a drive pushed into the trees on the right, a choppy recovery, an underclubbed approach, and three more to get down from the apron. I lost that hole, too. The thirteenth is a short par 4 that doglegs sharply to the right as it falls down a hillside to a ticklish little green. I was weak with my second, and when I stubbed my chip, I had lost three holes in a row and gone from 1 up to 2 down. Jones left at this point. As he later told my father, he felt that his presence might have led me to try too hard. After treating him to that splendid run of bogey, double bogey, bogey, I managed to settle down, and won two of the next four holes to square the match. Then I lost it on the eighteenth when I hit my tee-shot into heavy rough and couldn't get home with my second. Gardner played it perfectly, an excellent drive and an excellent fairway wood onto the green, and that was that.

My next meeting with Bob Jones took place some two years later when he spoke at the banquet held in connection with the 1957 International Jaycees Junior Championship, which was played on the Ohio State University course. (We had our picture taken together, and it hangs today in my game room.) Then, another two years later, I qualified for The Masters for the first time, so I was able to get together with Jones that spring—and in the springs that followed until 1962—at the amateurs' dinner on the Wednesday night before the start of The Masters. Sometimes we just talked. I remember, for example, his reminiscing about the 1926 Open one evening and recalling that the wheat field of rough by the eighth hole was so high that on one round, after his caddie had laid down his bag in the rough so that they could better help Bob's playing partner find his ball, they had an awful time finding the bag. Other times we talked a bit more seriously. However, the most helpful piece of advice I received from Bob came to me secondhand, through my father. "I think I was a fairly good young golfer," Jones told him one evening, "but I never became what I would call a really good golfer until I had been competing for quite a number of seasons. You see, when I first started to play in the big tournaments, whenever anything went wrong, I'd run home to Stewart Maiden, our pro at East Lake. Finally, I matured to the point where I understood my game well enough to make my own corrections during the course of a tournament, and *that's* when I'd say I became a *good* golfer."

When my dad relayed this conversation to me, it made a particularly strong impression because whenever something had gone wrong in a tournament, I had run home to Jack Grout. From the time Jack started to give me lessons, he wanted me to understand the mechanics of the swing and, for my part, I wanted to learn all about them—why you made this movement in the swing, or what effect that movement produced. I wanted to be able to take care of myself out on the course. Somehow, though, I was still always running back to Jack Grout to fix me up. This is why Jones' statement hit me so right. It made me much more determined to learn everything I could about my swing so that, to some extent, I could diagnose my own errors and put myself back on my game. I cannot tell you what a big factor this is in tournament play. It may be the biggest factor of all in shaping success or failure in the crucible of competition.

Bob Jones—I never call him anything but Mr. Jones—possesses the gift of intimacy and is always doing little things that make you feel that you are an old friend with whom he can be humorous, or frank, or spontaneous, as the case may be. One small illustration that comes to mind involved Bob only indirectly. In the 1959 Amateur, at Broadmoor, through the accident of the draw I came up against his son, Robert T. Jones III, in the first round. Young Bob is a very good player who has qualified for the Amateur quite a few times, and on his day he can give any golfer all that he can handle. That morning at Broadmoor when young Bob and I met on the first tee, he greeted me with a big, warm smile. "You might be interested in knowing, Jack," he said, "that my father was thinking of coming out for this tournament. Then when he found out who I had drawn as my first opponent, he changed his mind. He decided it wasn't worth a trip to Colorado just to watch me play one round."

More to the point was a letter I received from Bob Jones shortly after I had broken through in the 1962 U.S. Open. If my victory hinged on any one single stroke, it was the four-foot putt I had to hole on the seventy-first green to save my par, stay even with Arnold Palmer, and set up a playoff. It was an extremely tough putt: it broke a little left and then, near the hole, it broke back to the right off a little rise. The more I studied the putt, the more convinced I became that, especially under the pressure, I probably wouldn't be able to handle that double roll with the exceptional delicacy it required. My best chance would be to rap the ball so firmly that neither the left or right break could really take effect. I hit the ball hard, for the back of the cup, and it fell—and if it hadn't, it would have gone miles past, it was moving that fast. As I say, I thought this was the pivotal stroke of the tournament for me, so it pleased me enormously when Bob Jones gave it primary emphasis in a letter of congratulation he sent me shortly afterward. Watching on TV, he had recognized exactly what my problem was and the risk I took in trying to solve it the way I did. "When I saw the ball dive into the hole," he wrote, "I almost jumped right out of my chair." I can't recall a letter that made me feel as good as that one did.

Apart from whatever other talks we may have at The Masters each year, I generally get to see Bob out on the course. When you come to the most dangerous stretch, the passage from the eleventh through the thirteenth, Bob is usually out there in his golf cart, studying you closely. Quite often, he'll pick you up on the fifteenth and sixteenth, too. I have managed to play some acceptable golf in front of him, but I know he was also watching when I hit one of the rottenest shots of my life—an 8-iron on the short twelfth in the 1964 Masters that I shanked so beautifully I still had a pretty full pitch left over Rae's Creek to the green. (I got my 4, one of the best bogeys I've ever made.) Because of my admiration for Bob Jones, The Masters—the tournament he created, played on the course he helped design—has always been something unbelievably special for me. When I have been fortunate enough to win it, I have treasured not only the victory itself but the generous things he has said about my play at the presentation ceremony. When Bob says something about your golf, you know there is substance and sincerity in it.

Above and beyond this, you always feel that he understands what you are all about as a man, a well as a golfer. This gives everything a deeper meaning, and it sticks to your bones.

Looking back on my friendship with Bob Jones, I am increasingly aware what a lucky thing it was for me that he happened to win one of his Opens at Scioto so that from the beginning, despite the differences in our ages, there was always a bond between us. I have learned an awful lot from him. We all have. More than any other person in our time, he has served to give us a sense of continuity with the game's earlier eras and its earlier players, to make us feel a part of an immensely worthwhile tradition. In a word, he has embodied the spirit of golf.

—Jack Nicklaus

Preface to the 1953 Edition

Nowadays golf comes naturally. The young boy starts out as a caddy, or he is started out by an enthusiastic parent with Bobby Jones or some other star in mind; or he just starts naturally as he takes up baseball, or as he did take up baseball a generation ago. But nearly half a century before there were motor cars and movies and radio broadcasting and a number of other things now regarded as essential to existence, golf was a waif word—an odd little four-letter stray in the typography of the United States, something as yet unclassed as sport.

Specifically, the author of this narrative, in the beginning of the good year 1897, possessed a mind as innocent of golf as of the Einstein Theory of Relativity; a mind much taken up with serious matters such as baseball and the chance of making the "third team" in the town of Marietta, Georgia, to which my father and mother, with my brother Milton and me, had moved from Chicago when I was four years old, and in which city I was born. There were the approaching examinations of the third year in high school, a new bicycle, the exploits of the heroes of old, "Pop" Anson and "Bad Bill" Dahlen, and "Little Eva" Lange, and my own pet club in the old National League, Anson's Colts; all most absorbing as is the habit of youth in its 15th year.

But nothing of golf. A few months before I was 15, I stumbled on an article in a magazine about golf and fell flat. I do not remember the name of the magazine and of course I did not realize that this was Destiny. I vaguely recall some pictures that caught my attention with the idea that here was some sort of game, played out of doors, in which a ball, not in motion, was struck with an implement. The passivity of the ball, contrasted with the action of the ball in tennis or baseball, relegated the sport at once to the same class as croquet, palpably a game for girls.

But I read the article carefully; it had to do with the expanding interest in the old, old game of golf, new to this country and beginning to spread rapidly. I would like to read that article again to see if I could find what was in it that arrested and held the attention of a typical American boy, devoted to baseball and football, with a strong tincture of tennis in season. There must have been some germ of heroic enthusiasm that caused me to do something I kept a strict secret from my mates. I studied the picture diligently with my brother, who became languidly and rather cynically interested. We made ourselves each a weapon that we fancied resembled a golf club, a whippy green wood shaft that more or less fitted into a wooden head. In default of a golf ball (they were made of gutta-percha, the article had said) we used a hollow rubber ball, trying to propel it into a hole we made in the backyard.

And that was the first time I heard of golf.

The scene then moved northward to the southeastern corner of Wisconsin and the charming little village of Lake Geneva, where my mother took us to spend our vacations at the home of our grandparents. As we left the bright yellow train, nothing apparently was further from my mind than golf, that strange new/old game that had dealt me a single sage wink from the pages of a magazine; but before we had reached my grandparents' home, I saw a boy in a yard with an implement that I recognized with a start as a golf club. He was waving it back and forth over something in the grass, and as I watched, he swung the club back a little farther and struck. Up rose the ball, smaller than I had imagined, and flew along 20 or 30 yards, then hopped and rolled. Immediately I wanted to lay hold of that golf club and show him that I could do whatever he was trying to do better than he was doing it.

The first thing I asked my friends, kids we called each other in those days, was if anybody played golf around there. Gee, yes, they told me. Over on the south shore of the lake were regular links, the Walworth County Country Club. And there was money to be made caddying over there. Caddying? It was a new word. Sure, easiest thing you know. Carrying clubs for the players and watching the balls. Thirty-five cents a round. "Round?" Sure, 18 holes. That was a round. It was mysterious and baffling, but I was going to get into this game or know the reason why not.

The Sabbath day interposed between my new ambition and its realization. In our family there was a stiff Presbyterian prejudice against either gainful or sportive activity on the seventh day. But bicycling was permitted and my brother and a cousin and I rode around the rim of the lake southward and after five or six miles of pedaling we arrived at the links. As long as I live, I will never forget how bewilderingly beautiful that setting appeared to me even as a kid with my mind bent on the adventure of searching out a new sport. The lake was below us, its waters blue and sparkling through the trees on the bluff. I had never seen such turf as the closely cropped fairway presented, a lush carpet of vivid green spread up a gently sloping hillside to—why—that must be the hole in that even smoother and more closely cut space, with a little flag sticking out of it.

We were about to approach it cautiously when up the fairway toward us came a golfer, all by himself—the first golfer I had ever seen. He was carrying his own clubs, as the caddies did not work on Sunday, and was not garbed in the scarlet coat and white trousers that I discovered later to be a sort of uniform for the sport. A ball had preceded him, unnoted by us, and lay within a few yards of this small but absorbed gallery.

The golfer put down his bag, selected a club, squared off at the ball, and swung. Very likely he was embarrassed by our concentrated stare;

anyway he missed the ball and it scurried up the hillside 40 or 50 yards. I was absurdly excited and oddly enough not at all contemptuous of this failure. Conceivably I had a premonition right then that there was more to this hitting a golf ball than appeared superficially. But the golfer apparently felt humiliated and I gathered from his next move that he wanted the gallery to appreciate the difficulties of the game and the unseeming treachery of the innocent looking projectile.

He turned toward me as the largest of the group, held out a wood club, and asked pleasantly if I would like to try a shot. I accepted in mute astonishment. Immediately the flag seemed to retire an amazing distance; it looked easily twice as far as when I had discovered it. The club was strange and awkward in my hands. I do not recall my feelings distinctly, only that I was not comfortable and was morally certain that my brother and cousin were all set for a hearty guffaw. True to the tradition of the sport, I whacked the ball squarely on the roof. I recall this with a ghastly distinctness, propelling it not as far as our golfer had on his last effort. And I must say for my relatives that they forbore to laugh. This episode put us all quite at ease and the golfer put down another ball and we all whacked at it with varied and indifferent results, taking turns trotting up the slope and throwing the ball back.

After awhile, the golfer played on up to the green, one of us carrying his clubs respectfully enough, and we looked over the layout solemnly. Patently this was a magnificent game, and no child's play. I went home convinced of that and in the next quarter century, I became more and more certain.

On January 4, 1909, I definitely gave up trying to be a businessman after a steadily losing struggle of 10 years, walked up a long flight of stairs to the editorial rooms of the *Atlanta Georgian*, and reported for duty at 7:30 of a Monday morning, my first day's work on a newspaper. My contract at the moment was to work for nothing per week and furnish my own typewriter. It was my own proposition. I had never done any newspaper work. I had only been in a newspaper office but twice, once as a visitor and once to conclude the terms of the contract just started. I did not know whether I could be a successful reporter; neither did Dudley Glass, then city editor of the *Georgian*, or Edwin Camp, managing editor. But anyway, there I was with my typewriter, no experience of newspaper work whatever, a profound ambition to be a reporter, and the most ghastly assortment of forebodings mixed with stage fright I had ever imagined.

Percy Whiting was sports editor of the *Georgian* at that time, and in 1908 I started shooting poetry— sports verse anyway—at him, and he had been kind enough to print some of these. One day, when I was a cashier in a fire insurance office, I suddenly decided that bookkeeping was not my forte, and that I would just go out to the Chattahoochee River and throw a rock off the bridge, not turning loose the rock. But that, I reflected, would be that, so why not have a try at the newspaper game first? If I flopped, there would still be the good old river. So I went over and talked to Percy about it. He tried to talk me out of it, but when he found he couldn't, said all right, come on over and try it. And this I did on January 4, 1909.

I've been lucky. I was lucky right from the jump and I've been lucky ever since. That first morning Dudley Glass sent me out to the regular Monday morning meeting of the Baptist Minister's Alliance.

On this historic occasion, Dr. Len G. Broughton, then the flaming firebrand of Dixie ministry, elected to deliver an address on therapeutics—psychic healing of physical illness, if you please, a return to the laying on of hands for sickness in churches. Green as I was, I knew this was a sensation in that gentle era, so I galloped back to the office and told Dudley about it, asking him how much I should write.

I have never forgotten Dudley's reply: "As much as you can make interesting," said he.

I have never picked up a more valuable piece of advice. I have written yards more than was interesting many and many a time since—but I knew it. That story went on page 1. Lucky? When you make the front page with your first story—well, I was sold on the newspaper game then and there. The first day I was in this game, I knew surely that I would never leave it as long as I lived.

William Howard Taft, president-elect, came to town before my two weeks' trial was up, and when he departed, I was on the payroll. At the beginning of the baseball season, I went over to sports. I was writing baseball but thinking most about golf, which was just then beginning to emerge from the chrysalis, you might say, as a game to be written about. Talk about luck. There was a kid named Perry Adair, and a younger one, named Little Bobby Jones, beginning to be talked about, in a golfing way; and a redheaded girl named Alexa Stirling at East Lake, was precisely three years before winning her first of three national championships. Since then I have attended 45 major or national championships, 7 of them with Alexa and 27 with Bobby. I have traveled over 120,000 miles with Bobby, to Europe, to California, all up and down the United States. I saw him win all of his major titles. I wrote for the Associated Press the first interview with Bobby published in 1926 and for this the Associated Press made me an honorary member of their staff. I wrote the first interview the Prince of Wales ever gave out on golf at the international Walker Cup matches at Sandwich in 1930, and did not realize that it was anything unusual until the next day when the English papers all published it. Luck. Nothing else.

A telegram caught up with me in Rome, Italy, in 1930 and on that break, I was the first person to broadcast a sporting event across the Atlantic, the British Open golf championship of 1930, for the National Broadcasting Company.

I could go on and on breaking Dudley Glass' prescription for columns and columns, but I won't do it. I have met the greatest fellows in the world in this game, the newspaper game that Rudyard Kipling once called "The Press—the greatest game that all of a man can play." I found the best newspaper in the world in the *Atlanta Journal*, and in Major John Cohen the finest boss in the world to work for. So I'll just renew a pledge I've made many and many a time all to myself.

It's 'til death do us part.

Acknowledgments

Much of the material in this book first appeared in the *Atlanta Journal*, for which O. B. Keeler wrote for more than a quarter of a century, and in his columns syndicated by the Associated Press. Grateful appreciation is acknowledged for permission to reprint these stories.

Thanks is also extended to *Esquire* for articles of O. B. Keeler appearing in the January 1942, May 1942, July 1944, June 1945, July 1945, and May 1946 issues; to the publisher of *The Autobiography of an Average Golfer*, by O. B. Keeler, copyright 1925; to Harper and Brothers for *The Boys' Life of Bobby Jones* by O. B. Keeler, copyright 1931 by Harper & Brothers; to the North American Newspaper Alliance, Inc., for "The Bobby Jones Story" by O. B. Keeler; and to G. P. Putnam's Sons for *Down the Fairway*, by Robert T. Jones Jr. and O. B. Keeler, copyright 1927 by Minton, Balch & Company.

Grantland Rice (on the right) shaking hands with Bobby Jones.

Introduction

The story of Bobby Jones is one of the great stories of sports.

It is a story of youth, beginning at 5 years of age and ending competitively at 28—a story packed with raw drama from beginning to end.

It is the story of a great player, a great competitor, who was and is a scholar, a gentleman, and a sportsman of the highest ranking.

It has been written for you by a master craftsman, O. B. Keeler, who shadowed Bob at almost every stroke from journey's start to trail's end. No one in the history of golf writing is better equipped to tell the story of Bobby Jones' amazing career.

One of the star features of this career is that Bob in his early youth had a keen temper, almost a fiery one, when applied to golf. He was naturally a friendly, sunny young fellow off the course. At the age of 14 he was about as fine a hitter of a golf ball as you would care to see. He stood then with only one opponent to beat—himself. From the age of 14 to the age of 21 in tournament play he fought a long and desperate duel with one R. T. Jones Jr. Bob finally won.

From that point on he was a tornado turned loose—a cyclone unleashed.

For the next nine years he ran 1-2 in the U. S. Open eight times. He won the U.S. Open four times and tied for top place twice. He won the British Open three times, the U.S. Amateur crown five times, and the British Amateur crown once. Here was a marvelous amassing of 13 national golf crowns between 1922 and 1930, the greatest sweep in the history of the ancient green.

Bobby Jones was well equipped for this magic record. As a kid he was powerfully built, with big, strong hands. Mentally he was far above the general average, with abnormal power of concentration and unbreakable courage and determination. Concentration and determination are golf's two best assets. He had a vast capacity for making friends. And above all he had a golf writer named O. B. Keeler, a super-Boswell, with him to tell the story of his great years before he retired in 1930 from the competitive field. He played in The Masters at Augusta later but he was more host than anything else at this famous tournament.

It was a strange thing for sport—where anything can happen. A strange thing to see this young amateur meeting and beating the best professionals of his time.

And Bob happened to come along where I think the greatest played. Among his strongest rivals were the brilliant Walter Hagen, the able Gene Sarazen, Long Jim Barnes, Tommy Armour, Light Horse Harry Cooper, Wild Bill Melhorn, Wee Bobby Cruickshank, Macdonald Smith (the magnificent shot maker), Willie MacFarlane, George Von Elm, Chick Evans, Francis Ouimet, Johnny Farrell, Craig Wood, Jock Hutchison, and Horton Smith—these and many others who were stars. Bobby Jones came along at one of the strongest periods of golf.

How many golfers of today have won the U.S. Open, the British Open, and the P.G.A.? Hagen, Sarazen, Barnes, and Armour won all three. This was the high spot of golf in this country.

When you read again Jones' record from 1922 to 1930 you will be amazed. In 1922 he finished a stroke behind Gene Sarazen in the U.S. Open at Skokie. In 1923 he won at Inwood. In 1924 he ran second to Cyril Walker at Oakland Hills. In 1925 he tied with Willie MacFarlane at Worcester. In 1926 he won at Scioto. In 1928 he tied with Johnny Farrell. In 1929 and 1930 he won at Winged Foot and Interlachen.

In those days stray bookmakers accepted a few wagers. Jones was always around 2 to 1. Most of the others were 20 to 1. After 1922 neither Hagen or Sarazen, two of the finest players in all golf history, were able to lead until he finished nine years later.

In addition to other tournaments covered, this book also contains the stories of 13 winning performances. Reading these famous stories of Bob's famous days is absorbing. It is a different story, something the world of sport had never produced before.

It might be said that O. B. Keeler was lucky to have Bobby Jones appear on the scene while he was writing golf in Atlanta. Bobby was just as lucky to have Keeler around. O. B. Keeler was a magnificent reporter. He could cover any assignment given him. But golf was his big love. He knew golf thoroughly, so none was better equipped to write of achievements that surpassed anything the game had ever known. It took a combination of all the many things that happened to Bobby Jones to have the miracle come true.

In the early thirties Bobby Jones and his associates founded the Augusta National Golf Club, and in 1934 inaugurated The Masters Tournament.

Later he became a prominent Atlanta attorney with a distinguished war record earned in World War II. Bobby played his last Masters Tournament in 1948 and that was—coincidentally or otherwise—about the end of O.B.'s career. He retired as golf writer for the *Atlanta Journal* in 1950 and died that same year.

Hence, as Randy Russell wrote in the *Augusta Chronicle,* "He wasn't there in person but the spirit of O. B. Keeler was looking over the shoulder of President Eisenhower at the Augusta National Golf Club in the spring of 1953 when the chief executive presented Bobby Jones with a portrait of the great Atlanta golfer, done by the president's own hand. It was the sort of thing O.B. would not have missed. His 'boy' was being presented a portrait done by the president of the United States."

Bobby Jones was not one in a million persons. I should say he was one in 10 million—or perhaps one in 50 million. The combination of Jones and Keeler is one in a 100 million.

I think in reading this story you will find that it stands alone, for it happens to be fact beyond fiction any imagination could ever dream.

—Grantland Rice

Bobby Jones at age six.

1.

Little Bob

A toy cleek was the start of a career in golf for "Little Bob" Jones; beginning with a tow-headed little chap hammering a battered golf ball about a homemade course in his front yard. Bobby was a tiny, spindling figure in rompers at that time, just past his fifth birthday. He was in the yard of his home watching a friend, who was a member of the East Lake Club, putting and puttering about the yard as golfers will do when they are off duty.

"Like to try a shot?" he asked Bobby.

Bobby nodded solemnly. He would.

It must be recorded here that this first effort of the future champion was a distinct failure. The club was approximately the same length as

Bobby and poked him woefully in the stomach so that he missed the ball altogether.

"That won't do," said the golfer. He chose a discarded cleek from his clubs, sawed off the shaft below the leather, and presented it to Bobby with three somewhat used balls—treasure indeed.

In the neighborhood was another boy about Bobby's age. The youngsters laid out for themselves a golf course about the front yard, five holes that crisscrossed in defiance of golfing convention and at the risk of youthful pates; four holes in the yard and a "long hole"—all of 60 yards down the street outside, with a fairway of hoof-prints and wagon ruts and a rough of ditches full of stones. This was the ragged little homemade course on which Bobby Jones first played, with a fair prophecy of the rough trail, thick with the bitter dust of disappointment and defeat, on which he traveled to glory.

Such was Bobby's beginning in golf. Utterly untrammeled by advice or instruction, except he was told that a ball must be played wherever it lay and all strikes must be counted, he began his career—a career that progressed to the top of American golf with an orderliness almost as immutable as the orbit of the stars.

So Bobby Jones did not begin by cutting his teeth on a niblick or taking a Vardon grip on his first rattle. His first battle, too, was not on the links but a grimmer affair—a battle for life itself which golf helped him win.

Robert Tyre Jones was born in Atlanta on March 17, 1902, the only son of Mr. and Mrs. Robert P. Jones. He was named for his paternal grandsire, a sturdy North Georgian, who cared nothing for sports. The first five years of his life, Bobby was about as unpromising a prospect for a competitive athlete as could have been selected. About this time, his father, remembering his own rugged boyhood in the mountains of North Georgia, decided to give Mother Nature a chance.

The little family moved out from the city to a suburban town, East Lake. There they removed Bobby's shoes, and turned him out to grass. That was Bobby's first battle, the battle for life, and it may be that some hardy inherent fighting quality in the frail little chap asserted itself, for in a very short time, he was eating anything he could bite, and his dental equipment was adequate. Fatefully it may be that Bobby won his first fight at the very gate of the East Lake golf course; a tiny spindling figure in rompers pattering about the red old hills of Georgia, and peering curiously through the fence at white-clad grown people hitting a little white ball in a game just beginning to be popular in Atlanta.

The little boy in rompers was looking at historic ground—for him. It was there he was to acquire in this oddly fascinating game the style that later was to make him the glass of fashion and the mold of form wherever golf is played.

And not too long after this came the first big event in Bobby's golfing career—the biggest event perhaps. Stewart Maiden, a stocky little Scot from Carnoustie, came to East Lake to take the place of his brother, Jimmy Maiden, as golf professional. Late one afternoon, Bobby and his mother walked over to the gate of the club to meet Big Bob, and there they were joined by Jimmy Maiden and his brother, Stewart, who was to have so profound an influence on the little boy, just past six years of age. Bobby's father and mother and Jimmy Maiden did all the talking. Stewart did not say a word. And Bobby just stared at him— wondering in a vague sort of way if Stewart could talk.

Stewart Maiden's conversational style was always monosyllabic— but his golfing style was as fine and sound as ever came out of Scotland. And it wasn't a week before a little boy was following Stewart solemnly about the East Lake course, never minding in the least that the imperturbable Scot paid him not the slightest attention, but watching . . . watching . . . watching.

That was the way Bobby Jones began to play golf.

A young Bobby Jones with Perry Adair and Frank Medder in front of the old Mule House where he first lived at East Lake.

2.

The First Tournament

The generally accepted idea that Bobby's first association with Stewart Maiden was in the role of pupil is quite wrong. Stewart never gave him a regular lesson in golf. After Bobby acquired something of a game and began playing in tournaments, and finally achieved the position of a national figure in golf, Stewart was accustomed to coach him at times, when a club wasn't working for him, and he went with Bobby to a number of important tournaments. With his own perfect style and his unusual understanding of the fundamentals of the game, Stewart was almost invariably able to straighten out the kinks in Bobby's method, so exactly modeled on Stewart's own.

But that was years later. In those early days Bobby picked up his game as imitatively as a monkey, watching the man who played the best game at the club. Yet this gift of mimicry, as Bobby recalls it, never was suggested as a means to the end of developing a golfing style. It was often exploited by Bobby's father for the entertainment of his own friends on the veranda of their home on Sunday afternoons when Bobby was encouraged to get out on the lawn and perform imitations of this player and that—usually someone in the gathering. But Bobby's best imitation was always of Stewart Maiden. That paid off. And it was on one of these occasions that he caused great amusement by inquiring: "Dad, what do people do on Sunday who don't play golf?"

In the mild winter before he was seven years old Bobby, more or less equipped with a job lot of abbreviated clubs, was given permission to use the East Lake course except on Saturdays and Sundays. It is a curious fact that this amateur golfer began his career in practically the same way as the professional golfer begins. When he came from school in the afternoon he would take his little mashie and putter and a large cap full of balls, go down to the sunken thirteenth green back of the house, and there, all the afternoon, he would pitch to the green and putt out, pitch to the green and putt out.

He often played No. 1 on the old East Lake course, a one-shot hole of 160 yards with a wide grass trap a little more than halfway to the green. Swinging his small driver with all his might, Bobby could carry this trap, about 90 yards, and with a reasonable run on the shot, he was left with a fairly easy pitch to the green. Big Bob said it was surprising the number of 3s he made on this hole.

So Bobby traveled along the pathway of golf on a regular course and Stewart made for him a real set of juvenile clubs, and a little bag in which to carry them. He also began to play regularly with Perry Adair, son of George Adair, close friend of Big Bob's, a great sportsman and a true gentleman and the man who did more for golf in Atlanta than any other man ever did or ever will do. There began one of the most remarkable competitions in the annals of golf. And there was Alexa Stirling, another pupil of Stewart Maiden's, who also lived beside the course. At times the three youngsters played together. Bobby and Perry met at home and afield in invitation tournaments and friendly matches, and there is no way of knowing just how much this long and brilliantly contested struggle meant to Bobby's future development and career. But it is certain his association with Perry and his father, the encouragement given him by the latter, and the sharp battles accorded him by the former, were leading factors in his development.

The first championship won by Bobby Jones was at the age of nine years, and it was, as you may guess, not a very large or important one. Still, it was a formal tournament regulated in all respects like grownup tournaments: the Junior Championship of the East Lake Country Club. He did not meet Perry in this tournament as they were in separate brackets.

In the summer of 1913 Bobby shot an 80 on the old course for the first time. It may be explained that the old course at East Lake was an exceedingly tough scoring proposition. It was an odd affair, laid out by Tom Bendelow. There were only two par 3 holes on it, the first and the third; so after shooting three holes, a backbreaking stretch of 15 holes confronted the golfer, without a single short hole. You can understand that cards close to 90 were astonishingly good for a little boy of 10.

On this summer day, he was playing with Perry as usual, but for once—and for the first time—he wasn't paying any attention to what Perry was doing. He was scoring better than he ever had scored before and he had no room in his mind for anything else. At the last green, faced with a four-foot putt for an even 80, he must have wondered why his skinny little chest was so tight and why his hands were trembling as he stood up to that putt, not to beat Perry but just to score an 80. Down went the putt and on the card went the 80, with the signature of Perry Adair on the attested line.

And away across the golf course went Bobby Jones, setting off at a brisk trot to find his dad. He found Big Bob at the fourteenth green, and he walked solemnly up to him and held out the card—without a word—his hand still trembling. Big Bob took the card and looked at it. Then he looked at Bobby. Then he put his arms around him and hugged him hard. And so before he was a dozen years old, Bobby Jones had discovered a new adversary in golf, the Great Opponent whose tangible form is only a card and a pencil. He had played his first round against the toughest foe of them all—Old Man Par.

In 1915 Bobby had gained in weight and strength and Big Bob deemed him good enough to play in the Southern Championship which came that year to East Lake. His qualifying round was epochal. Bobby's own idea was that he was playing terribly, but he came in with a card of 83, a single stroke back of the medalist. Whether or not he was satisfied with his showing in this, his first grapple with the iron certitudes of Old Man Par, his score had won the team trophy for his club and he was second only to the man who was to win the title. At the age of 13 years and three months, he was in the championship division and he had established for himself a precedent—though he certainly did not suspect it at the time—of never failing to qualify in any tournament which he ever entered.

In the second round he encountered a famous figure in southern golf, Commodore Bryan Heard of Houston, Texas, the oldest man in the tournament—a rugged and experienced veteran of a hundred tournaments, a hard man for anybody to beat, although at that time he was well past 50. Indeed, he proved quite too hard for Bobby, though the youngster put up a desperate battle which went to the seventeenth green, where the Commodore, grim and impassive as a Chinese idol, ended the bout with a victory, 2–1.

Bobby started one of his most eventful years, 1916, by achieving the age of 14 and acquiring a good many pounds in weight. He met Perry in the semifinal round of an invitation tournament at Montgomery, Alabama, one of the most spectacular of their many matches and particularly interesting because it was in this season that Bobby gradually caught up with Perry to share with the little blonde gamecock from Druid Hills the ranking of Kid Wonders of Dixie.

In the Montgomery bout Bobby played the first nine holes in 33 strokes, a brilliant burst of golf which had Perry 3 down, and caused Bobby not unreasonably to feel that he had the match well in hand. What happened on the last nine was another notable contribution to Bobby's long education in golf. Perry came back in 33, including a stroke lost by a stymie at the sixteenth green, and won the match 1 up. There is nothing in the world like the fierce glare of competition to take the early dew off the turf. It was very likely the greatest match ever played up to that time in the South, and it was played by boys of 14 and 17.

The first Georgia State Championship was played that year at the Brookhaven Country Club in Atlanta and there was unusual interest since the Boy Wonders were entered. The stage was set for a great show at Brookhaven and the boys proceeded in an orderly manner to the final round of 36 holes. Bobby now was larger and stronger than Perry, but there was little to choose between their games and I am sure no two golfers ever met who were better matched in courage and determination. Bobby displayed greater power but Perry's superior accuracy in the morning round brought him in 3 up at noon. Starting the afternoon round, Bobby lost the first hole to be 4 down; and with that calamitous start, he buckled down to shoot a level 70 and to win on the last green to become Georgia's first amateur champion.

Bobby Jones' grip on the club.

3.
The Big Show

After such a fine showing during the summer, the two Kid Wonders of Dixie traveled up from Atlanta to play in the United States Amateur Championship at the Merion Cricket Club near Philadelphia in the fall of 1916. Such a magnificent and undreamed of game did this 14-year-old lad, Bobby Jones, play that the gallery, pressing eagerly over the links, went mad over him. Sportswriters all over the country acclaimed him the Boy Wonder and prophesied without hesitancy that soon he would take his place with the greatest of the stars. Who could blame the boy, if he kept hidden in his strong but unobtrusive boyhood the dream that one day he would win the amateur crown of the United States?

The spindling youngster of seven, reaching twice that age, had grown into a powerful, chunky, somewhat knock-kneed boy, 5'4", weighing 165 pounds; blue-eyed, rather towheaded; wearing long pants—he carried only one pair with him to the tournament, and one pair of shoes, his wardrobe being of the simplest and his mind untroubled with apprehensions of rain—and he regarded this expedition as the greatest lark of his life.

Until he got to Merion, Bobby had never seen anything but the comparatively coarse and harsh Bermuda greens of the southern courses, which by contrast made the Merion surfaces resemble billiard tables. And the change in speed was bewildering to the youngster, accustomed to rapping the ball firmly and decisively over the slower Bermuda. His first experience on these new greens included a most embarrassing episode. The sixth hole of the West Course was a short pitch to the green over a brook, the slope facing the player. In a practice round Bobby's ball was some 30 feet beyond the hole, which was in the middle of the green. Forgetting for the moment all about the faster pace of the Merion surfaces, Bobby struck his putt firmly with the little center-shafted Travis putter he used in those days, and was horrified to see the ball roll past the hole, and apparently gathering momentum, trickle over the green and into the brook.

At the end of the morning round on qualifying day it was suddenly discovered that Bobby's card of 74 was the best in the field. Word got about that the Kid from Dixie was breaking up the tournament, and when Bobby appeared to start his afternoon round, practically all the spectators had assembled at the first tee to watch him.

Now came the first lesson in the Big Show—the gallery, always a factor and often a terrific hazard in major championship play. Always the gallery follows a favored star, a leading contender, or a new phenomenon—as in this instance. The first gallery at Merion was watching Bobby and behaving in a very orderly and proper fashion. But the concentrated stare of so many eyes, all focused on him, afflicted the youngster with a stage fright, a ghastly and palpitant misery to which he was a perfect stranger. His fine power swing and his smooth putting touch suddenly and hopelessly tightened up; his shots strayed hither and yon; short putts declined to drop; and to his exemplary 74 of the morning round, he added a terrible 89 in the afternoon. The total of 163, however, was easily good enough to place him in the charmed circle of the championship. The highest score to qualify was 167. Perry Adair was tied at that score, won in the playoff, and lost his first match.

Bobby's first match was with Eben Byers, a former national champion. He went to the first tee that morning in a frame of mind that caused him, before the match was a minute old, to encounter what he regarded at the time as a rebuff. As Mr. Byers and Bobby walked off the tee after their drives, Bobby in the same spirit as he would have used in a casual match at home, offered the former champion a piece of chewing gum. Mr. Byers declined—without thanks. And Bobby, whose motive was entirely hospitable, felt somewhat abashed. This seemed to be a new way to play golf. He also wondered why Mr. Byers did not chew gum.

But he soon began to feel quite at home. Despite the absence of the gallery, due to that ghastly 89, he was playing badly. Mr. Byers was also playing badly and they had an exciting time. They missed shots frequently, and though Mr. Byers was one of the oldest contestants in the field, and Bobby was the youngest, they expressed their chagrin in exactly the same way. With the perfectly natural reaction carried over from early childhood, Bobby followed a badly missed stroke by throwing the club after the ball as far as he could. Mr. Byers did the same thing. Players in the match directly behind them said later that it looked like a juggling act on the stage. At the twelfth hole, Mr. Byers hurled a club over the hedge and out of the golf course and would not allow his caddy to retrieve it. Bobby explained whimsically that he had defeated Mr. Byers only because he had run out of clubs first.

Bobby's second match was against Frank Dyer, a state and district champion. Dyer started fast against his schoolboy opponent, winning five of the first six holes. Just here the Georgia boy displayed a faculty that was to be the determining factor in later years on many a hard-fought field—the ability to take a staggering blow on the chin and come back for more; the ability, in the slang of the game, to stand the gaff. Bobby buckled down and reeled off the next 28 holes in better than an average of 4s, better than the figures of Old Man Par himself. He set a pace that Dyer, even with his big lead and greater experience, could not stand. Bobby won 4–2 with the finest stretch of golf that the 1916 championship produced.

This victory revived the interest of the gallery and a huge crowd was at the first tee as he drove off in the quarterfinal round against Robert A. Gardner of Chicago, defending champion, who was working under the handicap of an infected finger. Having gone through his baptism of fire, Bobby had got over his stage fright before the gallery and he rather outplayed Gardner in the morning round of their 36-hole match, shooting a 76 to be 1 up. In the afternoon, the match was still even as they went to the sixth tee and here Bobby learned another valuable lesson in his golfing education. After being in serious trouble on the next three holes, Gardner pitched close enough to get down in one putt for a half on each of these holes. Ten years later it might have been a different story. Ten years later Bobby had learned the lesson he started to learn that day—that the iron pressure of par golf must break through the most spectacular procession of brilliant recoveries, even when an opponent's run of breaks seems endless. But this was not 10 years later. This was Bobby's first appearance in the Big Show and he had kept the iron pressure on his opponent as long as he could. And it was Bobby who broke. He lost the next seven holes and was beaten 5–3.

Early in life, early in his golfing career, Bobby learned to face defeat with a smile, and to take a beating as a sportsman should. Long afterward he told me that he never had learned anything from a match that he had won.

"I've learned what I know from defeats," he said.

Bobby Jones' swing.

4.

Seven Lean Years

So Bobby Jones was defeated in the third match of his first national championship, but in less than a week the Georgia schoolboy had become famous; more famous than he realized at the time. At 14, he became the outstanding youngster in the world of golf. And in a way this was a difficult situation. Never again did he present himself at a major tournament unheralded. The fierce glare of the spotlight was upon him as he went to the first tee of the first round. He was the pet of galleries and golfers alike. He was accorded a good chance to win every competition in which he took part. He was ranked higher and higher in the list of favorites; and through seven years, beginning at Merion in 1916, he played in 10 major championships—without winning one. These "seven lean years," as they have been called, constitute a chapter in the history of a world champion that very likely is without a counterpart in any sport; certainly in golf. Seven years of unvaried defeat in the Big Shows, and all the time regarded as one of the leading performers, would have broken the heart of any but a champion. The seven fat years, which came later, reversing the Scriptural order, bore no finer testimony of a real champion who first of all was able to take defeat.

Attending the tournament at Merion was the late Walter J. Travis, who had won the U.S. Amateur Championship three times, and the British once; a remarkable golfer who took up the game at the age of 35 and reached its front rank by accuracy and intelligence, and the deadliest putting stroke of his generation. Mr. Travis took a great interest in Bobby's performance at Merion. When asked what he thought of Bobby's prospects in the way of improvement, Mr. Travis replied: "Improvement? He can never improve his shots, if that's what you mean. But he will learn a great deal more about playing them. And his putting method is faulty."

A few years later, during an exhibition match in Augusta, Mr. Travis was in the gallery and saw Bobby do some putting which was even worse than usual. After the match I was privileged to be present when Mr. Travis gave Bobby, in the guise of a lecture, a lesson which so changed his putting in a single season that from one of the worst performers among the champions, he became one of the finest and most consistent putters the game has seen.

So that was all of golf for the eventful year of 1916, and the next spring, our country was in World War I, and no national championships were played in 1917 or 1918. The only important event that Bobby won during those years was the 1917 Southern Championship at the Roebuck Country Club in Birmingham. He was the youngest competitor ever to win this event.

In his second Southern championship Bobby trundled along like a little juggernaut through the field of 64, taking them as they came. Louis Jacoby of Dallas was the final victim. Trailed by a larger gallery than he had ever seen except at Merion the Atlanta youth shot a 76 and went into luncheon comfortably up on the stubborn and combative little man from Texas, always rated one of the best fighters in Southern golf. Jacoby rallied in the afternoon but could not break Bobby's stride, the match ending 6–4.

Bobby had won his first important championship. Suddenly the cool, determined little golfing machine turned into a red-faced, perspiring schoolboy, under the blast of cheers from the gallery. And when Jacoby, smiling broadly, extended his hand with a most cordial congratulation, all Bobby could think of to say was, "Much obliged!"

During these years, the Wright and Ditson Company arranged a tour of golf exhibition matches for the war chest of the American Red Cross, inviting four young players to take part—those inseparable friends, Bobby and Perry; Alexa Stirling of Atlanta, playing from East Lake, and Elaine Rosenthal of Chicago, two of the best of the female golfers of America. Miss Stirling had won one of her three U.S. championships in 1916 at Boston. And then came a series of matches which Bobby and Perry played against the leading amateurs. After that in the historic War Relief matches, Bobby found himself pitted against professional golfers in real earnest for the first time, which afterwards became so pleasant and fascinating a part of the game for him.

In all, however, Bobby did pretty well in this series of brushes with the professionals, and was the only member of the amateurs who escaped a defeat.

He learned one important thing in 1918, playing before great galleries in many states. The report of his club-throwing at Merion two years before had followed him; his temper was by way of becoming proverbial; and when he indulged occasionally in this method of blowing off steam after missing a shot inexcusably, the golf scribes took him to task—not always too kindly nor with the reflection that after all this brilliant golfer was only a boy of 14 or 15. They saw him play golf that any man would be proud of and that few could equal, but they also expected him to present to the gallery the imperturbable front of the case-hardened veteran—which, by the way, the case-hardened veteran does not always present in time of stress. It struck me as a bit unreasonable that so much should have been written on the gusty vagaries of one petulant youngster.

He was the most thorough sportsman as far as his opponents were concerned. It was not an easy matter getting his turbulent disposition in hand. The sportswriters loved to depict him as a hot-blooded southerner long after he had taken their criticisms to heart and had mastered his emotions, so far as any outward symptoms were concerned; a conquest which was an important part of his development in golf and otherwise. Bobby's later great poise and control on the links are all the more marvelous when you consider that a championship golf match is the most nerve-racking—physically and mentally—and devastating sports experience that exists. Such a match is far more strenuous even than a great boxing bout because the strain is constant and is pitched for hours at a time.

It is to be hoped that the uninterrupted rush of incident and action in this narrative will not engender in the reader's mind the idea that Bobby Jones did little or nothing except play golf; that impression would be greatly in error. His tournament season really was a brief affair. So keen a mind did he possess that all through his schoolwork he made almost as enviable a record as he did on the golf course.

The East Lake Golf Club.

5.
The Runner-Up Year

Bobby played in four championship tournaments in 1919—two sectional and two national events—without winning any, and because he finished second in three of them, this period was known as his "runner-up" year. He was runner-up in the Southern Open, the Canadian Open, and the United States Amateur Championships. At New Orleans in the Southern Amateur, he was stopped in the semifinal round by Nelson Whitney, many times winner of this event, so his defense of his holdover title from 1917 came to a somewhat sudden conclusion.

In the Southern Open, played at East Lake, Bobby came to grips with the professionals, this time for keeps. The young Georgian, at the age of 17, had been gaining inches and losing pounds. He was three inches taller and 15 pounds lighter than at Merion. His numerous bouts in the last two years had given his game a finish and an added consistency, and playing on his home course, the young amateur was considered a worthy rival of the professional experts, who assembled to play for a purse which was regarded as an important one in those days.

The confidence of the critics was not misplaced. Bobby proved to be the only amateur in the field capable of matching shots with the professionals in this lively and spectacular event. At the end of the second round of the 72-hole competition, Long Jim Barnes was leading the field by a single stroke—and Bobby Jones was running second. He and the tall Cornishman fought it out down the stretch but at the end of the 72 holes Jim Barnes was the first Southern Open champion. But Bobby was still just one stroke behind and this in spite of Long Jim's eagle 3 on the long 620-yard fifth hole, the only one ever accomplished on this difficult hole, in competition.

An incident that occurred at New Orleans is now one of the classic anecdotes of golf, and has been told many times, often inaccurately. Bobby's very first shot in this championship showed that, however the preceding two years had improved his golf, there was something left for him to learn about rules. The first hole of the New Orleans Country Club is a one-shotter of 150 yards. Bobby's mashie pitch from the tee was pulled off to the left of the green and the ball landed in a wheelbarrow, left there by some workman. Worse than that it landed in an old shoe, beside which the wheelbarrow contained another shoe, a lawnmower, some greasy rags, and a quantity of cut grass.

The rule of "upkeep" applied, of course. A player in this or similar position is entitled to lift the ball and drop it, not nearer the hole, without penalty, the wheelbarrow not being a part of the golf course. But Bobby did not know this rule, or at any rate he was not sure of its provisions and was taking no chances on disqualification. He studied the situation, which appeared remarkably gloomy. The only ray of light was the condition of the shoe, which was old and did not look as if it would hold together under a determined attack with a niblick. And indeed,

Bobby did take a niblick, planted himself as firmly as possible on the ground beside the wheelbarrow, and walloped the shoe as hard as he could. To his immense relief, the shoe was projected onto the green, where the ball rolled out, and he got a 4, losing only one stroke to par.

Thereafter I cannot recall a single predicament in his career in which he did not know exactly what the rules permitted and did not permit.

The story of the Canadian Open at Hamilton, Ontario, was that of J. Douglas Edgar, a little English professional, who had come to the Druid Hills Golf Club in Atlanta early that spring. Bobby, Perry Adair, Douglas Edgar, and Willie Ogg—then professional at East Lake, Stewart Maiden having gone to the St. Louis Country Club for a time—played many matches in Atlanta, and the four of them journeyed to Hamilton together. Bobby went to the tournament playing very good golf, and he played very good golf all through it, winding up in a tie at 294, an excellent figure for a national open championship, with the same Long Jim Barnes, who had beaten him by a single stroke in the Southern Open. Bobby came to the last green with two strokes left to become runner-up all by himself, but he took three putts!

But they were tied for *second place*, 16 strokes back of the amazing Englishman. Edgar's cards in the order of their performance were 72-71-69-66, for a total of 278, which remained for years the lowest aggregate score ever returned in a national competition in any country. Edgar's finishing round of 66 stood up for 11 years until 1930, when Tommy Armour in this same tournament and on this same course five strokes back of the lead as he went into the fourth round, went mad and touched off one of the lowest scores ever returned in important competition—64. With two holes left to play, Tommy was actually nine strokes under 4s, and after a 32 going out, he started home 3-4-4-3-3-3-3, but he finished with a 5 and a 4, and had to be content with eight under 4s.

And so little Douglas Edgar's cherished record went down under the scoring frenzy of this frenetic era, but his performance at Hamilton remains to this day the most conclusive drubbing ever administered to a crack field of contestants in an important open championship. He told me some funny things about his training for that famous tourney: how getting into Canada after a long dry spell in Atlanta, due to certain then prevalent prohibition laws, he went to a highly enjoyable party, remained in bed the next day until noon, then went out to the golf course and hit six shots with a jigger.

"Then my hands felt thin," he said with a slow smile, "and I knew I was 'right.' So I put up my clubs."

And he was "right" next day.

Edgar was the most temperamental of golfers. When in the mood—when he felt "right," he could play incredibly beautiful golf, a remarkable exhibition of perfect control and fancy golf, which rarely was played straight—often he was bending the shots this way and that, fading the ball, drawing the ball, and obviously amusing himself as a great musician exploits his fancies on violin or piano in lighter moments of practice.

His style was individual and somewhat unorthodox, in that he kept the club hooded, or with its face turned as much as possible toward the ball, during the stroke. The cardinal principal of his teaching was keeping the right elbow compactly tucked up against the right side until the ball had gone. Amplifying this tucked-in right elbow a trifle, Edgar's idea in keeping the right elbow close was to compel the player, easily and certainly, to bring the club head against the ball from inside the line of the shot. A great many years ago, bewhiskered teachers of the game, with no reference whatever to hitting from the inside, directed loose-armed pupils to put caps under their right arms and hold them there while the stroke was being made and until the ball had departed. That was the fashion for compelling a pupil to keep the right elbow close to the side in the days when the gutty ball, hats teed too high, hips, and peg-top pants were in vogue.

"Hitting through the gate," Edgar called it. And he made and patented a little device, and a book to go along with it, both very simple, known as "The Gate to Golf." This is still available in some sport shops.

Edgar met a tragic and mysterious death two years after the Canadian Open of 1919. So far as was known, or at all logically surmised, he was struck down and killed by a speeding motorist in front of the house where he was living in Atlanta. I wondered if the ghost of J. Douglas Edgar was not flickering around the fringes of the Hamilton golf course when Tommy shot that miraculous score.

And when Douglas Edgar was "right," I have yet to see the man who could step with him.

6.
The First Big Disappointment

The last tournament of the year saw Bobby Jones again in the Big Show, his second appearance in the United States Amateur Championship on the great course of the Oakmont Country Club, near Pittsburgh. In spite of the fact he had not won a title that season, Bobby's showing had been so good, especially in the Southern and Canadian Opens against the professionals, that he was regarded at Oakmont as having nearly as good a chance as the favorites, Chick Evans, holdover champion from 1916, and Francis Ouimet, winner in 1914.

Bobby had not been satisfied with his driving all season, and Big Bob had been even less pleased. So as the date of the championship drew near and Bobby continued to spray his big shots all over the place, Big Bob sent him out to St. Louis, for his first model and mentor, Stewart Maiden, to straighten him out. And for the first and, I think, the only time in Bobby's career, Stewart seemed unable to help him. After a couple of days of unmitigated and unsuccessful toil, Stewart decided to go with Bobby to the championship, and Big Bob joined them there.

The Oakmont course was a tremendous test of golf, and the first qualifying day was complicated further by the most impressive hail storm I have ever seen on a golf course, and resulted in the highest qualifying scores since the second annual championship, and never duplicated during the era of qualifying at the scene of the tournament. S. Davidson Herron, playing on his home course, was tied for the medal with two others at 158, Bobby was second with 159, and from there they soared all the way up to 172, the top figure to get in.

Bobby's driving had failed to improve, and after a seemingly fruitless session on the practice tee, Kiltie's advice was to go out on the course and hit the ball as hard as he could. "It will go somewhere," said Kiltie philosophically, "and if you get off the fairway, you'll be nearer the green anyway."

But in spite of his erratic driving, Bobby had a fairly easy journey to the final round where he met Davy Herron, who also had not met very stiff opposition, and who had been playing the best golf of the week. Bobby seemed at last to have found his game and at the end of the morning round, they were all square. In the afternoon, however, Davy's superior accuracy on the greens began to pay off, and on the twelfth tee, Bobby was 3 down. On this historic twelfth, a gigantic hole of 621 yards, Bobby for once was well out in front, and Davy had an indifferent recovery when his drive found a trap. But Bobby's second found a trap, he too recovered badly and went on to lose the hole and the match 5–4. It was on this "Ghost Hole" that Bobby turned back Watts Gunn in the amateur championship of 1925, when it looked as if Watts had him beaten in the final round. Destiny does seem to play no favorites in the long run, if the run is long enough.

The feature match of the 1919 championship was the amazing battle between those classic rivals, Chick Evans and Francis Ouimet, in the second round. Both were ill, and the terrible weather of the qualifying rounds had not helped them. Playing with superb nerve and courage, they traveled the morning round in a stroke better than par. Bobby's match was over early that day and he went out to watch the afternoon round of this battle of the giants, pop-eyed with interest and excitement. Francis went out in 34, and was only 1 up. Eventually they reached the eighteenth green all even, Francis' putt went down, and Chick missed. Next day he lost to Woody Platt on the thirty-eighth hole.

This was the first really bitter disappointment that Bobby had met. Through 1919, his "runner-up" year, he had played in seven minor and two major events, but beginning with 1920, he played only in the major tournaments. I have always regarded his debut in the open championship at Toledo as his real entrance on the world stage of sports. And before the "fierce white light" that plays upon a world figure should focus attention on Bobby Jones, the Champion, I have tried to give you a picture of Bobby Jones, a sturdy American schoolboy, through his formative years of study and play, of lighthearted battle and bitter disappointment, which went into the making of world champion, and what is far more worthy, the building of a character.

Bobby Jones and Harry Vardon in 1920 at Toledo for the U.S. Open.

7.
The First Open

As the tournament season of 1920 opened, Bobby was 18 years old, had completed his sophomore year at Georgia Tech, and was the leading member of its golf team. Early in the summer, he captured the Southern Amateur Championship at Chattanooga, with such an impressive performance, he decided to go on to Memphis the following week and play in the Western Amateur Championship. Chick Evans, perennial champion of the Western Association, filled the role of favorite. Bobby started the week of play as brilliantly as he had concluded in Chattanooga, setting a new qualifying record in the Western Association with rounds of 69 and 70. All the people in the Dixie delegation were sure Bobby was set to win, as he was more at home on the Bermuda greens than Evans. But Chick, an experienced veteran, the first golfer to win the U.S.

Amateur and Open titles the same year in 1916, and on his way to another national title this year, stopped him in the semifinal round, 1 up in 36 holes. Bobby's education in competitive golf contained few better lessons than this engagement, and he often said he never enjoyed one more. But Big Bob, when he met us at the station, lacked something of enjoying at least the result of the bout. Meditatively he uttered a prophecy, which lasted down the years. He said: "Well, Chick will never beat him again."

Chick and Bobby met twice more in national championships and Chick never beat him again. It is a somewhat curious fact that, as many times as Bobby was beaten in championship competition, the same man never defeated him twice. In the list are three champions who beat him once, Chick, Bob Gardner, and Francis Ouimet. He beat Evans twice, Gardner twice, and Ouimet three times.

The Open Championship of 1920 was held late that year, August 10–13, at the Inverness Club, Toledo. The clubhouse and course were simply crawling with distinguished professionals and amateurs. Whichever way one turned, he could get an eyeful of something worth looking at—Ted Ray, who weighed no small part of a long ton, Harry Vardon, Chick Evans, Walter Hagen, the defending champion, Jock Hutchison, Bob McDonald, Leo Diegel, a young professional playing in his first open. The Caledonian bur-r-r-r in the talk about the course resembled a battery of buzz saws working in a "wee hoose among the heather-r-r-r."

On qualifying day, the spotlight of the sporting world inevitably picked out to touch with its brightest beams the most romantically cast pairing of all the host—Harry Vardon of England and Bobby Jones of Atlanta; the classic golfer of this generation—and perhaps of all time, as history will see it—and the college boy who had come to be rated the peer of American amateurs; one playing with all the richness of a vast experience, the other with the rare power of young blood back of his perfect swing; one playing with his face toward the westering sun, yet at its brightest on him, the other on the morning side of the hill, his feet in the morning dew.

There was a singular appeal in this pair, the oldest and the youngest golfer in the tournament, were not age an ungracious fling at Harry Vardon's graceful and perennial youth. Harry was in his fifty-first year, and before Bobby was born, had twice set this country aglow with his perfect golf played with the old gutta-percha ball. Bobby and the lively ball arrived coincidentally, one might say in the year 1902, but Vardon had been the master of the gutty, as he was master of the rubber-core. Had he played with the "feathcries" with a shepherd's crook (craftily shortened, no doubt) Harry Vardon would have pitched round pebbles to the green with an accuracy more beautiful than all his rivals—and missed many of the putts, possibly.

Rain slowed up the Inverness course but the sun came out and shone on a large gallery that watched Vardon and Bobby play an even round of 75 strokes each in the morning. Bobby went out in a fine 34, while Vardon was four over par with 40, but affairs changed at the turn, Vardon striking a fast pace with a 35 in, while Bobby dug sand from traps and hooked his drives, finally taking three putts on the last green for 41.

Bobby was leading the veteran in the second round when they came to the seventh hole, an interesting, even exciting affair, laid out to be played around an angle of tall trees, which the bolder and stronger contestants were carrying with a towering drive from the tee, to place the ball in front of the small green. They both made the big carry successfully, and the balls lay some forty yards short of the green, Bobby slightly ahead. Vardon played a conservative run-up shot, close to the flag, and Bobby, though there was nothing in the line, elected to pitch delicately with a niblick—a pretty shot, when it works. In this instance it did not work. He half-topped the ball, which scuttled over the green like a rabbit into much trouble beyond. He played out with the loss of a stroke to par, and his ears flaming with embarrassment, walked along beside Vardon toward the next tee. Vardon always was a silent competitor when engaged in serious play. He had not spoken thus far in the round. Bobby, with an idea of breaking the ice, and at the same time alleviating his own embarrassment, decided to open a conversation.

"Mr. Vardon," he said bashfully, "did you ever see a worse shot than that?"

"No," said Harry. It was a simple answer but explicit. The incident was closed and no further conversation ensued.

In the first round of the championship Bobby, having qualified easily, started five over par in the first six holes. He was not playing championship medal golf, where you plod along in pars with here and there a stroke worse and here and yon a birdie to get it back. He was shooting the first part all right, but neglecting the second. It was a new strain bearing down on him of course, and he wound up with a lamentable 78, far down the list. In the next round he did much better with a 74, but at the halfway mark, still seemed well out of the chase.

With 152, he was seven strokes back of the leader, Jock Hutchison. He naturally concluded that he had no chance at all, and his mind thus relieved of the curious strain of the first two rounds, at the end of the third round, he had shot a fine 70. There is a lot of psychology in golf and most of all in the grim progress of a major medal play championship. Bobby looked over the board as his score of 70 was posted. Vardon was now leading the field with 218. Diegel and Hutchison were a stroke behind and Ted Ray was next with 220. Bobby at 222 was only four strokes out of the lead. With only one round to play, he had a chance. He did not know then as he learned later how the terrific pressure of the finishing round of an open championship can break down the game of even the best golfers and the most courageous competitors. He could not imagine that in the last round at Inverness every one of the men who were leading him would slip away from Old Man Par to a 75 or worse.

He had a chance! Now he told himself he must go out and do another 70—or better. And now the strain was on again. Once more his shots unaccountably strayed; once more the putts refused to drop. A misguided ambition brought in a card of 77. Bobby's real chance, though he was far from knowing it, lay not in a final round of 70 or better. It lay in stepping along with Old Man Par, while the pressure was breaking the leaders. A score of 72, even 4s, in the mode of Old Man Par, to total 294 would have won for him in the last round of the first national open championship he entered. But said Bobby years later:

"It was as fine a thing as ever happened to me. If I had won that first open, I might have got the idea that it was an easy thing to do. Better to have finished in eighth place with 299."

Bobby Jones' swing.

8.
Inverness

Edward Ray of Oxhey, England, won the Open Championship of 1920 because he stood the gaff best. He finished first of the half dozen leaders, who had a chance, because he cracked least under the terrific strain of the bitterest finish ever witnessed in an open championship. Golfers will argue that medal tournaments do not supply the thrills of match play but heaven preserve me from anything more devastating than the last hour of the Open Championship at Toledo. Somewhere in his huge system, the big Oxheyman carried the ultimate ounce that supplied the final punch—the single stroke by which he led Harry Vardon, his partner in the quest; and Leo Diegel and Jock Hutchison and Jack Burke. Had Ted Ray blown one more putt, missed one drive or one approach, there would have been five men in the most remarkable tie in the history of golf.

Ray finished with a 75 for a total of 295, the other four had 296. Under the final strain they cracked wider than Ray. That was the answer. Going into the last round, Ray was two strokes back of Vardon, who was leading the field with 218, Diegel and Hutchison, 219. And the tremendously dramatic ending—first Vardon blowing to a depressing 42 on the home stretch; then Ray making a perfect 4 to go one under Vardon; then Diegel having a twenty-foot putt for the 3 that would have tied and in five minutes more, little Jock Hutchison with exactly the same length putt for a 3 that would also have given him a tie for first place. More than 7,000 fans watched those heartbreaking, nerve-shattering finishes on the home green.

Never will I forget the manner in which Ted Ray took the news that he had a putt of four feet to beat Vardon. The big fellow was out in 35, but had gone 4 over at No. 17. He strode up to the last tee and banged out a tremendous drive of 300 yards down the fairway, but even Ted's smashing blow failed to reach the 322-yard green. He pitched on the green well away from the cup and his approach was short, leaving him more than a yard from the hole. It was here that he got the news that this putt carried the championship as far as Vardon was concerned. He was preparing to putt when he got it. He promptly handed his club back to his caddy; removed the habitual pipe from his mouth; and while the assembled thousands fairly sweated blood with anxiety, he calmly refilled his pipe, lighted it, puffed away two or three times, took back his putter from the caddy, and without any more to-do, sent down the putt that made him champion.

Ray demonstrated again and again his right to the reputation for long driving. In fact, it might be said that he won the championship on one hole—No. 7, as figured in all of his rounds. This is a trick hole, a doglegged affair bending to the left around a clump of high trees. The distance to the green via the fairway is 320 yards. A powerful driver who can hit both high and far can straighten out the distance to about 290. It is a terrific hole for the average golfer with a steep bluff at the left of the well-trapped green, but it was a sinecure for the mighty Edward. The big fellow never failed to pick up a stroke on this hole, getting a 3 every time he played it. Once his tee shot hit a foot from the cup and he almost got an eagle. He was easily the longest walloper in the tournament and there were many long hitters there. His longest shot was on No. 9, 492 yards, where he let out all he had, carried a tree at the corner of the boundary and went far past the road, 240 yards away—a shot of 340 to 350 yards. He was home with a mashie-niblick.

It was a gale of wind that blew Harry Vardon back from a certain championship. The grand old boy started out on the last round, leading by one stroke, and played like the world beater that he was. He always shot par and let the field come back to him and exactly par he shot for the first nine. He started home with a 4 and a 3, and we were all sure he was set for his second United States Championship, just twenty years after he had won his first. But the Old Master's gallant effort failed by a gust of stormy wind. As he played No. 11 with a beautiful birdie 3, a dense dark cloud was gathering in the west and a strong and rising wind straight out of the north began tearing at the neighboring trees. A fair gale was blowing straight against him on the tee of the twelfth, a 522-yard hole. This did not bother him too much as he had played against many a stronger breeze in his own country, but it cut his length and, when he came to his second shot, he saw that he could not carry the stream which flowed through the valley about 400 yards from the tee. His perfectly hit iron third, also held short by the wind, failed to reach the green and he finished with a 6.

He still was working on a surplus of four strokes on those last half dozen holes—but he blew them all, and one more which would have tied for first place, and finished in a tie with Jack Burke, who had posted 296 several hours before.

"I couldn't get the distance against that breeze," he said later, uncomplainingly—just in explanation. Harry Vardon was more than fifty years old, an old man for athletics. A championship makes the most severe demands upon physical and moral strength—in a word, upon the soul—of a golfer. Its exigencies are many and trying. Vardon was tired and the physical strain did what the mental strain could not do—unsteadied him. And as I judged by Harry Vardon's face, this either leaves a man a failure or a philosopher. Vardon's face was the most patient I had ever seen. It seemed rather the face of some quiet, placid old minister, resigned to the not too kindly usage of this world; thoughtful and reflective—and patient. Never a flicker of resentment crossed Harry Vardon's face, the natural resentful feeling that follows a bad break to a perfectly hit shot. No impatience was to be found there, when the play was slow and the course jammed. No trace of worry when his opponent was up and the end was near. Vardon was master of himself—thus he was master of the greatest of all games and I fancy his other contests with life were played out with the same quiet, patient fortitude that he exhibited in the game of his profession.

Twice on the last two holes of the final round, Leo Diegel had a chance to win the championship, a 10-foot putt on the seventeenth, and a 20-foot one on the last green, or either would have given him a tie. I picked up Diegel coming up the terrible twelfth, word having got around that he was out in 37, and coming back in par. Chick Evans was caddying for him and a tremendous gallery was pulling its multitudinous head off for him to come through and keep the championship in this country. One glance at Diegel showed that he was in a fighting mood and very cheerful. Withal he was nervous, one fan avowing that a farmer in an adjoining field putted an ear of corn, and sent Leo into hysterics, but it seemed not to affect his play.

On the fourteenth came a calamitous break. I am sorry to say that it was a well-meant but very stupid intrusion by a good friend of his that cracked him just when he had a grand chance to win. A frantic computation showed that he had a couple of strokes to spare on the last five holes to beat Vardon, and that par would, in all likelihood, beat Ray. It looked fine for Leo. His tee shot just cleared a bank that confronts the fourteenth green, leaving him a long brassie shot down the wind. As Leo was getting set to play this critical shot, a friend came running up to him and said: "Leo, Harry Vardon just got down a 4 for a 78."

Down went Diegel's own club on the ground and up went his arms toward the sky.

"Good Lord," he said, "Don't tell me things like that."

Keyed up as he was, the smash of this startling information shook him fearfully. He took a 6 on the hole and his margin was wiped out. To pass Vardon he still had one stroke to spare over par, but Ted Ray was looming menacingly. That is the savage thing about medal play. It is not only the one opponent that you must beat but all those still out on the course. He played badly on the next two holes and lost a shot on each. After his drive on seventeen, which caught the rough, word came that Ray had finished a stroke under Vardon, and this meant that Diegel would have to get a 3 and a 4 to tie.

It must be said that this information stimulated Diegel to a supreme effort. Out of the rough he came with a full iron shot ten feet from the cup, and 3,000 fans held their collective breath as long as they could and then gasped, and held it again as long as they could as Leo and Chick walked over the ground and stopped and consulted before Diegel took his stance. It was a perfect putt. Unwaveringly it ran to the edge of the cup—then switched as it hit the rim and stayed out by three inches. Leo again threw up his hands in a gesture that was more sincere than dramatic. Then he trudged slowly up the hill to the tee for his last effort—to get a 3 on the 332-yard home hole.

The gallery now consisted of everybody on the course, ranging from the tee to the green and banked solidly around both. Diegel drove down a lane of thousands of persons—getting a perfect shot. Then his approach came floating up, dropping lightly on the green, 20 feet from the pin, with a slope down which to putt. Why draw out the agony? He missed the putt by an inch. He did all he could. He gave it a chance.

After one long sigh, the hand-clapping crashed out and rolled and echoed through the green valley of the eighteenth fairway and about the clubhouse veranda for a game finish and a close call.

Within five minutes came Jock Hutchison, the fiery little Scot shooting the last six holes in even 4s, banging out a 300-yard drive down the eighteenth fairway with a 3 to tie for the title, the last contestant with a chance. We went through it all over again with Jock. He, too, was 20 feet from the pin but it was not downhill. Walter Hagen, far out of the running, was playing with him. He ran down a putt from the edge of the green and the gallery laughed. Hagen laughed, and said.

"Wish I could give it to you, Jock."

Jock gave the ball a chance, but it ran just past the hole. At that Jock had the best last nine of the day—38. And again came thundering applause for the little fighting Scot who had failed so narrowly—and such a gallant effort.

The memory of this, the greatest of the open tournaments, holds hundreds of sharply cut reminiscent pictures, outlined with all the clearness lent by the most absorbing interest. I can shut my eyes and see again scene after scene, or crisis after crisis, pass in swift review; the perfect swing of Harry Vardon; the tremendous lunge of Ted Ray; the well-cut pitches stopping dead to the pin; the billiard table putting greens, framed with a thousand eager faces. Memories we carried away from Inverness.

*Bobby Jones
leaning against
his car.*

9.
There Is a Destiny

Less than a month after the stirring battle at Inverness, Bobby Jones
went to play in the U.S. Amateur Championship at the Engineer's
Country Club on Long Island. This was his third appearance in this
tournament and I think the last time he engaged in any major competition with the carefree and lighthearted attitude of his earlier boyhood in
golf. After 1920, Bobby took his major golf engagements more seriously.

Our British cousins like to criticize us good-naturedly on the serious attitude of Americans toward competitive sports. They say we try
too hard to win; that we make too much of a business of our preparation; that our efforts are of so severe and even grim a determination as
to rob the sport of all or most of the enjoyment it is designed to afford.
It is true that Americans tend to specialize in sport, rather than to play a

number of games acceptably; and I fear that it is also true that sometimes American competitors give the impression of being too eager to win. After all, no cosmic catastrophe impends, no national calamity, even, should our crack relay team take second place, or even third in an Olympiad; or should some alien disc thrower hurl a spinning platter a whole yard farther than our best endeavor.

But certainly I am not apologizing for any American's giving his best efforts to win in any competitive event, against other Americans or against international adversaries. Rather, I think, there is a measure of discourtesy to a worthy foe in giving less than the best. A true sportsman can never appear offensively eager in his quest of victory, or to gloat on its attainment; or to brood too much upon defeat. This, of course, is nothing but proper manners.

How much good manners in sport may temper British criticism of American keenness to win is shown by the astonishing popularity of Bobby Jones in the British Isles, where he got away on the wrong foot in one of his first appearances and later went on to win four major national tournaments and to help win two international matches for the American side. Certainly no competitor, American or British, or of any other nationality ever tried harder to win championships in Britain, or with more uniform success. Yet on the replica of the great silver cup emblematic of the British Amateur Championship, presented to him by fellow members of the Royal and Ancient Club of St. Andrews, after he announced his retirement from competition, this legend is engraved: "A Golfer Matchless in Skill, and Chivalrous in Spirit."

The Amateur Championship of 1920 offered a marked international aspect. Among the entrants were Cyril Tolley, Amateur Champion of Great Britain, Roger Wethered, and a clever Scottish amateur, Tommy Armour, who, it turned out, was the only one of the trio to qualify.

Bobby qualified in a tie for low medal with Freddie Wright of Boston at 154, and they agreed to let this ride on the match when they met in the quarterfinal round. They were both about the same age, both rather cocky youngsters, but I do not recall another match in which I beheld as many 3s as these two boys produced in this morning encounter. Mr. Wright committed the fatal error of getting a 3 on No. 1, and winning the hole. He would have done much better to have taken a 7. Mr. Jones liked the looks of that 3, and forthwith set about collecting 3s for himself. Beginning with No. 2 over a stretch of 14 holes, Mr. Jones collected seven 3s—just half the 14. Four of these 3s came in the stretch of seven holes immediately following Mr. Wright's misguided effort on No. 1. Had not Mr. Jones interspersed these remarkable holes with several 5s and one 6, all records would have gone by the board. Bobby was 5 up at noon, and although there were no fireworks in the afternoon, he won handily.

This victory put him in the semifinal round against Francis Ouimet, and Francis, in the most solemn and kindly manner imaginable, gave him a thorough workmanlike spanking. It was at the seventh green of the afternoon round that the boyish spirit of the Jones boy cropped out for the last time, so far as my observation went, in an important competition.

Ouimet had finished the morning round 3 up, and Bobby, playing desperately, was unable to close with the tall Bostonian. Ouimet's ball lay above the flag at the seventh green, some 20 feet away, Bobby's somewhat farther. There was also a bee on the green. He was penned in by the assembly of human beings and did not know how to get out. Bobby was the only person who was moving so the bee decided he was the cause of it all and came zooming over to him, just as he was getting ready to putt. Bob shooed it away. As he stood up to putt again, back came the bee. He shooed it away again. The persistent insect then settled on the green a couple of yards from the ball and in the line of his putt. The referee then took a hand and cleverly covered the bee with a megaphone.

The gallery was beginning to giggle and it roared lustily when the bee at once emerged from the small end of the megaphone, and began looking for Bobby once more. Bobby, laughing, took off his cap, swung at the bee vigorously and chased it off the green. Everybody in the gallery was laughing. I think even Francis smiled a bit, but I am not sure. Anyway, Bobby, his concentration fairly destroyed, took three putts, and lost the match 6–5. The bee of course did not cost Bobby the match, but I have always fancied that insect flew away with a lot of Bobby's juvenile attitude toward what we are pleased to call serious golf.

The next day, Chick Evans gave Ouimet the most severe beating the Boston star ever received in a championship event. Chick was 2 up at the end of the morning round, but in the afternoon, he cut loose with all the golf that reposed in his remarkable system, and fairly rushed the usually steady and reliable Ouimet off his feet. He went out in 34, increasing his lead to 7 up and ended the match on the twelfth green, not very dramatically. Evans' golf had left little or nothing to chance or for a climax.

The object lesson for Bobby in this tournament came in the second round. His match finished early, and the marshals gave him a pretty yellow flag and sent him out to help with the gallery following Chick Evans and Reginald Lewis. In spite of his front name, Mr. Lewis, the plaintiff in the case, caused Mr. Evans to look very much like a defendant for several highly critical lapses. He was playing strong and aggressive golf and on the thirty-sixth tee, stood 1 up and 1 to play. Lewis had fairly outplayed his opponent toward the finish and Chick must have feared being put out by a comparatively unknown kid from Greenwich. For once his perfect swing flickered and his drive was trapped. Reggie was straight down the fairway. Chick came out with a powerful iron punch, but the ball hit a tree and rebounded, lying in the edge of the fairway.

It all looked to be up with the great Chick, but his pitch played with superb nerve and judgment caught the bank to the left of the green and trickled down to within ten feet of the cup, a magnificent shot. Lewis was a trifle strong with his pitch shot, which ran over the green and half a dozen yards up a steep bank, but he got a fine running shot down the hillside, inside of Chick. It all hung on the putts and Chick never looked better than he did sinking that curling sidehill putt that hit the cup fairly and dropped. He staggered off the green and dropped to the turf. He was that close to disaster—the ultimate champion was dangling on the turn of a ten-foot putt. But he was still in the match when Lewis just failed to get down the winning shot.

Thus began the longest extra-hole match in the history of the U.S. Amateur Championship. On the extra holes, it was Chick who was inside every time and Reggie who made the desperate recoveries. On the fifth extra, Lewis finally exploded and Chick won.

I think it was in this match that Bobby began to feel that there might be a destiny that shapes the ends of golf. The professionals have a way of saying: "It was *his* tournament."

10.
Far Afield

In the spring of 1921, Bobby Jones, in a happy and excited frame of mind, set sail for Britain with a jolly party of American amateurs, to play in the British Amateur Championship at old Hoylake, and in the British Open at St. Andrews. It was the first really organized invasion of the British championships by American amateurs, and the informal team match played before the tournament and won by the Americans was the forerunner of the Walker Cup international matches now played biennially in alternate countries.

Up around Liverpool were plenty of new things to see, and not a few new things to learn about golf. At the Royal Liverpool course, which was astonishingly dry for that tournament, Bobby learned that they did not have a system of waterworks about the great British courses. They are called links when beside the sea on real "links land"; inland courses are not properly termed links. He also learned that the huge greens were dry and lightning fast or wet and slow at the pleasure of the elements. He learned that one must have a variety of golf, to cope with British conditions; the sweeping sea breeze bothered him no end; his beautiful, steep pitch shots bounded from the baked putting surfaces as if from cement; and he had not acquired the deft and useful run-up approach that is an absolute necessity in dry and windy weather. The visitors were so dismayed by the greens that, as a concession, several buckets of water were poured about the pin on some of the driest surfaces, so a ball might be eased up and stopped somewhere near the hole until the water was absorbed.

Bobby was the first to start in the first round, purely coincidental as in Britain the pairings and starting times are drawn impartially from a hat. Bobby remembered less about the match, which he won easily, than the way the old cab-horse's hooves clop-clopped along the pavement in the very early morning air, as he went out to Hoylake.

His next adversary was a Mr. Hamlet, and so far as Bobby could tell, he was not a melancholy Dane and he was not at all a good golfer—at any rate on this occasion, which happened to be good luck for Bobby. It may interest a good many well-informed golfers to know that Bobby won this match in a national championship with a score of 86, defeating the hapless Mr. Hamlet 1 up on the home green, Mr. Hamlet's score being 87. Bobby played well the next day against Robert Harris, one of the best British amateurs, and was defeated in the fourth round. So old Hoylake, where Bobby won the last of his three British Open Championships in 1930, taught him in 1921 that he really knew very little about playing golf in a wind; or getting the ball on the greens baked hard and glassy; or putting on such greens when he did get there. All in all he did pretty well to get as far as the fourth round before elimination.

After watching Willie Hunter win the British Amateur Championship, mentioned especially because he and Willie had a prime argument to settle at St. Louis before the year was out, Bobby journeyed over to the Auld Grey City of St. Andrews, there to play in the British Open Championship over the Old Course, as they call it, alongside the North Sea under the changing skies and the yet more variable breezes of Fife.

If, as the great and wise Maurice Maeterlinck has suggested, the present and the future really are co-existent, Bobby Jones should have stepped out reverently upon the silken turf of the most famous golf course in the world. He should have loved it at once—for he was to love it beyond all other courses. And certainly he should never have behaved as he did in the British Open of 1921; for there in the future, superimposed upon the smooth pastel of the eighteenth green, is the same Bobby Jones carried high on broad Scottish shoulders above a gallery of cheering, scrambling thousands—winner of the British Open championship with the lowest score yet recorded.

Bobby couldn't have enjoyed the faintest prevision of this glowing scene. For what he did on the occasion of his first visit to St. Andrews was to hate the course enthusiastically; use up 46 strokes on the first nine holes of his third round; start the inward journey with a ghastly 6 at the tenth—and pick up his ball, withdrawing from the competition. This is the only instance in Bobby's entire career of giving up play in a formal competition before he was eliminated or the competition was ended. Of course there is no stigma attached to the withdrawal of a competitor in a medal play event when he is playing against the field. Every major open championship has withdrawals of contestants off their game and scoring hopelessly. I think it is the only real regret of Bobby's golfing life that he didn't play out the string in that first venture at old St. Andrews. And this is the only major competition or golfing event of any importance in his entire career of which the record is not complete.

Yes, Bobby learned a lot from that first journey so far afield. He was playing with Jock Hutchison, the brilliant Scottish-American, born at St. Andrews, in the first round when Jock had an ace on the 142-yard eighth, and then smacked a huge drive, with a beautiful draw down a quartering wind, clear on to the ninth green, a wallop of 303 yards, the ball touching the rim of the cup and stopping three inches away for an eagle—so near it was to being two aces in succession!

And the last round that the "Hutch" did in this tournament will forever be ranked with the favored candidates when the traditional debates begin as to which was the greatest round of golf ever played. Jock was set like a piece of flint to win this tournament. And he shot some miraculous golf, and some terrible, and he came up to the last round just as Roger Wethered had finished, confronted with the terrific problem of doing a flat 70 on the par 73 course to tie. And that problem is the very toughest in all golf; to know what you have to do, a whole round in advance, especially when the mark is better than par. Jock did just that. He did a 70 where par is a solemn 73 with only two par 3 holes on it—perhaps the greatest round of golf in the history of open championships. And he won from Wethered next day in the playoff.

So Bobby learned something from Jock, and something from Wethered, and something from St. Andrews. A lot from St. Andrews. He did not, it must be confessed, learn to love St. Andrews then. But he learned to respect it. And that, we are told, is the best foundation for true love.

11.
Home Again—and to the Battlefront

The British excursion of 1921 completed one phase of Bobby Jones' experience in the Big Show. He had now played in all four of the championships that compose it. At the age of 19 years, he had competed in three United States Amateur Championships, one United States Open, one British Amateur, and one British Open. And the golfing year of 1921 was only half over. Before Bobby was nearly through telling the home folks about his visit to Britain, he was starting out again on the long trail: this time to the Columbia Country Club, Washington, for the U.S. Open.

This tournament was remarkable for two things. Long Jim Barnes won it by the widest margin of modern times—nine strokes ahead of the field; and for the first and last time, a qualifying test of a single 18-hole round was played. Thereafter, until the present system of sectional qualification was adopted, the contestants met at the field of battle and played a test of thirty-six holes, the best sixty and ties qualifying. This was the only time Bobby Jones ever was close to failure in the qualifying round of any important competition. He got in but with not a single stroke to spare.

The battle for the U.S. Open Championship at Columbia developed into a parade with Long Jim Barnes of the Pelham Country Club, New York, doing the parading. He started off with a 69 and was never headed. He played well—grandly. And it was his time to win. Year after year, the tall, quiet Cornishman had been knocking at the door, and his entrance was a popular one. He shot the best golf of the tournament, if not the steadiest. His total of 289 was only three strokes above the record, and he spread-eagled the field by nine strokes.

Seated in a box at the eighteenth green, as Long Jim came up to sink his last putt for a final round of 72, were President Harding, an ardent golfer, and Vice-President Coolidge. The cameramen were torn between conflicting emotions. They wanted to get Jim Barnes, sinking his last putt, and they wanted the President in the picture. It being ethically impossible for the President to descend to the green and make a background for Long Jim's putt, they moved the battery down to where they could shoot Jim sinking the putt, which he did very obligingly, and then they coaxed the new Open champion over to the President's box, and shot them shaking hands and smiling. I stood within three yards of the President and after a mild altercation with a Secret Service man, I made a very good picture of him myself.

In a pleasant and graceful little presentation talk, Mr. Warren Harding, president of the United States, and a confirmed golfer, presented the gold medal and the cup. He congratulated Barnes on his victory and commiserated with him on the sad 6 he had taken on the eleventh hole—asking him all about how it happened. Then Jock Hutchison was brought up and the president said he was proud of Jock for bringing the British Open championship to the United States, and thanked Barnes for keeping the United States cup from making another trip across the Atlantic.

And once more Bobby Jones dashed madly up the heights of golf and fell back repulsed. On the last day he began the most brilliant round of golf seen in the tournament. He was going at top speed. He never looked better. He was hitting with tremendous power and confidence. He looked set for a record round, which might even catch Barnes, if he should falter. Three 3s out of the first four holes. He laced out a fine long drive on the distant fifth, 560 yards. I knew just what happened then. Bobby was in high feather. He was feeling right. The ball was rolling for him. He was master of his game, and he lashed into that second shot with the full intention of getting it on the green, 275 yards away, or so close he could get another birdie. Hence the hellish hook which pulled out of bounds. Now he must make up the distance, so he put his back into another—and hooked out of bounds. In the face of this smashing upset that left his friends speechless, Bobby kept his temper and regained his better judgment. Not a flicker of anger did he show. He eased up on his next shot (it was his sixth), played straight down the middle of the fairway, pitched on in seven, and took two putts. The path of glory led but to a 77 and a tie for fifth place.

Bobby had used very bad judgment and had learned something from it. I firmly believe that this tournament at Columbia was the ultimate closing of one chapter in the development of this remarkable young golfer. Bobby gained final control of his temper. That is a blunt way to put it; but it is just as well to say it that way, by reason of the number of things that had been written about this failing in the past; too many comments I always have considered, and too severe. Bobby had got a name for club throwing, and as everybody knows, any kind of a reputation constitutes a colored lens through which the future performance of any celebrity is viewed. Did Bobby but toss his putter to a caddy after taking three putts, it was immediately said he was throwing his clubs again. Did he but pick up his ball and retire from the British championship and it was heralded afar that Bobby should be furnished with an indestructible scorecard for his next start. Infinitely less comment was made on the retirement of Abe Mitchell, a famous British professional, under the same circumstances at the Columbia tournament. And it gave me great pleasure that not one glimmer of annoyance marred Bobby's whole performance at Columbia. Bobby had control of his temper now. The critics would have to dig up something else to criticize.

And when you come right down to it, fifth place in the National Open Championship is not to be scorned. Four men ahead of him—Barnes, Freddie McLeod, and Walter Hagen tied for second place, and Evans, one stroke behind Jones; Alex Smith, another former open champion, tied with him at 303. And back of him a long line of the best golfers in the world: George Duncan, 1920 British Open Champion; Jock Hutchison, current British champion; and Joe Kirkwood, current Australian champion.

I rode back to the city that last day with Walter Hagen. Walter said: "Bobby was playing some great golf in spots. He's got everything he needs to win any championship, except experience; and maybe, philosophy. He's still a bit impetuous. But I'll tip you off to something—Bobby will win an open before he wins an amateur."

This was a prophecy.

Bobby Jones' swing.

12.

Old Glory and the Union Jack

Bobby Jones wanted very much to win the 25th Amateur Championship at the St. Louis Country Club. This was the fifth Amateur in which he had played, as well as three National Opens. He was now a veteran at the age of 19. It was time he won something that counted. He started blithely enough, qualifying in 151, seven strokes back of the medalist, Francis Ouimet; won his first two matches handily; and in the third round met Willie Hunter, British Amateur Champion. Willie had won earlier in the season at Hoylake, where Bobby had been the victim of a bewilderingly dry course and British breezes.

Old Glory and the Union Jack floated above the first tee as they drove off, and the fore caddies were armed with flags to mark their drives, Jones' caddy with Old Glory and Hunter's, as a pretty compliment, the Union Jack.

On the first eight holes of the morning round, Bobby shot exactly par figures, and on the long ninth got a birdie. He was out in 34, but was only 2 up on Hunter with 36. He was beating the little Englishman by 30 to 60 yards from the tee and was out in front on ten holes of the morning round and eight in the afternoon. Hunter was hanging on with true British tenacity and was still only 2 down at noon.

In the afternoon round par golf gave way to a fighting brand in which each alternately was good or bad, but fighting every inch of the way. The heat was terrific after a fairly cool morning and the gallery, growing like a snowball, was reasonably well controlled on a golf course where the American eagle screamed and the British lion roared. Still only 2 up at the twenty-sixth hole, Bobby had a brilliant idea. The hole was played from a very high tee on a hillcrest to a small green hidden behind tall trees in a sharp angle to the right, 347 yards.

In practice, Bobby had been experimenting with a long, towering drive straight over the trees toward the green, and several times had been on the putting surface for an easy birdie. It was an extremely perilous maneuver, as a deep, wide ditch guarded the green on the side toward the tee, and the ball had to go all the way in the air. Bobby knew that Hunter did not have the range for such a shot, and insensibly irked by the Englishman's persistence, he tried the big jump, a towering drive straight over the tallest tree in the angle. Caught at the peak of its flight by the topmost branch of the tree, the ball came down like a wounded bird into a ditch full of stones and underbrush. Jones gave the ball a mighty wallop and dislodged a shower of stones, called rocks south of the Mason and Dixon line, but no ball. He studied the situation and took another poke. Out came the ball straight on the green, and out also came a frightened brown rabbit, ears turned back, scuttling across the course and out of bounds. The gallery cheered and laughed. Bobby laughed merrily but Hunter contented himself with a wan smile. Bobby then took three putts, and naturally lost the hole. It was suggested that to the terms *eagle* and *birdie*, be added *rabbit*, meaning two strokes over par. Hunter also won the next hole, while Bobby was still reflecting on the mutability of fortune. The match was square and Bobby's play never regained its smooth mechanical precision.

On the long thirty-first, 545-yard, back-breaker and score-wrecker, Bobby went out in front again, in this grueling match of many changes, in which Jones had never been down and it looked as if he might be on his way, 1 up and five to play. On the short thirty-second, Hunter sank a 30-foot putt for a par, after neither drive had been on the green, and Bobby's putt had rimmed the cup. On the fatal thirty-third, Hunter out-drove Bobby for once and had a fine second just short of the green. Bobby's iron second, usually one of his strongest shots, broke off to the right, and only stayed in bounds by hitting a spectator in the dense line along the road. He played a good shot to the green from the rough and putted up within 18 inches of the hole. It was a fatal moment although we did not realize it for the time. Hunter on in three sank another long putt, this time ten feet. Bobby missed and there went the ball game for fair. Until this thirty-third hole, the little Briton had never been up and never more than 2 down. But now he was up to stay. Another long putt on the thirty-fourth for a par, and an uncanny pitch on the thirty-fifth a foot from the pin, and Bobby had been overhauled and beaten by the plugging little Englishman and his deadly putter.

No excuses and no alibis from Mr. Jones.

"I blew a short putt, and there went the match," he said simply.

Low moans of anguish from the gallery broke into a storm of applause for a well-earned victory by the lone invader. The British champion played like a champion, 72 in the afternoon round, and fought like a champion. Bobby started the morning round with a rush of golf that was enough to send any man out of the tournament with the smallest weakness in his game or any base metal in his fighting spirit.

That night I told Bobby he had lost the match on the twenty-sixth hole, when 2 up, he had taken a chance. His reply was: "I can play this game only one way. I must play every shot for all there is in it. I cannot play safe."

Bobby liked the old maxim: "When you get him 1 doon, get him 2 doon; when you get him 3 doon, get him 4 doon."

In this tournament, Bobby learned another theory of the game. At St. Louis, as on many another field, his bold, dashing play endeared him to galleries and critics alike. He was the D'Artagnan of golf, the fiery young cavalier ignoring his guard to drive home the finishing thrust. He was defeating many a worthy foe brilliantly, but he was not winning any championships. But he was beginning to learn and take deeply to heart, the wisdom of an older cavalier, who told him: "The best shot, Bobby, is not always the one to play."

Big Jess Guilford, the Siege Gun of Boston, brought the title back to the East, which had been without one since Francis Ouimet, also from Boston, won in 1914. Jess played against Bob Gardner as a champion should, winning 7–6. Jess' opening nine holes would have closed out anything human; four birdies in a row; one putt per green on four successive holes, putts of incredible lengths. On ten of the thirty holes played, he used only one putt. The putting he threw at the hapless Bob in the afternoon has probably never been equaled.

In the semifinal round, Guilford and Gardner were a sort of combination of Oliver Cromwell and the French Revolution. They took a couple of golf kings out and on the thirteenth and fourteenth greens respectively, chopped off the heads of those kings in a most emphatic manner. The notable regicides in the roll of victims were Chick Evans and Willie Hunter.

In all golfing history there has been no day in which more royal blood was shed, nor more rain fell upon the sodden multitudes. Thunder roared as the morning round got under way. Lightning sparkled against the drab sky at dazzling intervals, and over near the fifth green struck like a celestial snake, knocking over an inoffensive policeman and his friend who was holding an umbrella over him. Uninjured but badly jolted, the officer said he thought Jess Guilford had hit him with one of his gigantic drives.

The wildness of the day abated somewhat with the coming of the gray evening across the low, green hills, and against the weeping skies, the blood red Union Jack, defiant to the last, went down before Old Glory and the new champion would be an American.

13.
The Last of the Lean Years

When the season of 1922—the last of the lean years—opened, the curtain rose on a scene in an Atlanta hospital. Bobby Jones, tired of the painful annoyance of sundry patches of swollen veins in his legs, which had given him much pain for several years, went for an operation less than a month before the tournament program opened for him with the Southern Championship at East Lake. Bobby was an extremely busy young man at this time. He was graduating from the Georgia School of Technology, and planning to enter Harvard in the fall in quest of a Bachelor of Science degree. In all probability he would not have entered the southern tournament, even at his home club, had it not been for the George W. Adair Trophy, put in play for the first time. This great silver trophy had been given by the Atlanta golfers in memory of George Adair, a great gentleman and a great sportsman, who had done incalculable service for golf in Atlanta and in the south, and had encouraged Bobby's career from the beginning. Bobby wanted very much to have his name on this trophy dedicated to his dear friend.

His practice for the tournament consisted of four hours, spread over suitable intervals, and one excursion of nine holes. If this unusual preliminary training was responsible for what happened in the tournament, we could think of a number of other events where an operation and a hospital sojourn would have been beneficial. He went on to win the championship without being threatened in a single round and his name was the first to go on the trophy. Bobby never played in the Southern Championship again, but the next year at Birmingham, Perry Adair won; and through the golfing generations to come, side by side, will stand the names of the two young golfers that George Adair loved best.

"There are more things in heaven and earth, Horatio, than are dreamed of in your philosophy." Perhaps so. Perhaps no. But there was something back in the hot summer of 1923 at the Roebuck Country Club of Birmingham, which will forever give me a long, long pause, when the skeptics insist that every result beneath the sun is due to a direct material cause. Perry had gone to the final round, battling for his life in every match. His iron nerve and his deadly putter had saved him, taking up the slack of a long game, which was never of great range. Frank Godchaux had also reached the final round and he was one of the longest wallopers in the game of that era; a powerful chap who had played football at Vanderbilt and was playing spectacular and brilliant golf in this tournament. This was the one round in Perry's life when inspired golf would count the most. He was devoting more and more time to his family and to business and would not be playing serious golf very much longer.

Godchaux went out in front at once, and at the eighteenth tee he was 4 up. Perry won the eighteenth hole, but the little gamecock from Druid Hills was 3 down and seemed hopelessly beaten. What happened in the second round that afternoon is outside of and beyond golf. I will merely say this—par on that long first nine at Roebuck was 37, and little Perry was out in 33. From a position of 3 down he proceeded in 12 holes to go to a position of 6 up, and to win on the next green, 6–5. I will always think that some supernal hand touched the blond head of Perry Adair. Such miracle golf is shot only once in a lifetime. And Perry was fighting not alone for the championship but that his name should be graven on the cup dedicated to his illustrious father.

At the dinner at Druid Hills, honoring Perry, I told the story of another dinner in that lofty hall, this time for the Georgia Tech football team. George Adair was speaking for the moment of Buck Flowers, a member of the varsity team who was a great football player but very light. That season Buck had tackled a giant speed man of the opposition and had been taken from the game with a fractured arm. George told of a man who fancied game chickens, especially the strain from a certain Blue Hen, and more than all of the others, the smallest and gamest, the Blue Hen's Little Baby. In the little battler's first fight, he had been terribly gaffed, and the handler of the other bird advised that he be taken out. He was apparently beaten.

"Take him out! Never!" was the reply. "That bird is never beaten. That is the Blue Hen's Little Baby."

George Adair, who idealized courage, said an order should be formed, the "Order of the Blue Hen's Little Baby," and that Buck Flowers should be the first member. And at Perry's dinner, I asked to name another member for the mythical Order of the Blue Hen's Little Baby—Perry Adair, champion by virtue of as bright a flash of golf and of golfing courage as ever gilded a championship crown; and whose name added luster to the silver trophy.

A few weeks later Bobby, Stewart Maiden and I set out for the U.S. Open Championship at the Skokie Country Club outside of Chicago. On the train Bobby was plugging away at Cicero's *Orations Against Cataline*, getting ready for Harvard. Once he said: "This bird Cicero was a long way from hating himself. I wish I could think as much of my golf as he did of his statesmanship. I might do better in these blamed tournaments."

At Skokie, it was little Gene Sarazen, who finished one stroke in front of him and won the 26th National Open Championship, with a score of 288, two strokes back of the record 286 shot by Chick Evans in 1916.

Bobby's game was right at Skokie. He shot the first three rounds in 74-72-70, and going into the last round was tied with Wild Bill Mehlhorn with 216. John Black, a California Scot, a grandfather and one of the finest shot-makers who ever came out of Caledonia, after leading at the halfway mark, had slipped to a 75, and a total of 217. Hagen, who had just returned from winning the British Open Championship, was 219, and Gene Sarazen, four strokes back of the leaders, seemed pretty well out of it. Bobby felt sure that he could do a 68 in the afternoon to bring his score down symmetrically. And that, he was warrantably certain, would be good enough to win. It was. But it was Gene Sarazen who shot the 68. A 68—that meant 288. Gene finished early and his score went on the board just as Bobby was turning with a 36 out. That meant that Jones must hit a 35 on the last nine, one under par, to beat Gene. He was hitting his shots marvelously well, but a 35 on that long side of Skokie, with two mean finishing holes, was not an assignment over which to give three rousing cheers.

This is where the iron certitude of medal competition bears down. You know what you have to do in that last round. It is not one man whom you can see, and who may make a mistake at any moment, with whom you are battling. It is an iron score, something already in the book. Bobby lost a stroke at the tenth where he needed so desperately to pick up one, and then another at the twelfth by pitching over the green. Stewart Maiden and I looked at each other under the long moaning sigh that the gallery exudes on such occasions. Bobby was working as hard as he had ever worked in his life, and as I was trudging dejectedly down the fairway, someone came up behind me and said: "Don't let your chin drag. It is not as bad as all that."

And there was Bobby, grinning bravely, and I did my best to grin back. His face was gray and sunken and his eyes looked an inch deep in his head.

The 17th hole of the afternoon round, the 35th of the match, ruined Bobby, as it stopped John Black, and as it stopped Walter Hagen, the lion-hearted. That tragic link had much to be blamed for in that tournament; a grim tableland in a desert of trouble, on which hope after hope went down. A slightly elbowed two-shotter on which a big, bold drive straight over a towering mound and bunker would be rewarded by a simple shot to the green. Bobby needed 4–4 to tie Gene as he stood on the seventeenth tee and par on these holes were 4–5. As always Bobby went for the bold shot and brought it off perfectly, the ball carried well over the bunker and disappeared as if on a ruled line toward the green. It was one of those fatalistic shots where luck plays you false, and the ball wound up in a sort of dim roadway under a tree. That was the break. A 5 there left him with an eagle 3 on the last hole to tie. He went for it fearlessly, ending in a tie for second place with John Black, who, apparently headed for glory with a 33 on the first nine, found ruin on the miserable seventeenth as Bobby had.

In this championship, the old guard went down before the rush of youngsters and the gallant veteran from the Golden State. Hagen, Barnes, Hutchison, Duncan, names to conjure with; only Hagen finished in the first five. The rest were trailing far behind. It was in this championship, too, that Bobby Jones forged definitely to the front among the amateur contestants in open competitions. Chick Evans, who nosed him out by a stroke at Inverness and again at Columbia, was 13 strokes behind at Skokie; Jess Guilford, National Amateur Champion, 13 strokes behind; and Willie Hunter, 17. No amateur ever finished ahead of Bobby again in any open competition.

Bobby was also moving up slowly in the open championships. In 1920, he was in eighth place; in 1921, fifth, and now he was in second. But there is a lot of difference between second place and a championship. This championship quest was getting a bit thick. And we all felt tired and discouraged as we rode back to Atlanta. In every open championship there would be more than 300 entered. And of these, maybe two or three, or even half a dozen, would be shooting at top form. And there was only one of Bobby. If he wasn't at top form, he was out of luck; and if he were at top form, there were also others at top form, and the breaks would settle it.

The new champion had made his debut in the Big Time at Toledo in 1920, at the same time Bobby made his, and they were the same age. Gene, an Italian ex-caddy, was a remarkable young golfer; chunky, 5'5" tall, bold, and tremendously confident. He played a fine game, supported by good nerves and determination, and showed clearly the masterful golfer he was to become, for many long and successful years.

Another view of the East Lake Golf Club.

14.
A Miracle Round—Not Bobby's

Of all the journeys home after golfing pilgrimages, the dreariest one was the long journey back to Atlanta from Boston in September, 1922. Oddly enough it was the last homeward journey from defeat in the last of the seven lean years, in which Bobby Jones had played in 10 major championships without a victory. The next time he started back to Atlanta from a tournament in the Big Show he would be bringing a large gold medal and an old silver cup, emblematic of the Open Championship of the United States. But of course Bobby didn't know this when he boarded the train at Boston. What he did know was that in his fifth start in the National Amateur Championship, Jess Sweetser had given him the most decisive beating of his career.

With all his indubitable talent for catching golfers at the very top of their game and being stopped in a national championship, Bobby had never caught one like Jess before; I doubt if there ever was another like Jess. As long as it has to be told, we will get it over with. Bobby Jones turned 6 down in the first nine holes, something I never saw before, something I had never expected to see at all, and certainly would never see again. And right here Bobby started an achievement in golf that is unmatched. Six down to an opponent who was a stroke better than par, his own game not going well, and the breaks black against him. Bobby set his jaw and started out to do the impossible—to catch up with par in 27 holes and be 6 up on him. And he shot the next nine holes two strokes under par. Seven holes he shot in par figures and two birdies—and he gained back one single hole. The next seven holes were halved, five in par figures and two in birdies. Hole by hole Jess Sweetser stepped with him for seven mortal holes and an eternity in strain until the seventeenth, where, showing the first and only symptom of strain, he took three putts. Jones had traveled 16 holes before winning one. The rest is briefly told but not easily. Bobby went out in the afternoon to break Jess if he could, but all Jess did was to step 11 holes in par figures for every hole. In short, Bobby rammed his bloody but unbowed blond head against the brick wall that had risen across the fairway in every major championship in which he had played; and this time it was Jess Sweetser playing in an unbeatable style.

Jess was the youngest amateur champion of modern times, a month younger than Bobby Jones. Francis Ouimet was 21 when he won the National Amateur in 1914, after winning the National Open the year before. I think Jerry Travers was younger than either of them but that was long ago. Jess Sweetser of New York and the Siwanoy Club, and Yale University, where he was their star golfer in his collegiate days, blond, handsome, and cocky, was the most complete amateur champion ever crowned. He won through the greatest field ever assembled by defeating the stoutest opponents that could be expected to oppose him. And to realize what a worthy champion he really was, take a look at what he was called on to beat in the order named: H. E. Kenworthy, 10–9; Willie Hunter, 11–9; Jess Guilford, 4–3; Bobby Jones, 8–7; and Chick Evans, 3–2. Any golfer who could beat these last four on successive days over the 36-hole route deserves to be a champion.

My old eyes were hopelessly dazzled by his brilliance. He won by playing better golf than anybody else in the tournament or possibly better than any amateur had ever played. He had smashed more course records that year than any other amateur ever had, and he added that of Brookline to his string with the 69 he shot against Bobby in the morning round. Deadly ability to keep the line in pitching was Jess' strongest point at Brookline. The course suited his game exactly, half the holes were of the drive-and-pitch variety, and Jess' pitches were so amazingly accurate that he was hitting the flagstaff frequently. In all, Sweetser was credited or charged, according to how you see it, with holing six shots from off the green, during the week; the longest of which was against Jones early in their match. He was consistently inside of Jones and Evans, who were by no means the two golfers one ordinarily would pick out to beat on the greens.

Sweetser's favorite pitching club was a heavy, ample mashie-niblick on the spade pattern for short and steep pitching. He pitched from all sorts of distances and places, including an occasional though infrequent trap and patches of rough. I never did get the complete story of the two miracle shots Sweetser uncorked against Willie Hunter in the first few holes of their match. Jess is a reticent chap as to his own achievements, and Willie was still speechless at the end of the round.

"He holed one from the rough and another from a trap," said Willie, manifestly aggrieved.

"What can you do against that sort of thing?"

Jess was also accounted a remarkable "stymieist." He laid Jones three, the last one on the sixth green of the matinee round, giving the

Atlanta boy the chance to win undying fame with the large gallery that was following them. Jones' ball was about 15 inches from the cup and Sweetser's putt left his an inch from the cup, each lying three. The stymie was mathematically perfect. Jones sighted it closely and then exchanged his putter for a mashie-niblick. He electrified the crowd by playing the shot with the beautiful accuracy displayed by Joe Kirkwood in his trick exhibitions. The ball, crisply struck, jumped over the intervening ball and landed plump in the cup. This probably was the prettiest stroke of the tournament although it had no bearing on the general result.

And I shall always believe that the Jones-Sweetser match was settled on the second hole of the morning round. After a half on the first hole, Jones slightly outhit Sweetser on the second hole, the balls being in about equal position. Sweetser, 80 yards from the pin, played his favorite mashie-niblick. It pitched just right. It ran just right. It dropped into the cup for an eagle 2. The roar of applause had hardly died away, when Jones, his nerves like chilled steel in spite of the jolt, played his pitch and run.

It pitched just right.

It ran just right.

But it stopped ten inches from the cup.

And there was another roar of applause for a great effort and a birdie 3 that was not good enough to cope with the birdie's daddy, the old Eagle himself. Now I shall never be able to settle which was the greater shot. It is a great thing to play a perfect shot that drops for an eagle from many yards away. And it is a very great thing to play a shot after such a shot that wants less than a foot of the reward of the first. They were two great shots and I never hope to see their like again.

When Bobby came back from the long eleventh hole, where the match ended, I saw something that made my eyes sting. The gallery had gone chasing off after the victor, as galleries have done since time immemorial. All but 30 little boys, caddies at the Brookline club. They were trooping along with Bobby as they always did wherever he played and whether he won or lost; some of them squabbling over which should carry his clubs.

And one more champion lost his chance to make it two in a row when Sweetser defeated Jess Guilford. Guilford, who had won by his putter the year before at St. Louis, lost by it at Brookline. Guilford told me that Jess had laid him 11 stymies in all, either complete, or partial, so he had to putt wide. It should be borne in mind when getting excited about the crime of the stymie, that it usually is the man who is playing the best golf up to the green that lays the stymies. And it is a fact that Sweetser was consistently inside all his opponents. Had he been as consistently on the outside after reaching the green, he might well have been as greatly stymied against.

And these stymies were repaid with interest the next year at Flossmoor.

In the final round, Chick Evans, the coolest, craftiest amateur in golf, nine times a semifinalist in the National Amateur Championship, and twice a winner, went behind at the first hole and never was square but once, pulling level at the tenth hole of the morning round with a fine birdie only to fall away at the terrible eleventh with a wretched six. Three down at luncheon, the play was exactly even in the afternoon, Jess just retaining his lead of the morning. Sweetser's golf was utterly destructive.

When Bobby went up to congratulate Sweetser on his victory, Jess said a very kind thing.

"Thank you, Bobby, I beat the best man in the field yesterday."

But it hurt Bobby. The thorn was beginning to rankle in earnest. There was that increasing insistence—a great golfer but it was time he won something. What was the matter? Was he a great golfer? He could hit the shots well; everybody knew that. But was he one of those hapless mechanical excellencies known as a great shot-maker, who cannot connect the great shots in sufficient numbers to win? Nothing seemed any use. Big Bob and I agreed thoroughly on that on the way home in the gloom of the Pullman.

Shortly after we got home, Bobby was playing at East Lake with his father and two friends. On this waning September day, the patron saint of golf, St. Andrew, took a good look at Bobby as he started out, and he said, said the good saint:

"Bobby, this is your day."

The course record at East Lake had been set by Bobby at 66. Four times he had equaled it but he never could break it.

And as night drew round about the match, Bobby stood on the last tee with a par 3 to make a 63. A 63. Nine under fours. Nine over threes, if you prefer to put it that way. A miracle round. It was Bobby's day. St Andrew was right. And so was Bobby. And I think the good old saint himself must have smiled, as he rarely had smiled before, as the youngster with the tousled hair above his steady young face tapped the ball into the cup. Here is the card with par:

Par (out): 434 553 435—36
Jones: 324 443 434—31
Par (in): 434 455 443—36—72
Jones: 433 454 333—32—63

Nine birdies. Nine holes in par. Not an eagle. Not a bogey. A little pitch, a bit too strong on the fourteenth, costing his only five of the round. On this long and difficult 6,700-yard course, the toughest in the Southland, he shot the lowest score he had ever made on a full-sized course. And it remained to the end of his career the lowest score he ever shot.

All Bobby said was:

"The place for that round was at Brookline—or Skokie."

A few days later, Bobby entered Harvard in quest of a B.S. degree and his golf was over for the last of the lean years.

Perhaps it would have been just as well not to let Jess Sweetser know that he was going to Harvard that fall. This might have excited Jess' Yale spirit to a marked degree. Chick Evans was more diplomatic. Playing Rudy Knepper, the slashing, brilliant youngster of Sioux City and Princeton, Chick donned an orange and black necktie, and naturally Rudy couldn't be awfully rude to anyone wearing his colors.

Bobby Jones the lawyer.

15.
The Long Lane Turns

The premier golfer of the South, and indeed of the country for the nonce, Robert Tyre Jones Jr. returned to Atlanta in February 1923 from Harvard University having finished his B.S. course there, and acquired his degree, along with a Harvard sweater with a large "H" thereon, voted him by the Athletic Council, despite the fact that he was not permitted to play golf for Harvard inasmuch as he had previously played for Georgia Tech.

He was placed at the top of the athletic role of honor, only four other names appearing on this distinguished list, all the others being three-letter men.

On March 1, Bobby entered the office of the Adair Realty Company of Atlanta, where he found his old partner of the links, Perry

Adair, ready to stand gallantly beside him while he studied the new business with his customary patience and intelligence, as he started out on his business career.

And in June, Bobby and I once more set out for the National Open.

They said Bobby Jones could not win because he didn't have the punch. They said he was the greatest golfer in the world but he lacked the punch. We had heard it a thousand times, but we never had to hear it again. One stroke settled that little matter for ever and ever. At the same time it settled the crown of the United States Open Golf Championship on Bobby's blond head. On the evening of July 16, 1923, Bobby sat on top of the world at the Inwood Country Club on Long Island, as the sun sank into Jamaica Bay, off the marshy coast of Far Rockaway. And it was one punch that did it—the greatest punch ever seen in a golf championship. Out of the rough, a full iron bang of 190 yards to six feet past the pin, with the score a tie, and the last hole guarded by water on two sides, traps and bounds on the other. That was the punch. And it settled the championship, and the most spectacular playoff of a tie yet seen in the United States.

I thought that would be the easiest story I had ever written. But it seemed an impossible story to write. I did not know just what to say. Bobby himself had little to say.

"I don't care what happens now, ever," he said as he sat on the steps of the Inwood clubhouse, waiting for the presentation of the trophy of the Open Championship, and the gold medal that only four amateurs had won: Francis Ouimet, Jerry Travers, Chick Evans, and Bobby himself. Bobby did not need to care what happened. I knew what he meant when he said it.

"The greatest golfer in the world," they had been saying, "but he can't win."

From the fastest field ever assembled on the hardest course over which the championship had been played, Bobby Jones broke through;

tied for first place, and then beat game little Bobby Cruickshank in the playoff, as conclusive a victory as could have been arranged. And Bobby Jones beat more than Bobby Cruickshank at Inwood. He was good enough to win any of the four championships in which he had played. He was good enough to win this one. But he was playing against something besides famous professionals and amateurs, and narrow fairways and terrible traps. He was playing against a grim fate that in every start had ridden him and crushed him to the turf in tournament after tournament when it seemed his time had come.

When little Bobby Cruickshank, as courageous a little golfer as ever stepped on a golf course, finished the seventy-second hole of the tournament with a birdie 3, when it was a 100-to-1 shot that he could not do it, and shot himself into a tie with Bobby, my hat came off to Cruickshank, and my heart caved in before the inevitable tramp of fate. I am as certain as possible that no other golfer but Bobby Jones, the greatest and unluckiest golfer who ever lived, would have been caught by a finish like that of Cruickshank. It was the tramp of fate on the hollow floor of the halls of doom. Bobby had finished eighth at Inverness. He had finished second at Skokie. There was only one place left—and that was first place—and when he reached it, there was Bobby Cruickshank with him, on the wings of a miracle 3 on a long and perilous two-shot hole.

The gods of golf used all they had to keep Bobby Jones from winning. Three times they managed it, and it had also taken a miracle round at Skokie to bar the door the year before. This time Bobby stood up under a smash of fate that would have sent a weaker man into the discard, and he met the gods of golf at their own game and defeated them. I shall never feel that it was Bobby Cruickshank that Bobby beat in that last round. It was fate itself. And it takes more than a great golfer to do that.

And now that he had won I could say things that had been locked up in my heart for four long years. I could not say them before. They would have been misunderstood as alibis by those who did not know Bobby as I knew the boy. And one of the things I had wanted to say was this: all those years he had been the victim of too keen a mind and too fine an imagination. It was never his heart that was at fault. In his breast beat the heart of a lion. And the world knew it now. But to me, Bobby Jones was no greater on that day than he was the day before, or than he was last year. He had showed the world—that was all. And so long as the records of golfing champions endure, the world will never forget.

And now it is time to write something of how it happened.

Bobby Jones, his greatest chance just ahead, was three strokes in front of the field as he started his last round Saturday afternoon. He went out in 39, nicked a birdie 3 at the tenth hole with a six-yard putt, and began a tremendous run of pars and birdies that carried him through the dangerous fifteenth hole two under par, leaving him 4-4-4 to finish with 72, and shut off all chance of being caught at the wire. Not once had he taken over twelve strokes on these holes and I fancy this circumstance let down the tension under which he was playing. He swung his iron second out of bounds on the sixteenth, and finished 5-5-6, with a card of 76, and a total score of 296, leaving the door wide open for the one pursuer who might be going at a par clip.

"I'm afraid I finished too badly," said Bobby, as he walked off the green, "I had a great chance to shut the door, and I left it open."

And once more, just as at Skokie the year before, a fast-flying contender started up from behind, and for a time it looked as if Bobby Cruickshank would breeze in. I told Bobby I felt sure none of the others could shoot the golf needed to catch him, but back in my mind was the recollection of this same Bobby Cruickshank in the St. Joseph tournament in 1921, when with eight holes to play, Hutchison had a lead of nine strokes over him, Barnes a lead of eight, and he caught both of them in a triple tie and beat them in the playoff.

I set out to find Cruickshank and Hagen and to learn the worst or whatever it was. It was none too good. The little Scot was coming with a rush. At the turn he was a stroke under par, and at the twelfth hole, he had a margin of two strokes to waste on par and still win. This was serious. He looked fearfully like a winner. The breeze that had started to blow an hour before had moderated; the sky was bright; and I was good and sick and utterly empty. I had passed up breakfast and luncheon and was rattling like a gourd. Also my feet hurt. If there was any less happy person in the world than I, he inevitably was looking for a red barn with a rope over his arm.

But the strain was taking its toll from the wee Scot too, and he cracked on the thirteenth, again on the fifteenth, and blew wide open with a six on the sixteenth, leaving himself a 4 and 3 to tie Jones on holes measuring 405 and 425. I felt as if the burden of the world had rolled off my shoulders. I walked to the clubhouse, dead tired all of a sudden, and went up to Bobby's room. Ouimet and several others were already there congratulating Bobby. I asked Ouimet if he thought Bobby was safe.

"Absolutely," said he. "No man on earth could play those two holes in seven shots under these circumstances. Bobby has earned at last what he has been deserving a long time."

And then came a U.S. Golf Association official and told Bobby to get ready to come down and be presented with the cup.

"Not me," said Bobby ungrammatically, but emphatically, "I'll wait until the last putt is down."

Bobby Cruickshank had broken under the cumulative strain and had fairly collapsed on the sixteenth. And yet—and yet—I decided to go down and watch the finish. I heard Cruickshank had his par 4 at the seventeenth. They had already driven from the eighteenth and Cruickshank was preparing to play his second shot. He used a mid-iron as they were called in those days, and it came on a ruled line, splitting the pin all the way, hit 20 feet short of the cup, and stopped 6 feet from it. The cheer of the gallery crashed out like artillery. Bobby Cruickshank had a chance. The 100-to-1 shot had dwindled to an even bet. I knew

Cruickshank was going to sink that putt. I saw it going into the cup before he hit it—and after it, too. And then came the roar for as gallant a finish as ever was made in a golf championship, and Bobby Cruickshank deserved it.

So the two Bobbies were tied, the first tie between a professional and an amateur since the famous triple tie in 1913 between Francis Ouimet, Harry Vardon, and Edward Ray. Each had broken in the last few holes and tossed the title away, only to get an even grip on it again, when the grinning gods of golf, for their own delectation, ordained a dogfall.

Saturday was a day of fasting and prayer and blasphemy, and I told the Reverend Plato Durham of Atlanta that very thing, and he understood and never even shook his head in reproof.

Bobby Jones and his father, Colonel Robert P. Jones.

16.
Champion

After that horrendous Saturday, when Bobby Jones dragged his sagging frame from the last green, and I went out to watch Cruickshank make his bid, it was hard to tell which was the greatest ordeal, watching Bobby in the last round, or watching Cruickshank catch him, or watching the duel Sunday with a raving mob of 8,000 insane golf fans.

Francis Ouimet had Bobby in charge and Sunday morning he reported that Bobby had slept well, but when I saw him my heart sank, stopped for a second. The boy's face was drawn and pinched and his eyes were far back in his head, and introspective, with the look of a chess player exerting all the powers of his mind. He said he was feeling all right, but he always said that.

I was not feeling all right nor anywhere near it. I was sick with a nervousness that had my stomach gripped in a vise. I could not sit still and my legs shook when I tried to walk. I got Francis Ouimet and Francis Powers and Sol Metzger and suggested that we go out on the links somewhere and sing or something. We sat on the bank by the third green and we talked a little and tried singing, but it wasn't much of a go. It was silly, of course. But there was an utterly indescribable tension in the close air; the sky was overcast. I could not get it out of my mind that fate was closing in. I felt numb and idiotic. My thoughts were in a curious jumble and in my head a line from one of Kipling's poems kept repeating itself, over and over and over.

" 'I'm dreading what I've got to watch,' the color sergeant said."

Over and over again. The reiteration was maddening. It is impossible in cold type to depict the strain and tension of that round. Nothing could exaggerate its importance to either player. To Cruickshank it meant a fortune. To Jones, something dearer still—he must clear himself to his own rigid satisfaction of the memory of how he had left the door open when he could have closed it, for Bobby is the last golfer in the world to deceive himself as to how he lost or won a match or a championship. If Cruickshank had not made that wonderful birdie 3, and Bobby had been left champion, it would have been less winning the title than Cruickshank losing it. So the game young Georgian set himself for a battle that he welcomed as a chance to get square with his own severest critic—himself. I knew better than anybody else what that round meant to Bobby. Maybe I knew better than Bobby.

It seemed that 2:00 would never come. The gallery began to assemble early and got thicker and thicker. Anything might happen. The general opinion was that the strain promptly would prove too great for one or the other; that one would blow early; that the round would be a parade. Yet—under the fiercest strain that can be laid on any competitive athlete, both golfers were so far from blowing that they stepped the first nine holes in exactly par. It was the first time that Jones had gone out in par since the tournament started. It was Bobby Ding and Bobby Dong all the way around, and the gallery nearly expired with hysterics as Jones closed with the flying Scot and passed him, going two strokes in front with a birdie 2 at the twelfth that was within inches of a hole-in-one. Losing them back to brilliant play on the fourteenth, where Cruickshank nearly holed an eagle 3, and at the fifteenth. Jones gained a stroke lead again at the sixteenth and lost it at the seventeenth, where Cruickshank made another grand recovery, and was down in one and they were all square again.

All square just as they had stood on the first tee nearly three interminable hours ago—the two young gladiators stood on the last tee of the playoff, and the fairway, 425 yards to the home green, was banked with an enormous gallery, and around the green was a mass of humanity, a blur in the distance.

It was Cruickshank's honor and he missed his tee shot for the first time since the tournament began, and a low, half-topped hook went shooting through the rough to a roadway so far from the water hazard in front of the green that there was no chance to carry it or even to reach it from where the ball lay.

It looked as if fate had voted for Jones—for once.

But his own drive, evidently hit with flagging muscles, wheeled off a bit to the right and stopped in the rough, at least 190 yards from the pin, and a water jump in between. The decision was up to Bobby. From a somewhat dangerous location he could play safe with Cruickshank and try to out-pitch him or out-putt him, with the most probable result a drawn round and another play-off. Or he could go for the green, risking the championship on one bold shot, almost certain to win if the shot came off, perfectly certain to lose if the ball found the water. It was a terrible gamble, the question of a championship, the question of a life-time ambition. What would he do? Play it safe or go for it?

If there was the least hesitation in the mind of the boy from Dixie, his actions did not betray it. He took one look at the ball, drew an iron and without a single flicker of hesitation or uncertainty, he spanked it out against the sky as perfectly hit and as bold a shot as ever came off a golf club. From the gallery came a rustle and a murmur and a cheer, and then one crushing roar. For the ball, climbing up the pathway of its own backspin, hovered over the big water hazard over the green and dropped and curled up six feet from the pin.

I knew at last the long, long lane had turned; that the quest for the golden fleece was over, and that the gallantest young Argonaut of them all had come into his own.

Bobby Cruickshank did his best. His pitch found a trap. His fourth shot was far over the pin and when he putted and missed, that great little sportsman walked over to Bobby and held out his hand. There was an odd solemnity on Bobby's face back of the smile it wore.

It was all over.

Bobby Jones had come through.

And the man he had defeated had this to say:"Bobby Jones is the greatest of them all. Man! It was a bonnie shot. There never was such a golfer, and I'm proud to have stepped so close to him. He is now what Harry Vardon was at his very best—the greatest golfer in the world."

It was a grand and glorious feeling coming home with the championship, especially since it was the first time it had ever come to the South. And the cup looked mighty good sitting up in a corner of the drawing room. Bobby had brought home many cups and bronze medals, and silver medals, and honor and esteem and love and affection. But this time it was THE CUP. Every now and then I would catch Bobby cutting his eyes around at it and a grin spreading itself over his face, which hadn't been smiling much in the last ten days. And every now and then I would surprise Stewart Maiden—Kiltie, the King Maker—taking a peep at the cup, and, while Kiltie wouldn't exactly loosen up enough for a smile, he wore an expression similar to a cat that had just swallowed a pet canary.

"Kiltie," I said, "what were you thinking when Bobby stood up to make that iron shot out of the rough that meant victory or defeat?"

"I didn't think," said Stewart.

"Well," I insisted, "why did you bust your new straw hat over Bobby's caddy's head when the ball hit the green?"

"How the - - - - should I know."

Stewart's contributions to the conversation were not numerous but emphatic.

And then that beautiful, roaring reception at Brookwood station.

Nobody there will ever forget it. It was Atlanta taking Bobby Jones straight to her heart, almost as Bobby's mother took him to her heart as he jumped off the train, and as his father Big Bob embraced the boy who had so honored the fighting blood of all the Joneses from John Paul Jones down to date. And by their side stood Mary Malone, Bobby's boyhood sweetheart, and his future wife. Bobby hesitated just a second and then he kissed her too.

And there were speeches and smiles and laughter and more than a few tears the next week as this man and that spoke at the great banquet at the East Lake Club. And Bobby himself, when they gave him a wonderful silver service as a token of the club's appreciation for the honor he had done it— Bobby, in his little speech of acknowledgment, came out in one line that rang like a deep silver bell with the sincerity he put into it. "You gentlemen have said some beautiful things about me and what I've been fortunate enough to do. But one thing they all have absolutely wrong. They spoke of my honoring the Atlanta Athletic Club. No man can honor a club like this. The honor lies in belonging to it. I am prouder of being a member of this club than I could be of winning all the championships there are."

And Big Bob said much the same thing: "It wasn't all for the boy that I dreamed this dream and had this vision years ago when he was trotting about this golf course. It wasn't all for the boy, and certainly it wasn't all for me. Some way it is, and always has been, inseparably mingled with this dear old club, forever in my heart."

17.

Flossmoor

Everything proceeded as usual at the 27th National Amateur
Championship at the Flossmoor Country Club, outside of Chicago.
Bobby Jones ran up against a brace of miracle rounds on the third day
and bounced back and out. The tournament thus far was entirely conventional.

Max Marston's march to the championship after 12 years of
unavailing struggle had all the hallmarks of a predestined victory. He
reached this position over the prostrate forms of three of the greatest
golfers in the world; Bobby Jones, Open Champion; Francis Ouimet,
who had won both the open and amateur titles; and capped the climax
by beating Jess Sweetser, defending champion, in an unparalleled final
round that went to the thirty-eighth green. It was a great record, greater
if anything than Sweetser made at Brookline the year before in beating
Willie Hunter, Jess Guilford, Jones, and Evans. It was a big year for
Marston, 31 years old, after years of thwarted endeavor, mixed with
spasms of champion busting. He shot some magnificent golf and some
ragged golf, but he always matched his opponent and a bit more. And
that is the answer in match play. He never had a bad round against a
good one.

So Bobby passed out of the championship rather earlier than usual, but at the instigation of another of those inspired golfers, who went perfectly mad at the very name of Jones, and shot their heads completely off. To the list that included S. Davidson Herron, Willie Hunter, and Jess Sweetser, we now add the name of Max Marston. Sweetser was only two under par to beat him at Brookline. Marston was four under at Flossmoor. The performance apparently was progressive.

For a little while in the morning round I was foolish enough to fancy the jinx had been busted. Even when Marston with a brace of birdies took back two of the four holes he had lost and went into luncheon only 2 down. I felt that Bobby had at least an even chance. But no. All Bobby had done was to shoot a round of 70 on a par 74 course and all he got by it was 2 up. Still, 2 up was 2 up. At least it was 2 up until Max began running off birdies in the afternoon. The match broke on the sixth, seventh, and eighth holes, where Max fired 3-2-3 at Bobby, all birdies, and suddenly Jones was 2 down and was beaten, 2-1, just as Max had stopped the great Jerry Travers at Detroit in 1915 with a run of five birdies, two more than he had against Jones, when Travers was grimly trying for the double crown.

In the playoff for the qualifying medal, for which Bobby and Chick Evans had tied at 147, Bobby shot a delectable 72, two strokes under the somewhat liberal par of 74, to win by four strokes. This brought on the reflection that if Bobby Jones ever was to win a national amateur championship, we would just have to call it medal play and start the lad out playing the card instead of his opponent. When Bobby was playing the card, his concentration rarely wavered. He had a grim and implacable opponent before his eyes, and as has been suggested, Old Man Par makes no mistakes. He never gets down in one putt and he never takes three. Human opponents make their own mistakes and they seemed to influence Bobby.

And lest I was so pestered by mosquitoes and other things as not to do Max justice, permit me to say that beginning after a bad sixth hole in the morning round, Max shot the next 30 holes to the end of the match 6 strokes better than par. It was the best golf that I had yet seen in an amateur championship. Does it strike you odd that this super golf should be shot so often against Bobby? Well, I was getting used to it.

The only bright spot in that drab day was the discovery of a guy with a bottle of citronella. Up to the luncheon intermission, the mosquitoes had been working on me until I was lopsided. If they would only fight man to man, or rather mosquito to man, it would not be so bad. But they ganged me. I slew them by the hundreds anti there were thousands ready to take their places. Weak from loss of blood and temper, I welcomed the boy with the citronella like an angel from heaven, though I fancy he smelled differently. He said it would keep the mosquitoes away. I begged to be anointed with it, and he obliged copiously. That afternoon I went about the course practically alone. The only joy that came into my harassed life during that terrible round was watching brigades of man-eating mosquitoes charge me furiously until within the citronella zone and then recoil and retreat with screams of mingled rage and horror. Through clouds of mosquitoes all afternoon I walked like the Israelites through the Red Sea and they parted before me. I should like to see a citronella before they extract the oil from him, but I should like to see him in a glass case.

Marston beat Ouimet with a combination of mediocre and miraculous golf, mixed with the ministrations of the angels and the intervening forms of several Boy Scouts, who must do a good deed every day, the flagpole on No. 9, and Ouimet's own putter.

The gallery was swarming all over the place as the other important matches of the day had finished, when this match turned in the afternoon round, Marston 1 up. Boy Scouts supposedly used in herding the spectators out of the way and usually contriving to be underfoot at all critical junctures, were rimming the green of the thirteenth hole, a pitch of 115 yards. Ouimet was evidently set for a finishing punch and his shot hit four feet beyond the cup with a drag that pulled it back to

30 inches—apparently a safe deuce. Marston cracked under the strain and his shot was long and out to the right. It looked as if it would not hit the green at all, but it just touched the edge and was hopping cheerfully over the bank of a trap when it struck the legs of one of the trusty Scouts and was deflected back onto the green. Still the break seemed immaterial. Francis was up there for a deuce, and Marston's ball was 40 feet away with a downhill putt. The match was square and Francis was coming up like the traditional finisher that he was. Max started the long putt on its way and stepped back. Six thousand hearts skipped a beat as the finger of destiny guided the ball straight into the cup. This of course was the break. Before the startled applause had ceased to echo, Ouimet stepped up to the cup, tossed the ball to Max, and without wiping the mud from his own ball, putted hurriedly and the ball rolled off line. Marston won 3–2.

Each man broke three separate and distinct times during the final match, fairly collapsing and missing shots that indicated an utter loss of nerve control. And every time after losing a hole or two, each rallied like a game though groggy pugilist and came back. It looked three times as if Marston had Jess Sweetser on the run, and three times as if Max had broken past repair. And yet, reeling under the strain, they came up after Marston's final break by which he lost the fifteenth and sixteenth and went from 1 up to 1 down with two to play, they played incredibly brilliant golf on the two long finishing holes, Max getting a birdie 4 on each, and Jess being stymied out of a 4 on the seventeenth and having to sink a dangerous curving putt for a 4 on the last hole to stay in the match.

"He who lives by the stymie shall perish by the stymie" was the refrain in the press tent that night, remembering the five stymies Jess had laid Guilford at Brookline and the two he laid Bobby Jones the next day. And truly it did have a smack of retributive justice when on the thirty-eighth green, Marston ran his putt straight at the cup, taking care not to go past it up a slope. The ball curled off right at the rim and stopped four inches from the cup in a mathematical line with Jess' ball—a dead stymie, full in the face, cut Jess off completely from the chance to drop a six-foot putt for a half. Marston had outplayed him from the tee, driving to 16 feet from the cup, while the tired champion of 1922 sliced his spoon shot off to the right of the green.

It was Marston's tournament. It was in the book.

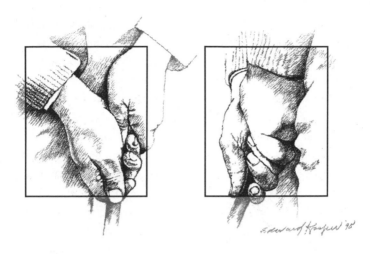

Bobby Jones' grip on the club.

18.
Oakland Hills—Dethroned

The season of 1924 began for Bobby Jones, National Open Champion, in June when he set out for Oakland Hills in an attempt to win two open championships in succession. This he did not accomplish, but he did prove himself the worthiest wearer of the crown since far back in 1911 and 1912 when the ill-starred Jack McDermott achieved the incredible feat of winning the Blue Ribbon twice. It was not quite so much of a show in those days, and latterly, a man wins one year and the next he is out of the running, but Bobby retained his enviable reputation as a medalist by finishing in second place at Oakland Hills, three strokes behind the winner, Cyril Walker, a little English-born professional of Englewood, New Jersey. Bobby won like a sportsman and a gentleman at Inwood, and he lost like a sportsman and a gentleman at Oakland Hills.

All hail Cyril Walker! A wizened little Englishman, who weighed 118 pounds soaking wet, and who outfinished a great field with the four steadiest rounds of golf yet seen in an open championship. His steady pace stood out as the marvel of the tournament. He shot 74 in the first round, 74 in the second, 74 in the third, and with the great prize blazing in his eyes and a powerful wind whooping about his ears, he shot his way to fame with a 75 in the final round. Any golfer who could finish 3-3-5 on that course in that situation was a real champion.

Oakland Hills, 22 miles out of Detroit, was the largest golf course I had ever seen. It was 6,880 yards around from the tournament tees, with a par of 36–37, and with all this territory in play, the surroundings were so ample that in only two places was it possible to go out of bounds, and there was no excuse for such a misadventure on either. There were 11 holes of more than 400 yards, the most difficult length on which to get a par. The vast ranges of the course, and the prevailing winds, favored Bobby. He had the distance and he was in good physical condition. We all thought that a card of 300 would be good enough, but Cyril was going too well, even for Bobby. Yet it is hard to say he lost when only one man finished ahead of him out of 80 who sought to supplant him.

Cyril was a methodical, thoughtful little Briton from the windswept downs of Lancaster, and the brightest exemplar of modern times of the old Scriptural adage that the race is not always to the swift. The slowest golfer in the world, the wonder was that he had not been slaughtered long before by a niblick in the hands of an infuriated opponent. It was as if each hole presented a problem, the only problem of the day, of the tournament, of his whole existence.

Driving with a wonderful snap in his full shots that gained distance, and with no breaks in luck, he came in with a par 37 for that perilous last nine, a finish not devoid of courage or even reckless boldness. His last real test was on the sixteenth, a par 4 hole of 380 yards, with a lake edging the front of the green, and a huge, yawning bunker behind, leading as he was by three strokes. If he plumped his second in the lake, as Hagen had done a few minutes before, he might easily take a six and have a fight on his hands. His drive was a good one against the wind, but it left him a long iron shot over the water, if he wanted to shoot for the green. He did. Like a champion, he squared away, and after deliberation that left the gallery ready to drop in its collective tracks, he let fly. Back came the crackling rattle of applause, louder and louder as the climbing ball fought its way into a head wind, and dropped on the green. Cyril Walker had won.

When he came to Oakland Hills, Cyril had said: "I could not win this tournament. This course is too big for me. Twenty-eight thousand yards of slugging would be too much for my game. I haven't the physical endurance, and I only hope to play well."

All hail Cyril Walker!

Bobby Jones and his wife, Mary.

19.
A Wedding

Call it Bobby's wedding in this book because it's his book. On the society pages, the best the groom gets is a little less than an even break. Golden lights across a dark lawn. How heavy green grass looks in the glow. There's a moon, too. There would be a moon, when Mary and Bobby were married. And the golden glow over the dark green lawn. What a pretty idea. The wedding on the lawn. And the lights on the broad veranda. Orchestra starts an arrangement of that lovely old love song in *Samson and Delilah*. Frank "Wop" Roman is in the orchestra. Roman has been connected with Georgia Tech for 20 years or more, Bobby was a Tech student—not very long ago.

House filled and a million more people on the lawn and on the veranda, waiting for the wedding march. Folks beginning to close in on the white ribboned lane. I've got my place. I can just see Big Bob's face. He looks pretty solemn. Reverend Plato Durham comes in. He explains why he was not at Oakland Hills—he simply could not get there. You may be sure of that. He was at Inwood all right. Until the playoff which was on Sunday. Must be tough to be a minister. Still, I don't know. I never want to see another playoff.

Eight twenty-five. Everybody here now. Glad I got here early. Gee, it's a great crowd. Feminine voice: "I never saw so many *men* at a wedding in my life." Come to think of it, neither did I. There's Perry Adair. How young he looked under the glow.

Eight thirty. Lady in front of me makes a frantic gesture at the orchestra leader, and the wedding march begins. Here comes the bride. Only it isn't. One of her attendants. How slowly they march. Must be quite intricate, keeping time so slowly. Here she is now, on her father's arm. They say that a girl looks more beautiful at her wedding than at any other time in her life. It must be true. It's easy to understand at one glance why Bobby always was the loyalest sweetheart.

Wedding march stops. Ceremony begins. Everybody on tiptoes. Queer what vagrant thoughts get in your mind at times. I catch myself thinking it is a well-behaved gallery, but packed awfully close. Will the players have room to swing! A glimpse of Bobby's face. I have looked at him many times over other people's heads, and I've seen him look pretty serious, too. But not like this. Happy and solemn at the same time. Another vagrant thought. At Oakland Hills, all Kiltie Maiden would say about his pupil's play: "He's studying well."

Bobby seems to be studying well now.

A short man hasn't much chance here, but there's one trying mighty hard to see. Kiltie himself! Of course he would be here. Hard man to find. I did not see him four times during the championship at Oakland Hills. But he seemed to see every shot. He looks as if he is just about to cry now. I thought only women cried at weddings. And here is old Tess Bradshaw—that wasn't your noble brow you were mopping, Tess. You know darned well it wasn't! And now my glasses have gone and fogged all up.

Orchestra again—it's all over! Crash of music and congratulations, and the gallery is all over the green—no, confound it all. Not so unlike that home green at Inwood at that. I was afraid they would kill Bobby there when that last putt went down. I got to him first at Inwood but not this time, not by several hundred. Hard gallery to get through. But I can see them standing there, young and radiant and beautiful, both of them. What a wonderful couple. Takes a long time to get to them. Wonder what I'll say. Wonder what Bobby will say. Old friends always say something supremely foolish at important junctures.

"Hello, Bobby."

That's foolish enough. And:

"Say, O.B. I found your belt in my trunk when I was unpacking. It just got there."

That's true sentiment for you.

I know it is customary to congratulate the groom and wish the bride happiness, but this is one of the exceptional instances where it is essentially proper, if not conventional, to congratulate both, and to be certain of their happiness. And looking from Bobby to Mary standing there together—really together, under the flowers—I wished I knew words delicate and happy and graceful enough to say something fitting of the culmination of this charming romance. There is something beautifully old-fashioned and tender about it; something of a quiet garden and the fragrance of roses.

Bobby deserves his great fortune. He is so much, so very much more than a national open golf champion. There have been many champions; there will be many more. There has been only one; there will be only one Bobby Jones. And here the few feeble words run out, that presented themselves with so little hope of expressing the love and esteem of the thousands of people all over this country, all over the world, to whom this wedding is of deep and sentimental interest. It is not a matter for words, perhaps, but rather for the thoughts and hopes and emotions that never are spoken but lie deep in the heart. God bless them both!

From left: George Sargent, Bobby Jones, Charley Yates, and Errie Ball at the East Lake Golf Club.

20.

The First Amateur Championship

Bobby Jones came back to the Merion Cricket Club in 1924 where in the autumn of 1916 he had made his modest bow to the world of golf—came back to Merion, longer and more beautiful and with a hundred more traps. "White faces," Chick Evans named them, bunkers faced with glittering white sand to the very brim, staring every time a shot was off line; staring menacingly; ready to catch a missed shot.

Dreams began for Bobby at Merion. Eight years they took to come true, but at last they did come true, as dreams seldom do, and Bobby won his first national amateur championship at Merion. Looking back, it seems that winning a national amateur championship was, and should have been, the easiest thing Bobby had ever done. But looking farther back, along the way is one of the ruggedest trails in the history of sport. A great golfer and a great sportsman had come into his own at last. As the professionals say, it was his turn and his tournament—the lucky seventh in which he had played; the tournament that found him ready and fit, physically and mentally. All through it some way he was set to win. And no champion ever traveled to glory in as steady a march or by as decisive a series of victories.

Not a close match did he have in his rush to the top: W. J. Thompson, 6–5; Corkran, 3–2; Knepper, 6–4; Ouimet, 11–10; and Von Elm, 10–8. The only time a finalist had been so largely defeated as Von Elm was 30 years before in the first amateur championship ever played, where C. B. McDonald beat C. E. Sands, 12–11. Bobby was never down after the first round.

Persistent par, that invisible, immaterial, terrible opponent that never eases the pressure, was what Bobby gave his opponents to fight all through the tournament. The great medalist of his time shot medal golf at last, and the great match-players of his day were as children before it.

In the evening following his match with Knepper, Mr. Jones announced a discovery: "I have discovered," said he, "that if you just keep shooting pars at them, they will all crack, sooner or later."

And this, by the way, came as near being an immodest statement as I ever heard that young man make. At this exact juncture, I began to feel that Bobby was on his way. Because you see it is no small trick to keep shooting par at them. Bobby meant that you did not have to make birdies; that the old card was good enough. Besides, birdies have a way of coming home to roost. At last he had the idea. At last he had begun to realize the power of his own game, to believe what I had tried to tell him at St. Louis in 1921: "Bobby, you will win championships just as soon as you come to believe that when you step out on the first tee with any golfer in the world, you are better than he is."

But Bobby was too modest. He still was too modest to believe that, but he had come a bit closer to the realization than ever before, and he had won his first amateur championship.

The night before Bobby played Francis Ouimet, his dearest friend in golf, he was miserable. He could only say that he hoped the man who won would win the tournament. I told him: "Try to forget that you are playing Francis. Remember that you are playing the card. Play it as close as you can."

Francis was not on his game. Weary and worn, he won only two holes all day, one the eighteenth of the morning round, which left him 8 down. With his luminous honest smile, he said: "Bobby, you could afford to lose that one."

Bobby looked less like a victorious golfer when this match was over than anyone I had ever seen. He looked far more like a man who had just been notified that his bank balance was overdrawn.

Maybe it was inevitable that Bobby should come back to Merion, eight years later, and win his first amateur championship. He was the most formidable looking golfer I ever saw as he walked out on the first tee; bulky and powerful and trim; cool and confident and businesslike; even before his perfect swing began operating, it must have been a severe test of nerve to walk out there as his opponent. I never saw him look just like that before. George Von Elm, a formidable golfer himself, broke and fell under the fire, and on the tenth green of the afternoon round, he stopped Bobby as he was about to putt, held out his hand and said: "Don't putt that one, Bobby, I've had enough."

When asked what was the greatest match he has ever seen, Bobby Jones always includes the match between George Von Elm and Roland McKenzie at Merion in 1925. George was making his first great bid for the amateur title at Merion and in the first round, he met Roland McKenzie, a 17-year-old lad from Washington, D.C. Von Elm, playing airtight golf, was 7 up at the end of the morning round. In the afternoon, Roland started by winning the first hole with a par. George promptly retaliated with a birdie at the second 523-yard hole. He also won the third, which put him 8 up and 15 to play. Consider this as an abstract proposition. George Von Elm, ranked as one of the greatest match players in the world, making a bid for his first amateur championship, is 8 up on his first round opponent after the third hole of the afternoon—8 up and 15 to play. What are the chances that the opponent, a 17-year-old lad, will square the match and carry it to the thirty-sixth hole? Not much of a chance.

From what George told me later, his face drawn from the strain after the thirty-seventh hole, he must insensibly have eased up; but Roland, insensible or otherwise at the same juncture, began to shoot superb golf. At the afternoon turn, Von Elm was only 4 up, having dropped the fourth, fifth, sixth, and seventh holes in dizzy succession. He was fighting desperately now to regain command. He took back a hole at the eighth, but an 8-foot putt for a deuce at the ninth left Roland with half his deficit accounted for, and George was struggling.

Iron par was all Roland shot on that last nine, par at every hole. And George slipped ever so little at the tenth and fourteenth by taking three putts, and at the seventeenth where his tee shot missed the green. And at every slip, the tall kid from the capital snapped up another hole.

At the home hole, Roland, 1 down and 1 to go, half missed a drive at last and the ball, hit low, plumped into the steep bank across the quarry and stopped in a fairly cocked up lie, nearly 300 yards from the green. George had a good drive and could easily get home with his second. And Roland? That boy hit a wood shot that I am sure had never been quite equaled under the circumstances. I'll never forget it. I was far back of him, and saw him slash into the shot with all his tall, lithe frame. I could not see the green but I could trace the flight of that Homeric shot by the rolling roar of applause from the gallery, terminating in a sudden furious crash, as the ball rolled onto the green.

After that historic shot, George took three putts and the match was square. Frenzied fans in the gallery began shouting to Roland that he was a sure winner; they even started to cheer "the new champion."

The rest is history. The rampaging gallery, the sudden news, the foolish slaps on the back, all took their toll, along with the furious strain of a last round. George won and deserved to win at the first extra hole. Roland had done enough for fame.

"Don't take any credit from the kid," said the Utah tiger. "He shot great golf at me. A 71 on this course will step out with anybody. I must have eased up a bit after I was 8 up and then I couldn't get going again. But I learned my lesson. The next time I ease up will be when I shake hands with my opponent."

Of course Atlanta did just what Atlanta would have been expected to do when Bobby came home, wearing the Blue Ribbon of American amateur golf, with Tom Paine carrying the grand old trophy of championship. The last dozen miles of the journey, with No. 37 a bit behind and roaring along at better than 60 miles an hour, the ring of the wheels blended in the tune of an old operatic chorus, The Soldiers' Chorus in *Faust*, and the words began to sort themselves out:

"Now home again we come, the long and fiery strife of battle over; rest is pleasant after toil as hard as ours beneath a stranger sun. . . ." Pleasant was right. And there we came, with old No. 37 swinging along in the gray dusk with a spatter on the windows, and the big welcome awaiting at Brookwood Station.

At Brookwood, this young man, the cynosure of all eyes at Merion—heralded as the greatest golfer who ever lived—became a palpably embarrassed and blushing, but happy withal, boy. I wish everybody who had seen Bobby on the golf course could have seen him under the fire of a welcome like that at Brookwood; and that everybody who saw him blushing and speechless at such a welcome could have seen him walk out on the first tee in a championship, with acres of tip-toeing spectators lining the fairway from tee to green, thousands of faces turned on him. Both pictures would have had to be seen to realize how many sides there were to this remarkable Bobby Jones.

A few days later, 300 guests gathered at the East Lake Club to honor the man who had brought the National Open Championship to his club in 1923 and the Amateur Championship in 1924, the only time either had been south of the Mason and Dixon line. Twenty-eight names were already on the Havemeyer cup, but they fittingly found a place for Bobby's at the very top, before they added a base for future names. Bobby and Mary were given a dozen silver dinner plates in the same design as the silver service presented the year before.

Telegrams were read from all over the world; from Jerry Travers, four-time Amateur Champion and once Open; from Charles Blair McDonald, first Amateur Champion, and many others. After the speaking had died away, the lights were dimmed and on the screen appeared brilliant studies of the master players in golf, a triumph of the ultrarapid cinematograph. Bobby and Alexa Stirling, who was present, were shown, the two who had brought five national championships to East Lake; Perry Adair, Bobby's first golfing pal, who was also at the dinner; then shots taken at Merion. Between these shots, flashes of the scurrying galleries at Merion were seen, and once or twice I saw a somewhat lanky figure in gray limping after a gallery and I knew that Bobby was in that match. I could feel my collar getting tight and my hands beginning to sweat as they always did when Bobby walked out on the first tee.

It was great to be young and a champion and to live in Atlanta. And it was great to come home with a champion—and the Big Cup—when you lived in Atlanta.

Bobby Jones and Alexa Fraser Stirling, Amateur Champion in 1916, 1917, and 1920.

21.
Alexa Stirling

Alexa Stirling, daughter of Dr. Alexander W. Stirling, British consul in Atlanta, was the first golfer to win a national champion from the town that was later to be known as the Golfing Capital of the World. The little red-haired Alexa was three years older than Bobby Jones and was winning her first United States title in 1916, the same year that Bobby won the Georgia State Championship and went on, at the tender age of 14, to play in his first United States Amateur at Merion. This quiet little Atlanta girl won her three successive national championships in 1916, 1919, and 1920 before Bobby had broken the spell of the seven lean years.

Alexa was a neighbor of Bobby's at East Lake and they played together in their first tournament with Perry Adair and Frank Meador, four kids from six to nine years of age. Frank's mother arranged the tournament, six Boles at medal play for a silver cup, three inches tall. Bobby always had believed that Alexa won that tournament, but since Frank's mother was putting on the show, the kids considered Frank as having something of a plenary connection, so the cup went to Bobby.

I saw Alexa win her first U.S. championship at Belmont Springs just out of Boston. That was the first time I had seen the Atlanta star in competition, although she had played in two previous nationals. Then came the first World War, and three Atlanta kids, Alexa, Bobby, and Perry Adair, and Elaine Rosenthal of Chicago, toured the country, playing exhibition matches for the Red Cross War Chest. This charming young mixed quartet turned in a large amount of money for the cause, and Alexa and Bobby naturally acquired a lot of golfing experience that was useful in their subsequent careers.

Alexa won her second national in 1919 at Shawnee-on-Delaware and her third at Mayfield Country Club in Cleveland. I saw her win that one too, her third in a row, counting out the war years, and Bobby himself never was able to pick off three U.S. amateur titles in succession, though he had two chances. A particularly bright memory of the little Alexa ranges back to this Mayfield tournament. It was one of those curiously brilliant midwestern seasons in the early autumn, when the woods sparkled with crimson and orange against the first touch of Jack Frost. Alexa was playing the finest feminine golf yet produced in America. Without the power of the great Glenna Collett or Helen Hicks, slight of stature, and rather frail of hands, her shots were the finest I had ever seen a woman present. Her irons especially, prima facie evidence of Stewart Maiden's influence, were as crisp and as firm as Stewart himself ever let fly. She was winning matches smartly and handily until she reached the semifinal round, where she encountered a traditional rival, Mrs. Clarence Vanderbeck.

Starting as smoothly as a Rolls-Royce, Alexa went quickly along to a position of 4 up through the seventh hole. The eighth hole at Mayfield was a firm five iron shot for a woman, a good pitch for a man. Both girls were well on the green, and Mrs. Vanderbeck, with that curious air of certitude that characterizes the predestined strokes in golf, stepped to her ball and holed it for a deuce. And starting with that deuce, she clicked off the next nine holes with a total output of 11 putts! This was rather drastic in any competition, and was enough to take up the margin and catch Alexa at the fifteenth green.

From 4 down, Mrs. Vanderbeck was square. And Alexa, as game a little golfer as ever planted a set of hobnails in the turf, had been compelled to see a commanding lead wrenched from her, the most devastating thing that can happen to any golfer. But instead of folding up under this unexampled attack, Alexa hit the ball harder and harder, and smacked the irons closer and closer as Mrs. Vanderbeck's putts went down. Waiting for the break, if it ever came.

The sixteenth at Mayfield was a par five for women and a tough one. Mrs. Vanderbeck, feeling at last the grim pressure of Alexa's increasing power, was on in four, 25 feet from the pin; Alexa was on in three, 20 feet from the flag. I had not seen Mrs. Vanderbeck miss a putt in so long that I had become hypnotized and was certain that she could not miss. I whispered to Bob Harlow, who was with me, that she would hole this one, too.

"If she does," whispered Harlow, "it's in the book that Alexa will sink hers."

Now that is the plain truth, call it coincidence, if you please. Mrs. Vanderbeck did sink that putt of 25 feet, and so help me, St. Andrew, Alexa did sink hers for a win, and ended the match on the eighteenth green. She went on to win handily next day from Mrs. Dorothy Campbell Hurd. This was Alexa's most brilliant win of a national championship. She went to the final in 1923 at Westchester-Biltmore. Then she was married to Dr. W. G. Fraser of Ottawa, Canada.

In 1925 at St. Louis, out of a not very distant past, stepped a little auburn-haired woman with the very finest golfing style in all the feminine world, and over the long and arduous course of the St. Louis

Country Club, Alexa Stirling Fraser showed the way to a great field in the qualifying round of the national championship with a card of 77, a new record. It was the second time a score under 80 had been recorded, Glenna Collett having had a 79 the year before. Thinner than I had ever seen her, and prettier, too, I found the matchless crispness of her iron play as fine as ever, the same power in her woods, and apparently a recently acquired putting touch and confidence about the greens.

Alexa and that Stewart Maiden swing marched on gallantly to the final round, winning one close match after another, until she was in the final round with Glenna Collett. And there Miss Collett shot the greatest round ever played in the United States Championship up to that time. She had a card of 75, four over men's par. Alexa did not have the endurance, but despite Glenna's amazing golf, she was still in the running up to the last two holes of the morning round. She began to slip on those holes, finished with a card of 81 and was 4 down. Glenna started the afternoon round with three birdies on the first three holes, and the match ended on the tenth green.

I saw Alexa play in eight national championships, the last one at Cherry Valley in 1927, where she was beaten in a great match in the semifinal round by the ultimate winner, Marian Burns Horn.

In a stretch of 15 years, from 1916 to 1930, Alexa had led the way for Atlanta to hold at least one golfing championship in every one of those 15 years, except 1921 and 1922. Alexa won three and Bobby 13 in 15 years, which is a record that no other city in the world can approach. And certainly no other club. Atlanta was indeed the Golfing Capital of the World.

Bobby Jones and his daughter, Clara.

22.

A Marathon

On the first 36-hole playoff in the history of either the United States Open Championship or the British Open Championship, Bobby Jones and Willie MacFarlane were all square after 107 holes of play at the Worcester Country Club; Jones, losing at the thirty-sixth green of the double playoff by his bold and determined effort to end the proceedings right there; MacFarlane coming back on the last nine in 33 strokes after being 4 strokes behind at the turn. What can you ask of drama?

One thing must be said about golf professionals. They decline to part with an open championship in favor of an amateur without a struggle. For the second time in three years, Bobby Jones' name was at the top of the board after the last hole had been played in a United States championship, and for the second time, he shared this position with a professional. This time, it was Willie MacFarlane, a Scotsman, 35 years old, born in Aberdeen.

Of all the supernaturally and exasperatingly persistent Caledonians that ever practiced the Scottish national industry, this MacFarlane was the most persistent. He never seemed to realize that Bobby Jones could beat him playing golf.

When Bobby was four strokes up and nine holes to play on the last lap of the marathon and Willie had lost these four strokes by weak and erratic putting, we thought Bobby was in. And I have never yet seen a golfer, so evidently weakening, get such magnificent hold of himself, and haul down four strokes and one more, against such a golfer as Jones. The weakening Willie slapped in a 10-foot putt for a deuce on No. 10, and another of the same length on No. 13, and came in in 33. The tall, lean pedagogical Scot played himself a strip of royal golf to win his crown, and I have never counted another Scot out as long as he was on his feet.

Bobby missed only two shots in that last round, and he paid for both of them. Only one stroke ahead at the long fifteenth, 555 yards, after a prodigious drive he set out to reach the green across a wooded angle with his second. It was a good shot and had plenty of length, but he was bunkered for his boldness, and Willie gained back the last stroke.

Going down the seventeenth fairway, waiting for Willie to play his second shot, Bobby came over to me and said: "This thing is getting funny. Still tied after 106 holes."

I could not deny it.

"Looks like a third playoff," I said.

His face hardened a bit: "There won't be another playoff," he said, "I'll settle it one way or another in this round."

He did. They halved the seventeenth. The eighteenth was a drive and pitch hole of 335 yards, uphill, to a small, shelf-like green notched into a hillside with a steep bank behind and a deep bunker in front, the pin very near the front edge. Bobby hit a big drive far in front of

MacFarlane, who played a safe, conservative pitch to the back of the green for a safe par. Then Bobby, as he had said, settled the playoff. Staking all on a brilliant thrust, the shot was aimed to pitch a mere foot beyond the front edge of the shelf, so the ball might trickle up close enough for a birdie 3. It missed—by four inches—and rolled back into the bunker. He had made the magnificent gamble just as he did at Inwood, but this time the gods of golf turned their backs, and Bobby was runner-up for the third time in four years in an open championship.

Bobby said reflectively, "One trouble with me is I seem always wanting to gamble on the shots and go for more than I really need. However, that is the best way to learn. You can't learn anything from a tournament that you win. Then everything you have done seems right and justified. It's from the ones you lose that you learn."

Bobby had not started well at Worcester. He had been greatly pleased with his qualifying scores at the Lido Country Club on Long Island, a seaside course that is able at all times to protect its maiden reputation against the rough assaults of brutal golfers accustomed to ravish scores of 67 and 68 from tender links. In his first round, under a sunny sky with the gentlest of zephyrs blowing, he turned in a card of par 72 with eight 3s on it. But in the second round, with slashing rain on the wings of a biting wind, it was grim, hard, unremitting work, and only a great workman could have scored. Bobby does not talk much about his rounds, but after he had fought the Lido course for three mortal and drenched hours, and came in with a card of 70, he said he had never played so fine a round.

It was surprising and not pleasant to see him in the first round at Worcester with the game on top of him and about to pin his shoulders to the turf. With a card of 77, he was perilously near disaster in a championship in which he had never been as high as 80. Another round of 77 would put him out, and he would have failed to qualify for the first time in his life. His driving was superb, his pitches were fine, and his putting was good enough, but his irons were ruinous. On the eleventh hole, a sour iron cost him two strokes, one of which he called on himself. The ball was in long grass to the left of the green, and as he prepared to shoot, the ball moved out of position. Neither the officials nor the spectators thought he had caused the ball to move, and it was generally felt that he was too harsh on himself. But at his insistence, a meeting of the U.S. Golf Association officials was called. He said he had touched the grass with his club and the penalty was imposed. I said that day if it turned out that one stroke stood between Bobby and the championship, I would be prouder of him than if he had won. It happened exactly that way. With that stroke off his card, there would have been no playoff. There are things in golf finer than winning championships.

At the end of the first round, he stood thirty-sixth; at sunset of the second day, he had pulled up to tenth place by a tremendous burst of golf that netted a 70. After another 70 in the third round, he was in a tie for fourth; and at 6:00 his name was leading all the others, except only Willie MacFarlane. Bobby was pretty lucky to get into the second playoff. He had to execute some miracle shots to catch up with the lanky Scot in the first playoff. Right at the start, Willie showed how he could make scores of 31 and 33 on nine holes by ramming down a 10-foot putt for a par on the first and one of exactly 69 feet for a 3 on the third hole. Coming to the eighteenth hole all square, Willie missed a putt of five feet with the championship in his pocket.

All square again in the Turkish-bath temperature that New Englanders call summer, and the galleries were nearly dead, and the players too. After the two hottest days on record in seventeen years, Worcester decided to show her guests what a really hot day could be. As Bobby and MacFarlane trudged down the blazing fairway starting the second play-off, Bobby said: "The papers say it is over 100, in the shade."

"Yes," said Willie, "but fortunately we do not have to play in the shade."

When the count was once more squared at the fifteenth hole of the same round, Willie quipped: "Marcus Loew would give us a lot of money for this thing as a continuous performance."

"For my part," rejoined Bobby, "I'd rather we got a job as a couple of ice men."

Reams of ecstatic copy could be written concerning the finish of this most furiously close of all U.S. Open Championships, with even more competitors having a chance to win than in the legendary tournament at Toledo in 1920, when Ted Ray won, and Vardon, Burke, Diegel, and Hutchison were tied for second. The gracious hillsides of Worcester echoed and re-echoed on that last day with reverberations of exploding golf stars as candidate after candidate, under the deadly tension and the heat, blew apart at the seams and lost the precious shots that would have brought anyone of at least ten striving experts to victory.

It was left to Walter Kennon, locker-room boy at East Lake these many years, and probably the most idolatrous of Bobby's admirers, to give the best definition of the United States Open Championship as it had appeared for the last four years. After the news came in of Bobby's defeat at Worcester, Walter sat brooding in a corner as only he could brood. Then he wandered over to a group of club members and spoke respectfully, but firmly: "You-all want to know what this here 'Open Championship' really is?" he inquired.

Seeing he had something on his mind they told him yes, they did want to know.

"Well, I'll tell you," announced Walter. "This here 'Open Championship' ain't nothin' but a great big invitation tournament, which they has every year, and invites all the big professionals to come to it and see if one of them can beat Bobby Jones."

In New York the next day, the heat was intolerable. Sixty-seven persons died, and I was ready to make it sixty-eight, when Patterson McNutt, playwright and producer, invited Bobby and me over to the Players Club. There after a fine luncheon, we sat in the wonderful library, surrounded by statuary and paintings and rare first editions of books and plays, framed old playbills, and the original letter written by Edwin Booth to the people of the United States regarding the assassination of Abraham Lincoln by his brother, John Wilkes Booth . . . a most wonderful place.

And so to home. Bobby had lost 12 pounds in the last three days so he had a neat and trim waistline to take back to Atlanta with him; but I did want him to take that big round gold medal back to little Clara Malone Jones to cut her teeth on.

*Another view of the
East Lake Golf Club.*

23.

More Glory for Old East Lake

Dreams do sometimes come true. The impossible does sometimes happen. The beautiful plans we formulate in the early hours of the morning, between waking and sleeping, usually go to smash like the iridescent bubbles—too lovely to last—that we blew from the clay pipes of happy childhood. But once in a lifetime, they may come true and crystallize into a reality that makes up for a lifetime of disappointment. Sure, there is a Santa Claus and a pot of gold at the end of the rainbow, and very possibly Easter rabbits lay eggs.

An all-Atlanta final. I can believe anything now that Bobby Jones and Watts Gunn went to the final round of the 29th U.S. Amateur Championship at Oakmont. Robert Tyre Jones, for the first time in a dozen years, repeated as national champion, and retained the crown he won in 1924 at Merion Cricket Club; and Watts Gunn, Georgia Tech student, playing in his first national championship, dipped his mashie in the golden sunlight, somewhat tinctured by Pittsburgh smoke, and inscribed his name in imperishable letters in the annals of golf.

The giant Oakmont course stretched its perfectly groomed and barbered length along the peaceful valley of the Allegheny among hills that are fair to see, 6,900 yards. Two hundred and seventy-three bunkers in grim array festooned the fairways, and keen, sloping, deceptive greens challenged the contestants with its par of 72, the severest test yet devised to settle the question of championship. And to add to its already insuperable difficulties, for the first and only time, the U.S. Golf Association tried an experiment at Oakmont—the qualification of 16 competitors instead of the customary 32. Two rounds of 18 holes each were played. Bobby qualified with a satisfactory 147 that went into second place when Roland McKenzie, an 18-year-old schoolboy from Washington, finished with 145. Watts Gunn was tied with George Von Elm for fifth place with 154.

When the two Atlanta boys were drawn in separate brackets, a staggering thought came up, the brilliant mathematical possibility that Atlanta might supply both finalists. Let the welkin reach out and ring for ice water—the millennium could be on our heels.

It seems odd writing a story of golf and not writing it about Bobby Jones. I have never done it before in an important tournament, but this time the little dark Atlanta pony, Watts Gunn, who suddenly grew overnight into the dark horse, must be the basis of this astounding narrative. Watts Gunn, a Georgia Tech student, and former state champion, had never played in a big championship before, and had never tackled the fast, keen greens of the eastern courses, and yet in his first flight from the old home had gone to the finals. Watts was a quiet youth, who always appeared to be exceptionally well balanced. I do not know what got into him at Oakmont. The boy's game simply defied any description at my feeble command. He played that fearful golf course

More
Glory
for Old
East
Lake

107

like a man in his sleep; he seemed not to be aware that he was shattering precedents and records and stouthearted opponents. After watching a brilliant round of golf in the state championship, Bobby and I had called on Judge Will Gunn, Watts' father, and urged that Watts be allowed to go to the U.S. Amateur Championship. Judge Gunn did not think him good enough but yielded to our importuning.

In his first match with Vincent Bradford, West Pennsylvania Champion, Watts shot the first nine in a sorry 42 and was 2 down. With a great chance to win the long 621-yard twelfth, he had deftly steered his third shot into a trap. It was at this precise juncture that young Gunn was spiritually renewed, or in some manner, made over from a nervous little neophyte, sputtering shots about the scene, into a cold, precise, grim, and implacable golf machine, clicking off birdies and pars to the utter destruction of Bradford, and Jess Sweetser, and Dicky Jones, and finally, giving Bobby the hardest run he had in the tournament.

He devastated the luckless Mr. Bradford by the unprecedented method of winning 15 consecutive holes, going from 3 down to a 12–10 victory—a record that still stands in match play competition. At that, Vincent was not so hopelessly bad after the first few holes of this appalling onslaught. He was simply hypnotized. Outdriven on every hole from 20 to 50 yards, if his second shots were on or near the green, Watts' irons were banged like rifle bullets straight for the pin, hopping backward as they landed.

If you want my honest opinion, I think Watts was hypnotized too. You may take it from me, St. Andrew had touched with the tip of his wing the brow of the dark boy from the South, and if I ever saw inspired golf played, it was in those 15 holes against poor Vincent Bradford.

Three years before at the Country Club of Brookline, I had seen Jess Sweetser on his way to the championship trample all over the prostrated form of Bobby Jones, turning the first nine 6 up. I saw Bobby, his face set like bronze, reel off the second nine in 34 and gain back only a single hole. I saw him go out on the eleventh hole of the afternoon round in the most crashing defeat he ever met. At Oakmont, I saw this same Jess Sweetser, blond and handsome and debonair, go out with this kid from Georgia, and I saw him go down to the severest defeat of all his brilliant record. I saw him fighting like the game golfer he was, going farther and farther down against the dark little juggernaut that we had called the Atlanta pony. I saw him 7 down at the end of the morning round, and in the afternoon, saw him fighting courageously but helplessly against an invincible foe, who shot his way through par after par to a final birdie on the twenty-seventh, where Jess smiled and held out his hand.

More
Glory
for Old
East
Lake

109

At the end of the morning round, I asked Watts how he was feeling. He looked at me a moment, the curious faraway look slipping from his deep eyes, and as speculation returned, said: "Gee, I'm hungry. I am so hungry my pants are about to fall off."

Bobby asked Watts questions about the play on four different holes and he did not get one of these holes properly located. He remembered only one thing—that the wind was against him on the long twelfth. As a matter of fact, the wind was directly with him all the way on this hole. In 31 holes, he had won 17, lost 2 and halved 12, and had brought in the greatest match player in amateur golf 7 down. But what he realized was that he needed food.

In his semifinal round with Dick Jones of New York—odd how these Joneses seem to take to golf—Watts began to regain consciousness and was continually having to fight for the pars that had come so easily in his first two matches. He was only 1 up as they went into lunch. This was evidently preying on his mind, as Jess Sweetser met him on the stairs.

"Hello, Watts," said Jess cordially, "how are you coming?"

"Gee," said Watts, "I got a tough one today. I am only 1 up."

This to Sweetser, whom he had brought in 7 down the day before, and who as a club mate of Dicky's, was accustomed to start him 3 up.

Jess got a big laugh out of this bit of naïveté.

After Watts came off the thirty-third green where his match with Dicky ended and he knew that the next day he was to play Bobby, his guide, philosopher, and friend, he spoke as follows: "I'm scared stiff. I'm awfully hungry. This Dicky Jones is a tough one. I enjoyed the match. I am tickled stiff to be playing Bobby. He gives me four strokes in our matches at home, but I reckon he won't do that here."

Odd, whimsical, and greatly attractive was Watts Gunn. And how the galleries admired him, as much for his personality as for his golf. Unobtrusive and modest to a degree of bashfulness, so quiet in his manner and in his dress, he won the esteem of 10,000 golfing fans and scribes.

After this match, Watts, who had been standing around in somewhat of a daze, suddenly spoke up: "Say, I ought to telegraph Dad that I am in the finals."

"Don't bother," said Bobby. "He knew it long before you did."

As for Bobby's trek to the final round, he was never pushed. In his match with Von Elm, their second encounter, one single comment will tell the tale. Von Elm, the youthful Uhlan, won only five holes in the match, four with birdies and one with an eagle.

24.
Way Down South in Dixie

An almost flawless combination of rhythm, power, and perfect style, the inimitable Bobby Jones still wore the coronet that he won at Merion in 1924. For the first time in 12 years, since the double victory of Jerry Travers at Chicago and Garden City, an amateur champion had successfully defended his title. The first time in the history of the championship two golfers from the same club met in the final, in fact, the first time two contestants from the same city. "Atlanta *uber Alles*" was the word, as it never was before. No wonder the joy bells rang out against the red clay hills of Georgia. No wonder Atlanta pressed her claim as the golfing capital of the bunkered world.

A hundred times we answered questions:

"How do they get that way in Atlanta?"

"What sort of town is it that produces such golfers?"

"Why didn't they play this at East Lake and save carfare?"

Bobby Jones versus Watts Gunn, as they had been on display so many times at East Lake when nobody bothered to go out to watch. As thousands of fans scrambled after them at Oakmont, I thought of what this match meant to each of them—these great battlers from East Lake.

To Watts, it was his maiden effort, a new and interesting excursion into untried and unfamiliar fields. He could shoot the works. He had nothing to lose. He had reached the final round of his first Amateur Championship, and he could bang away at a blazing chance for incredible glory.

And what of Bobby, with his enviable reputation at stake, playing this match against a boy to whom he was accustomed to give four strokes; the spectacular kid he had coached, played with, and brought to the tournament? There is nothing sure or safe in golf. There are too many slips twixt the ball and the lip of the cup. For the first 12 holes of the forenoon, Jones had faced a tidal wave of pars and birdies with young Gunn moving at a terrific pace. And I could not help feeling that after all these years of careful preparation and gallant courage and inimitable shotmaking, Bobby Jones was in grave danger of losing to this strangely able youngster, who did not realize how hard a thing he was doing. After 11 holes had been played, Bobby was a stroke better than par and still 1 down. Also he was up to his neck in the bunker to the right of the twelfth green, the long "Ghost Hole" at Oakmont, 621 yards, with his third shot, and Watts was neatly on the green for a sure par 5.

Bobby said afterwards: "I could not help thinking, as I climbed down into that trap, of the eloquent speech I had made to Judge Gunn, begging him to send Watts to Oakmont. And here he was taking the championship away from me. He was playing inspirational golf of the most devastating kind. He should have been 2 up at the eleventh, for I have never seen a putt come so near to dropping. He was playing better golf at the long twelfth. And if I had not managed to get that pitch up and the putt in, the chances are that I would never have seen Watts again. He would have gone away from there in a cloud of dust."

Bobby squared on the next hole, and calling out the ultimate resources of his game, he stepped off the next six holes, 3-3-4-3-3-4, running him out to a lead of 4 up at noon, and a card of 70, a record for match play in this tournament.

In the afternoon, Jones started with two birdies and Watts responded with two to cut down the lead again but he couldn't shoot birdies on every hole. Gunn held on firmly and bravely through the first seven holes, but no man could face the unbelievable fusillade that Jones laid down and the battle ended on the twenty-ninth green, 8–7. The presentation was a scene not to be forgotten. The spectators were banked in solid masses, row above row on the sloping terraces. And Watts' little speech when he was called up, wriggling with embarrassment, to get his silver medal.

In effect, he said: "When I came up here, I didn't expect to qualify, and everybody was so good to me that I wanted to stick around as long as I could. So I did stick around as long as I could; that is, until I got to Bobby. You know nobody can beat our Bobby."

In the locker room, Bobby said: "I don't think I will urge Judge Gunn to send you to another championship, Watts."

And in a boyish imitation of the eastern links, Watts said: "Jones, you are a tough kid."

And they shook hands all over again with no movie cameras about.

Scott Hudson, president of the Atlanta Athletic Club, wired us to stay on the train until it reached the Terminal Station. That was totally unnecessary. I personally would have obstructed any movement to block a mob scene. I love mob scenes and the larger the mob, the better. These two young heroes deserved all the mobbing and all the tumult and shouting that could be given them.

It was the greatest sporting achievement any city in the land had ever accomplished.

It was after this tournament that Bobby told me, in strictest confidence, of his ambition in competitive golf.

"If I could be a national champion of the United States, either open or amateur, six years in succession," he said, "then I'd feel that I could hang up the old clubs."

Of course it did not seem possible, though he had already accomplished half of that ambition. And we didn't speak of it again for years. It seemed the dream of a D'Artagnan, who, you remember, was a Gascon.

Bobby Jones' swing.

25.
The Tide Sets In

The year 1926, which was to be the biggest year of Bobby Jones' career up to this time, started inauspiciously with a severe drubbing and ended on the same sad note. Walter Hagen gave him the first drubbing and the most complete. Bobby was in the real estate business at Sarasota, Florida, and Hagen was president of the Pasadena Golf Club, a few miles away. Bobby, regarded as the leading medalist in golf, was Amateur Champion of the United States, and Hagen, rated the leading match player of the game, was Professional Golf Champion of the United States, having won in 1924 and 1925. A 72-hole match was arranged between the two champions, 36 holes to be played at Whitfield Estates Golf Club, and the other 36 at Pasadena; thus to be settled the much discussed question as to which of the two was the better golfer.

The admirers of these two great golfers had been wishing for just this encounter for a long time. Probably never in the history had the same interest been aroused by a set match. This was easily understood in view of the widespread popularity of the principals; the fact that Bobby was rated the greatest amateur in the game, and Sir Walter, the greatest professional.

The margin was somewhat absurd, considering the known merits of both golfers. Hagen won 12–11, stopping Jones with a half in a birdie 3 on the twenty-fifth hole at Pasadena, which half of the match he started 8 up as a result of absolutely marvelous play on the last nine of the Whitfield section. The explanation of the outcome is by no means hard to reach. Hagen played superb golf. He was more on his game, especially about the greens, than I had seen him in six years. He finished the match four strokes under par on two severe courses and he deserved to win. I think, indeed, that Hagen would have defeated any other golfer in the world in that match, playing as he did. And this is not the shadow of an excuse offered as an alibi for Bobby. The only thing I would say is that Bobby was badly off his irons, and that looseness there and at times about the greens, caused the margin. Cards of 76-74-73 were not exactly Jones' regular game, any more than cards of 71-70-69 were Hagen's. The extreme happened to coincide in this one match; the 12–11 margin was the answer.

The Florida encounter of these two champions afforded a curious study in the psychological differences between the problems and tactics of a golfer confronting a single human opponent, and a golfer competing against the grim specter of the card and pencil, whose opponent is that unalterable opponent—Old Man Par.

Incidentally, it is unfair to both Sir Walter and to Bobby to intimate that either was lacking in proficiency at either style of golf. Walter had won the United States Open twice, and the British Open twice, both medal competitions. Bobby had won the United States Amateur Championship twice in succession; yet Hagen was persistently regarded as a match player and Bobby as a medalist. In the last six United States Opens in which both had competed, Hagen finished ahead of Jones once and Jones ahead of Hagen five times. The inference is, then, that Jones was a better player than Hagen against the card and pencil. But Hagen's impressive record of losing only four set matches in the last five years, topped by his second consecutive win of the Professional Championship, and his sound drubbing of Bobby in their one formal match should establish him as our greatest match player.

There is much in golf besides mechanics; even besides the patient courage and undaunted morale needed to play under the shadow of the card and pencil, generally regarded as the highest type of golfing competition. Walter Hagen unquestionably had something in his game beyond the ability to stroke a ball correctly. Indeed up to the vicinity of the green, a dozen players might be adduced who were his equal, but around the greens, within chipping and putting range, Hagen very likely was the greatest. Hagen was also celebrated for his recovery shots, which reputation collaterally implied an inclination to wildness. This implication is accurate. Walter was one of the wildest of all the front-rank golfers, and this disposition to wallop the ball off the visible confines of the course, not to mention the fairways, cost him more than one medal play championship. Hagen was a hard man to beat in match competition for two principal reasons, and one oddly enough, was this very tendency to wildness. The other was his super showmanship; his histrionic talent; and for making of some special shot a ceremony on which the gallery hangs with hypnotic attention—and which his hapless opponent regarded with a distinctly disadvantageous concern, not to say exasperation.

On the sixth hole of the afternoon round at the Whitfield course Bobby, who had just won the fifth hole and cut Hagen's lead to 3 up, had a beautiful drive down the alley. Walter, who had missed every drive but one in that round, shoved his tee shot out to the edge of the rough, where a tall pine stood inconveniently near the line of his pitch to the well-trapped green. He hit as wretched a shot as can be imagined, topped it so that it fairly rolled along the turf straight to a wide sand trap guarding the front of the green.

See now how the complexion of a hole and the match can change and change again in a few seconds. As Hagen missed that shot any sane spectator would have concluded that Jones had won a hole, was only 2 down, and about to stage a rally. But the topped ball ran on through the trap, wriggled up on the green a dozen feet from the pin. Jones' perfect pitch left him a couple of feet away, and his putt rimmed the cup and stayed out, right on the edge and almost a complete stymie for Walter. Now it appeared that Walter had a lucky half—instead of which, putting with incredible daring and accuracy, he tricked the ball delicately past Bobby's and it toppled in for a birdie 3. Bobby was 4 down instead of 2 down. That was the turning point of the match, I shall always believe.

Sir Walter could never be counted out, even with trees in the way. At the thirty-sixth hole at Whitfield, and the fourteenth at Pasadena, Hagen hit a tree with his drive and the ball bounded out into the fairway and each time he won the hole with a birdie against a perfectly played par. These shocking upsets do not affect the card and the pencil; but they do work havoc with the equilibrium of a single human opponent—which is one of the reasons Sir Walter was accounted so formidable at match play.

Willie Park, a long generation ago, said that the man who can putt is a match for anyone. And Hagen could putt. In this match, he used 27 putts in the first round, and 26 in the second. Bobby, a fine putter himself, took 31 putts in the first round, and 30 in the second; eight more than Walter and he was 8 down at the end of the 36. Bobby needed 11 more putts than Walter as far as he went, though it should be explained that Walter also was playing his irons better than Jones; and in justice to them both, in Bobby's last rally at Pasadena, he shot the concluding 25 holes in par and went 4 down to Hagen's amazing golf.

Now for the other factor—showmanship. The gallery had no effect whatever on Bobby, so long as it kept out of his way. It didn't bother him and it didn't inspire him. He didn't care if its component members hung with bated breath on his next shot or read a newspaper, so long as they did not walk about nor talk when he was making a shot.

Not so Sir Walter. If Hagen were not a great golfer, I fancy he would have been a great actor. He loved to do his stuff for the gallery—and for an opponent when it was match play. His cold, confident, deliberate personality impinged on a single human opponent with such effect that so good and game a player as Leo Diegel said to a friend in the gallery following the match between him and Diegel in 1925 in the Professional Championship, where Hagen picked up a deficit of five holes and won on the fortieth green: "Bill, I never want to play him again; he's killing me."

I remember once when Sir Walter was playing a quiet practice round the day before a tournament. On the last hole, his second shot went into a simple sand trap by the green. Without an instant's consideration, he picked a mashie-niblick from his bag, went down into the trap, chipped the ball from a clean lie to a couple of feet from the pin. The next day, his ball behaved in precisely the same way, hopping into the shallow trap with a clean lie, almost in the same place. But this time there was a gallery.

And Sir Walter did his stuff.

Walking slowly into the trap, Hagen studied the position of the ball carefully, and considered its relation to the position of the pin. Then he chose a mashie-niblick and returned to the ball, which he inspected again with the utmost care. Then he went back to the bank of the trap and exchanged the mashie-niblick for a niblick, returned to the ball and resumed his study. The gallery by this time was on the verge of hysterics and on the outskirts frantic units were semaphoring to distant friends to hurry hither and see the sights.

After another painstaking examination, Sir Walter regretfully shook his polished head and went back to the caddy for the third time, changing the niblick for the mashie-niblick he had chosen at first. Armed with the original implement he returned again to the ball, once more studied the situation, took his stance, addressed the ball—and played exactly the same shot he had executed in three seconds the day before. And the gallery, convinced that it had witnessed a golfing miracle, split the welkin up the back like a patriarchal locust.

In the match with Jones, on the way to the ninth green at Whitfield, Hagen's drive was in the short rough in a sort of valley below the green, resting against a twig about the size of a pencil. The twig could not be moved without moving the ball and incurring a penalty. But Walter, with the gallery close about him, and Bobby standing none too well at ease after an indifferent second shot, consumed all of a minute that seemed an hour, studying that twig. At last he got up from his knees and played the shot, a very good one that won the hole.

Sir Walter's golf, plus showmanship, plus psychology, had pretty well flattened out the opposition those last few years so far as match golf was concerned. Bobby's own pet system went to smash against the Hagen psychology in Florida. After Marston had defeated him at Flossmoor, Bobby discovered that by playing the card in match competition as well as in medal, he could win matches—and he won nine of them in succession, including two championships. But in Florida he made the fatal mistake of going back to his original plan and playing Hagen instead of the card. Walter was a calamitous opponent, when you tried to match shots with him. He made such odd shots from the tee—and he took so few shots about the green! He could be so shockingly wild and so distressingly precise, all playing the same hole. He was the great match player, was Sir Walter!

The old Haig was keyed up. There has never been anybody with Hagen's ability to rise to the most tremendous situation; to produce according to the difficulty of production; to meet the toughest problem with the coolest head, the steadiest nerves and the most masterful shot. Neither golf nor any other sport has produced a champion with so invincible a reserve of nerve, gameness and sheer, cold determination as Sir Walter. He was the greatest competitive athlete I have ever encountered. And one other thing, Walter never forgot for one instant what he owed to the public. I have seen many a lesser champion become snobbish in the moment of opulence and glory; but never the old Haig. Winning or losing he was just the old Haig himself. And that is sufficient. There are worse epitaphs than that in Carrara marble and bronze.

I think the greatest line ever spoken on a golf course was what Walter Hagen said, on the way to winning his first of four British Open Championships. His beautifully placed drive on one of the trickiest fairways at Sandwich took an utterly reasonless bound into the deep gorse—a shot, maybe two shots gone.

Somebody in the gallery was moved to offer sympathy:

"Gee, Walter, that's tough luck!"

Chin up, grinning away, Walter Hagen said: "Well, *that's where it is!*"

That's where it is! Whether a bad shot or a bad break put the ball there, that's where you play the next one. Game of golf—Game of Life, it's the breaks that count. The breaks and how you take them. That above all.

Bobby Jones.

26.
Invasion

The United States Walker Cup team for 1926 left New York in a blaze of glory and bunting, under the blended emblems of Old Glory and the Union Jack, the most ambitious invasion ever undertaken by American golfers. Uncle Sam's favorite sons, setting forth to emulate the quest of the Golden Fleece on battlefields somewhat complicated by labor strikes and other complexities. The boys who were going to play for the Stars and Stripes against the British Lion were: Bobby Jones, the champion, the cynosure of all eyes, red-faced and a bit uncomfortable; Watts Gunn, the boy wonder, looking as if he wished he were back at Georgia Tech, standing an examination in whatever Watts had to stand at Tech; Francis Ouimet, easy and graceful and gracious; George Von Elm, composed and smiling and handsome; Roland McKenzie, the Washington schoolboy, a fair match for Watts in modest demeanor; Jess Guilford, calm, sleepy, maybe a bit suspicious; Jess Sweetser, confident and debonair. There you had the finest array of golfing talent that ever took the field since the first Scottish shepherd swung his crook at a round pebble among the hills and vales of St. Andrews.

It's quite a business, this sailing. The shores of your native land fading into the darkness, and the lamp of Liberty, enlightening the world, traveling back along its own path of brightness and disappearing into the night. After a number of sailings, it probably gets to be an old story. But there is only one first time.

Cason Callaway brought me down to the boat and there I promptly found Watts Gunn. We wandered around and finally got up on the boat deck, which corresponds to the roof of the ship, and there we stood, high above the dock, and waiting for the time to come to shove off. It was dark up there and the *Aquitania* stood up like an office building above the mass of people down on the dock. Watts and I stood up there in the dark, at the witching hour of midnight, 50 feet above the milling crowd, and their voices rose steadily in waves of sound. One thin voice, a child's, intermittently kept sounding above them all. There was an odd, plaintive note in it, and suddenly I was homesick.

The steam whistle above us let loose its mellow roar, profound and of a soul shaking timbre, and Watts jumped: "Gee," he said, "what's that?"

"Twelve o'clock," I said, "here we go."

As I say, one doubtless gets used to it. But this was our first trip away from the old native land, and we both got an unforgettable thrill out of the splash of the line cast off from the pier, and the boiling water about the propellers, as the *Aquitania* backed slowly away, so steadily that it seemed it was the big dock and the piping crowd that were moving. Five minutes and the engines turned the other way and we really were going ahead.

And there was the Statue of Liberty, a great light up in the sky, the figure beneath only a darker shadow, the path of the lamp coming to us across the smooth water, and growing long and longer and longer. That was our last impression of America, the stretching and dimming pathway, leading to the Statue of Liberty. It was cold on deck and in some way my eyes were stinging. We went down to C-deck and to bed. I suppose I should say turned in, being now at sea.

Our gallant ship made a disappearing light blue furrow across the Atlantic at the rate of approximately 530 miles every day, or every 23 hours, which seems to constitute a day on a trans-Atlantic voyage eastward. We kept setting the clock up as we steamed along the cobalt trail toward the rising sun—hour after hour we lost out of our existence. Personally I did not miss the vanishing hours. An hour more or less per day was an easy matter on the *Aquitania*. Up on the boat deck was one of those cute little devices installed with a tethered golf ball, which flew around and around a registered contrivance when struck. And when the members of the golf team wearied of driving golf balls into the Atlantic, they amused themselves with this contraption. The ship's population gradually assembled on the roof in such numbers to watch this performance that I began to have apprehensions of the *Aquitania* becoming top-heavy, especially after learning that she burned fuel so rapidly as to raise her out of the water about seven inches a day, this lightening including food consumed by passengers who were not sea-sick of course—but nothing happened.

I became accustomed to life on shipboard amazingly fast. I learned to buy Bass' ale in British. It cost 8d. A florin is 2s. An 'arf-crown is an overgrown florin and comes to 2 and 6. One pound and ten shilling notes were of convenient size and slippery, especially about the bar, and notes of five, ten, or twenty pounds reminded you of miniature paper towels—a use that their value rendered virtually prohibitive. At that, they were the size of note paper, but I did not make any notes on them.

How could anyone ever weary of the ocean and its blue romance?

A flat world with a rim; a flat world of tumbling water with a bowl over it for a sky. And the water changes from cobalt to purple, and again to gray but the cobalt is the loveliest of all—Lord, when the rich blue is churned off the side of the ship into the glistening white spray with a stain of blue through it, you can stand looking down into it for hours, hypnotized. And what is below—what mountain peaks and deep valleys. What Spanish galleons with tall decks and rustling anchors, and bars of gold that will never rust, nor again see the light of day. What skeletons of tall ships and white bones of brave men, who went down with them, all deep and dark until the Judgment Day—under the cobalt blue sea. The overwhelming desire to go down to the sea in ships had been in my heart since I started remembering, and this was the first time. . . .

The Atlantic edition of the London *Daily Mail*, printed on the ship, gave us the news from the strike every day. W. C. Fownes Jr., president of the U.S. Golf Association, cabled the Royal and Ancient Golf Club of St. Andrews, that if it were inexpedient to carry out any or all of the golfing program, The U.S. Golf Association wished only to be helpful in this time of stress. The Royal and Ancient Golf Club, after true British deliberation, responded in true British fashion: "Shall try to carry out all of the program."

Those Britons—of all the nations, they stand the gaff best. The *Daily Mail* informed us that immediately after putting down a riot of rowdies with their batons, London police donned football apparel and played football against a team of strikers. A strike must be especially interesting in a country where they do things like that.

Looking out over the blue sea at sunset, a channel of glory to the rim of the world, a strike of five million men, or a revolution or a golf championship, seems little and inconsiderable. . . .

A hopelessly sentimental idiot—I confess it now—after having stayed up all night just to get a sight of a foreign shore as soon as it became visible. Of course there were mitigating circumstances. The *Aquitania* was an easy ship on which to stay up all night, especially the last night out. There were many people willing and able to stay up most of the night, but when it simmered down to the dogwatch, waiting for Cherbourg to come up out of the dark, there were just four of us. I had never before seen a strip of beach, or a tree, or a mountain top that was not a part of the United States of America. Once I had stood on the shore of Lake Erie at Cleveland and gazing northward, I had been assured that I was looking at Canada, but it was too far away to see, miles and miles over the curve of the earth. And that was the nearest I had come to seeing a foreign strand.

And now I was going to see France.

We went out on the sun deck. It was dark out there and cold with a touch of mist in the air, and yet not a hint of dawn in the east. Presently along the place where the rim of the world had been for a week, were four blinking lights, off and on, off and on. And that was France; four winking lights along the rim of a dark world far across the rush of black water. I'll never forget those four lights and the way we stood gazing at them on the cold, dark deck. Presently we were going along the English Channel, but England was not the first foreign country I had seen. There never will be another first one.

There was a growing air of concern as we approached the scene of the strike. We had been told that there would be no boat train to carry the passengers to London. Off the boat we came after a considerable wait, found our luggage, got past the customs officers quickly enough, and trundled away in a big motor coach. It was interesting to be on land again, and a foreign land.

The first 30 hours we were in Britain, we saw great happenings. We saw the British Lion at bay and we saw him on top. We saw armored cars and tanks and helmeted Grenadier Guards on the streets of London. We saw the British people standing the gaff, silent and uncomplaining under the stress of a portentous situation, silent and undemonstrative as the tension relaxed, accepting a solution of the gravest political problem of modern times with the same imperturbable patience and courage with which they had faced the problem itself.

And then the big news. The strike was terminated—that is the conservative British word. And our golf program would be carried out, even to the restoration of St. George's Vase competition. The Amateur Championship at Muirfield, the Walker Cup matches at St. Andrews, the Open Championship at St. Anne's—everything as scheduled.

Bobby Jones' swing.

27.

First American to Win the British Amateur

For the first time in its long and honorable history, the British Amateur Championship was won by a native-born and bred American in 1926—Jess Sweetser of New York. Sweetser, a star in his intercollegiate days at Yale, and U.S. Amateur Champion in 1922, defeated Alexander Simpson, 6–5, on the historic Muirfield course. Simpson, a braw Scot, was too new in championship play to bear up under the grueling 36-hole test against so fine a golfer and so relentless a competitor as Sweetser. Only once before had America's frequent challenges for this coveted trophy been successful. Twenty-two years before, Walter J. Travis, a native of Australia, living in the United States, had won.

This victory was a great triumph for the young New York broker. More than a score of Americans were entered, including the eight members of the Walker Cup team. It was the finest opportunity Americans ever had to come through with a long-sought victory, yet one after another they fell and it was Jess, who carried America's standard and finally wrested the much-desired trophy from British hands. And well indeed did Sweetser bear the responsibility. Drawn in the more difficult half of the bracket, Jess had a savage battle with his teammate, Francis Ouimet, which went the full route, and then was forced to go 21 holes before defeating W. H. Brownlow, a ranking British golfer. Jess had everything needed to win, his strong game was slowly coming to the crest, a break, when he got a default in his first match; and all the rest of the works, including a lion's heart and a rabbit's foot which he picked up on the Muirfield course.

The big gallery was delightfully fair and sportsmanlike. They rushed in unprecedented numbers to congratulate Sweetser, for a good golfer is a good golfer to these Scottish crowds. Jess was hoisted to the shoulders of his American friends and carried back to the clubhouse, a quarter of a mile away through a lane of cheering fans.

In presenting the trophy, Captain S. Gillen, of the Honorable Company of Edinburgh Golfers, said: "Our Amateur Championship has gone to a citizen of the United States. There is no doubt that the best man won. Mr. Sweetser is armed with every possible stroke a golfer should have. I hope he will come back and defend his title, and I hope we will beat him. My lords, ladies and gentlemen, are we downhearted?"

Cries of "No, no," came back from the crowd.

"I will come back, and I will be beaten," said the new champion modestly.

And right here I want to tell you something of Jess Sweetser's amazing courage and stamina in winning this championship. He was reluctant to interrupt his business career to make the invasion, suffered from a severe cold while crossing the Atlantic, and two weeks of heavy weather in England was far from beneficial. He was not himself during the tournament at Muirfield. On the day before the matches began, he was near collapse on the course. Only the withdrawal of his opponent the next day saved him. A day of rest and he was able to carry on but the nerve strain and illness gained steadily, and the night before the final round, he suffered much pain from a wrist sprained during the grueling 21-hole semifinal round with Brownlow. He went into the final round with Simpson on courage alone, a great demonstration.

Then came St. Andrews and the Walker Cup matches. Jess was greatly worried about his game and his physical condition. But the British Amateur Champion, and the former U.S. Amateur Champion, refused to lay down his arms. He was on the edge of a dangerous collapse, which indeed came within seven hours of the time he shook hands with Sir Ernest Holderness, his opponent in the singles match. On the morning of the foursomes match, he was suffering from severe nausea. He was not complaining, just merely mentioned this to me as he was preparing to start. Sweetser attended the cup presentation and formal dinner for the two international teams that night but he left early. About midnight he came into my room. He was white as a sheet and holding a blood-stained handkerchief to his mouth, but perfectly calm.

"What shall I do?" he asked.

Before I could reply he was seized with a coughing spasm. I helped him to bed, and went out and found some of the team, and a doctor. The doctor was pessimistic and told us privately that Jess should not be moved, nor should he think of starting home the next day. Next morning we got a second doctor in consultation, and they finally agreed that it might be best for him to start home. Jess never had any other idea. He was set on going and we thought the same courage that had carried him through the tournaments would carry him safely home.

On the train to London, Jess and I had adjoining rooms with the door open between. He did not complain or ask for anything and in the morning he seemed quite himself. His iron fortitude never wavered. Sweetser's courage on the golf course was proverbial, but it never glowed so brightly as in this longer, grimmer battle. So Jess Sweetser, the conqueror, returned home to be greeted by only a few close friends, the coveted cup on its first trip to America forgotten in the haste for a quick return to health.

It is at times difficult to understand how Bobby Jones managed to carry even across the ocean his uncanny faculty for catching opponents at the top of their game, and for inspiring hitherto unknown competitors to shoot rounds which left them more or less famous as the man who stopped Bobby Jones.

I had never seen Bobby so highly keyed up as he was for the match with Robert Harris, the British Amateur Champion. I had seen him go out and play par golf like a machine and crush his opponents with a ruthless pressure, but I never before saw him flame with the brilliancy he displayed against the luckless Scotsman. It was the first time an American and British champion had ever met in either country's championship, and Bobby went out and destroyed Harris most spectacularly.

Andrew Jamieson, whom Bobby met the next day in the sixth round, was an inexperienced lad, not in good health, for which reason he had taken part in little formal competition. He was a boy of pleasing demeanor and somewhat eccentric golfing habits. He rode his bicycle back and forth to the Muirfield course, and his brother caddied for him. He spent three hours the night before his match with Bobby putting on the practice green in front of his hotel. And all this untried youngster shot at the American champion was a string of 13 pars and one birdie, and Bobby, slack from his tremendous play of the day before, could not meet the blast. Jamieson never failed to get a chip close nor a putt down, and took the great Bobby off in the ratio of 4-3.

Exhausted and with shattered nerves, Jamieson passed out of the picture in the afternoon with a round of approximately 85.

I had felt that Bobby was really going to win this one, and after that long day's play in the sixth round, after his defeat by Jamieson, I went out on the old Muirfield course all by myself away from the tents and the players. The gallery had all gone and there was only the towering gray dunes with the gray and restless North Sea behind them; and the plaintive sound of those strange little birds called Peewits, from the cries they made, about the darkening links. In all my life I have never heard anything as lonely as the cry of the Peewit in that long English twilight on the rolling Muirfield course, nor was I ever so lonesome. But things changed in many ways and vastly, not long after that.

Later in the international matches at St. Andrews, Andrew Jamieson proved his mettle by defeating Robert A. Gardner, the American team captain, handily in the singles. Fellows named Bob seemed to be his specialty. His telegram to Bobby after he had won the British Open at St. Anne's was a model of modesty and good taste. It was written in Latin and as nearly as we could translate it, read: "Congratulations from a small nobody (nemo parvo) who was impudent enough to beat you."

It would be difficult not to like such a boy.

An American winning the British Amateur was not the only tradition that went overboard at Muirfield. After due felicitations to Sweetser, an historic scene took place in this old clubhouse, where they have portraits hanging on the walls of captains before the American Revolution, stately appearing old boys in scarlet coats, with the oddest of golfing implements and stances. The links are governed by the Honorable Company of Edinburgh Golfers, and they won't let you play on Sunday. After I had written my story of Jess' epoch-making victory, I went over to the clubhouse from the press typists' tent in search of— well, what they have in the lounge, which is entirely legal and proper over here. Long before entering the sacred portals, I became increasingly conscious of strains of extremely close harmony, and some not so close. And there they were—the singing Americans, announcing to the world that the gang was all there.

And there were Frank Carruthers and George Greenwood, British golf scribes, their eyes protruding, and members of the Honorable

Company, standing around in a sort of daze, but looking rather pleased, I fancied.

"A tradition is shattered," said Mr. Carruthers. "I never thought I should live to see this day. There never was a note sung in this sacred edifice before."

"My God, no," exclaimed Mr. Greenwood. "The members are supposed to wear felt slippers walking about this place. I am not superstitious but at this extremely melodious and ribald moment, I can see the ancient dead of the Honorable Company turning over in their graves. You amazing Americans! You win our championship, and then you sing songs in the Honorable Company's clubhouse!"

I'll say they sang, awakening the echoes among the Lammermoor hills. "Big White Moon," "My Honey That I Love So Well," "Mandy Lee," "Show Me the Way to Go Home," "Sweet Adeline," and in compliment to Jess Sweetser, "The Sidewalks of New York."

A member of the club asked me: "Would you mind asking them to sing 'Drunk Last Night'? It's quite the best thing they do."

It really was a wonderful picture and after all their fine sportsmanship of a week that had gone rather against them they now expanded their conventions to accommodate our troubadours and actually seemed to like it. They stood for Bobby Jones playing without a coat; they applauded Sweetser and gave him three rousing cheers at the thirteenth green, and let us sing in their clubhouse that had never been sung in before.

With the arrival at Muirfield of Bill McGeehan, Henry Farrell, Don Skene, Frank King, Bob Harlow, and other American newspaper men, we organized a great companion rival of the American Walker Cup team, entitled "The American Johnny Walker Cup team," which played its first match at the Marine Hotel in North Berwick. The match was a Scotch foursome.

First
American
to Win
the
British
Amateur

133

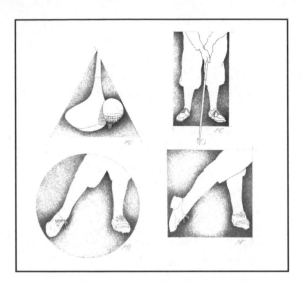

Bobby Jones' foot position during the swing.

28.
Back to the Home of Golf

The road from Muirfield to St. Andrews is 80 miles around the Firth of Forth and there was a Scotch mist, which in the United States would be called rain with the utmost candor, as we came over in motors for the Walker Cup matches. Rounding the turn of the Firth, I saw the first Scottish scenery that blended with my long conceived ideas of what Scotland would look like—the bald, bleak hills with a fringe of gorse and an occasional and wholly incidental little forest climbing skyward only to slip off the precipitous summit of black-rocked hills against the rainy evening sky.

Writing of St. Andrews, Lord Cockburn said: "There is no place in Scotland equally full of historical interest, and no place in this country over which the genius of Antiquity lingers so impressively."

Yet, I confess, my regard for St. Andrews was solely as the home of golf; the cradle of golf in the days when Parliament decreed that the game, which had brought a great international competition to St. Andrews in 1926 under the blended emblems of Old Glory and the Union Jack, should be "cryit doun and nocht usit." The idea was that golf, upwards of 500 years ago, had become so strangely fascinating that the people were neglecting the practice of archery, and thus lessening the powers of defense.

Of course there is a rather well-known golf course at St. Andrews, as well as the other historic points of interest. The Old Course it is called to distinguish it from the New Course, the Eden and the Jubilee, some 50 years younger. The Royal and Ancient Golf Club lives in a square and solidly built stone clubhouse by the first tee of the Old Course. Here is the supreme authority in golf and I think always will be. This is fitting. Golf is the game of the Royal and Ancient Golf Club just as baseball is strictly an American game. And I, a patriotic citizen of the United States, am convinced that whatever clever improvements we fancy we can make in the old game, St. Andrews should have the last voice. And be sure that St. Andrews *will* have the last word.

Bobby Jones played so well in the Walker Cup matches that he began to get a bit excited over playing in the British Open. He was disappointed in his play at Muirfield, he had left Mary and a little daughter, Clara Malone, at home, and frankly, he was homesick and had about decided to sail on the *Aquitania* with the team the day after the matches were finished. The Americans won three out of four bouts in the foursomes, unexpectedly, and even more unexpectedly lost four of the eight matches at singles, and halved another, so it really was the gallant play of George Von Elm against the gigantic Major Hezlett that saved a narrow victory for our side. That gave the Americans $6\frac{1}{2}$ points to $5\frac{1}{2}$. Bobby defeated Cyril Tolley 12–11 in the singles, and in the foursomes, he and Watts Gunn defeated Tolley and Andrew Jamieson, 4–3.

Andra Kirkaldy, celebrated in song and story, most famous of the Scottish professionals then living, held the flag at the home green all day for both days, and at the three-score-and-ten mark was one of the world's wisest golfers.

"Your boys won on their third shots," he said. "We can drive with you, hit long irons with you, but we cannot hit third shots with you. That is the shot that wins, a pitch, a chip, or a putt. You finish the hole better than we do. The art of finishing a hole is an American development."

At that Andra did not see the longest putt of the tournament—at the thirteenth green of the morning round in the match between Gunn and Jones against Jamieson and Tolley. Watts' long iron was just on the carpet of what is probably the biggest green in the world. It is a double green, containing both the fifth and thirteenth holes and measures about 230 by 175 feet, with at least 40,000 square feet of putting surface. A ball can be on the green and be 200 feet from the cup. Watts' ball was 120 feet away. He hit it firmly and it rolled and rolled and rolled and dropped into the cup for a birdie 3, probably the longest putt ever holed in formal competition. The gallery gasped.

But that was not the only dramatic incident in this conspicuous foursome. I recall with peculiar distinctness the seventeenth, or Road Hole. This famous, or infamous, hole is 467 yards, a sharp dog-leg to the right. The bold or reckless golfer can drive over the Auchterlonie drying sheds and have a straight shot to the green, that is, if he does not land in the drying sheds. Our side was comfortably up when they stood on the tee of the seventeenth hole in the morning round. Watts was driving against young Jamieson and he essayed to go over the sheds, missed the ball but luckily it got over into the fairway, from where Bobby hit a good shot into a swale a short pitch from the green. Jamieson attempted a sliced drive around the angle and went out of bounds. Tolley, playing three from the tee hit a powerful ball well to the left and Jamieson topped a brassie shot deplorably. Tolley, having no alternative, banged a great iron shot at the distant green and went over into the concrete road from which the hole gets its name, and which is not out-of-bounds. The Britons lay 5 and Bobby told Watts to kick the ball up on the green as they would then have four putts for a win.

But no. Watts in some mysterious manner actually shanked a chip shot and the ball scurried out into the road, farther away and in a much worse situation than the opponents. However, the Americans had played only 3 so Bobby decided to play safe and hammer the ball out of a rut, as a wide yawning bunker made it inexpedient to shoot for the green, leaving Watts another simple chip shot. Jamieson played a fine recovery from the road, 20 feet from the flag. Watts missed the pitch. Bobby, looking serious now, ran an approach shot 20 inches from the cup, their sixth shot, after circumnavigating the green. Tolley missed the putt, and Watts, after a palpable struggle, holed for a 7, and a win, probably the only hole ever won in big time with such Pompeian fireworks.

This celebrated hole some years ago cost J. H. Taylor, five-time winner of the British Open Championship, not only a flock of strokes but also a vast amount of esteem among the Scots, who consider St. Andrews the world's classiest course.

"It's the worst golf hole in the world," said J.H.

"Right," said Bobby and Watts.

But there it remains to this good day.

This wonderful course, in my humble opinion, has been much slandered of late years, and I came here in a critical mood. I had heard here and there that it was unlike any other golf course or links in all the world; and that comment is meticulously accurate, so far as I know. They said also that bunkers were scattered haphazard about the place with none of our cherished American design for what we call scientific trapping; that mounds in front of many greens destroyed an opportunity for scientific play of the American plan, and that all too frequently, the obvious line to the hole was one of the worst ways that could be selected.

Bobby Jones will tell you frankly and emphatically that the Old Course is a classic and one of the very finest he has ever played. He says:

"To an extent I have never found anywhere else you must place your shots differently, round in and round out, according to the wind. The fourteenth is 527 yards and one of the two longest on the course. In one practice round, I found a following wind at the tee, coming rather from the right. Using the wind, I drove off line to the left and got a big shot into the fifth fairway, where I was in a position to play a little fade with a brassie fairly against the slope of the green and stop well on for a birdie. In the afternoon, the wind was slightly against me, and from the right. No chance to get on in two, so I banged the ball straight down the fairway and played the brassie 50 yards off line to the left, which gave me a simple pitch the long way of the green and against the slope."

And so all the way around—St. Andrews changes with the wind, and the wind bloweth where and when it listeth. It may follow you all around the course, out and in, or it may oppose you all the way around, turning just when you turn. Or it may come across from the left or the right, constantly, or with a baffling variety.

There are only two short holes on the Old Course, No. 8 and No. 11. With a total yardage of 6,572, this means a lot of sound walloping if you would approach the par of 73. The greens are gigantic, providing plenty of use for the severest shot in golf—the long approach putt. Some of the greens have two cups in the one surface, as the combined fifth and thirteenth, where Watts holed probably the longest putt ever made in formal competition.

Bob Gardner, captain of the team, said: "When I first came to St. Andrews, I played one round and considered it the worst golf course I had ever seen. When I was here next, I played three days and decided it was a good golf course. Next time I played all week, and went away saying it was a great course. And now—I think it must be the most wonderful golf course in the world."

I also achieved distinction at St. Andrews. I determined to be the only American duffer who ever came to St. Andrews and did not desecrate the course by playing golf. However, I did make my contribution to golfing history by having my picture taken driving from the first tee.

The caddies occupied a lot of my attention during the British invasion.

Don't overlook the caddies, gentlemen. They fight and bleed and die for their "man." Some day I will write you a story of Luke Ross, the boy just Bobby's own age, who carried his clubs in a dozen national championships.

But this is of Jack MacIntyre, the Scottish boy who would not admit that Bobby could be beaten even after Andrew Jamieson had sent him out of the British championship. There is something to be said for Caledonian persistence, and Jack was a fair sample.

"I know he's the greatest of them all," said Jack MacIntyre, tears streaming from his eyes after Bobby was beaten. "You'll find me waiting at St. Anne's to show them all in the open championship."

Simple faith and maybe a bit of Scottish Presbyterian predestination! Jack was waiting for Bobby at St. Anne's. He carried his clubs like a conquering hero through those four tremendous fighting rounds on a windswept course, when Bobby, never in front of the field for a single round, turned up two strokes ahead when the chips were all in. I'll never forget the scene in the lobby of the Majestic Hotel at St. Anne's when Bobby, British Open champion, said good-bye to Jack MacIntyre. "Good-bye, Jack, old man," said he. "We won it together!"

Jack tried to speak and failed. He shook Bobby's hand hard and then suddenly let go and sat down on the floor, and sobbed like a child. Don't forget the caddies, gentlemen. The players get the glory or the sting of defeat. But they don't do all the fighting.

Bobby Jones swinging at impact.

29.

T. Stewart

The largest freight ship afloat could not carry in one cargo all the iron golf heads that have come out of one celebrated little shop at St. Andrews, the T. Stewart factory, entered through a sort of alley that runs along the side of the forge shop and the finishing room. Twenty hardy Scots toil like a platoon of Vulcans in the forge room and sixteen more at the finishing wheels next door. It is not the American idea of a factory or workshop, this curious little place where the T. Stewart irons are made, stamped with a clay pipe symbol.

The little shop never catches up on its orders, and of course a clever American with a business of such fame would long ago have had his efficiency experts and his engineers working out quantity production with the idea that every golfer in the world should really have a set of Stewart irons. And in place of the tiny, grimy shop along the alley, a vast factory would spread across acres, humming machines and modern ventilation and lighting; and labor problems, and other annoyances would go into the manufacture of a production that was once the T. Stewart irons.

Instead of which here was the hand-forged process with a force of about forty men, and old Tom himself, his eyes protected by black goggles, bending above a finishing wheel. You cannot go into that funny little shop and pick out a flock of irons. They make them to order at the T. Stewart shop, and quantity production never has been considered, if it had ever been heard of. And when old Tom himself personally inspects a club head and finishes it off there's a round dot punched in it. Bobby Jones had a lot of copies made of his favorite clubs and they all bore the little round dot.

Watts Gunn, Francis Ouimet, and George Von Elm all bought irons from the grimy little shop. You told Jock Stewart, who looked exactly like any of the rest of the hands, what you wanted, if on the heavy or light side, or regular, and any little eccentricity as to pitch or angle of lie. You went away and came back for the heads, all polished and shiny at five shillings and six pence, or about one dollar and a quarter. Hereafter when you see on the back of a blade, the mark of T. Stewart, St. Andrews, and the old clay pipe, you will know that this club, be it yours or another's, was forged on order in a little old shop innocent of efficiency or quantity of production. But there undeniably was quality to the Stewart irons, and no competitor need grow excited over this story for T. Stewart would not forge one single more head than he would otherwise have done. He had all he could do and orders ahead meant nothing in his sturdy life.

At noon during the Walker Cup matches at St. Andrews in 1926, when the singles were working to a fine finish, I slipped over to the shop to get a picture of Tom Stewart. Up to that time, none had ever been printed on this side of the Atlantic. There I found not only Tom but all the rest of the help getting out of overalls and into street clothes. Evidently they were going somewhere.

Old Tom obliged with the picture after a bashful little argument, and I photographed him standing by his little factory, without waiting for him to get his coat. I asked: "Where's everybody going this afternoon? Is it a holiday?"

"They are finishing up the Walker Cup matches. The lads will be wanting to see your boys play," he replied.

"And you, Mr. Stewart?"

"Aye, I'll be watching a bit of it, too."

Which may explain a bit more of the undoubted excellence of the T. Stewart irons.

Of peculiar interest also was the old Tom Morris golf shop near the eighteenth green on the Old Course at St. Andrews. And there was Old John Morris, "Jack" Morris, they called him affectionately, as old or perhaps older than the famous Andrew Kirkaldy of St. Andrews. This is a story of Old John, then 76 years old, and an active professional at Hoylake, and a club which came from his shop more than 30 years before.

The first club I ever owned was in 1897, when I was a summer visitor at Lake Geneva, and at the age of 15, worked as a casual caddy at the Walworth Country Club, later the Lake Geneva Country Club. The first club I purchased was a secondhand cleek, designed to handle the gutta-percha ball then in use. It was long, narrow, and graceful in the blade, and on the back of the blade was an oval line, and inside the line was stamped, "John Morris, Hoylake."

I have the original today. I had two copies made, cut down to putter length in the shaft; and a few years before when Bobby was worrying about his short chip shots, I asked him to try this little club. He played tiny approach shots from just off the green with such success with it, that he had Tom Stewart make up a dozen copies for him, all marked with his autograph.

But the story of Old John. At Muirfield in 1926, when Bobby was playing Robert Harris, British Amateur champion, in the fifth round, at the first hole, a par 5, Bobby was just off the green with his second and sent the ball into the cup, a superbly delicate shot from 75 yards away. John Morris was walking with me in the gallery. When the ball rolled into the cup, he turned back toward the clubhouse.

"The match," said Old John, "is over."

What a thrill he got when I told him the shot had been made with a copy of an old club from his shop, 30 years before. Incidentally, he was right about the match. Bobby won 8–6.

In this shop you could see in a glass case the very clubs used by Old Tom, the patriarch of the game, in winning four British Open titles. And if you seem probable, they will even let you take them out and handle and swing them. His son, Tom Morris Jr., "Young Tom," died at the age of 24 with four British Open Championships already behind him. Tom Morris Jr. is the first name on the beautiful old trophy, a pitcher that was put into play in 1872. The reason for the pitcher was, Young Tom had won the "Challenge Belt" three times and retired it from competition as his personal property.

Often the question arises, how good was Young Tom Morris? How would he have played under modern conditions; or how would our present day champions have held up under the conditions in which he won three consecutive British Open Championships by the time he was twenty-one years old. It is a fascinating speculation, but we have only the scantiest data on the subject, and for the rest we have to conjecture, as always, when champions of different eras are compared in any sport.

The Year Book of 1870 says Young Tom in winning the "Belt" for the third time had a score of 149 for 36 holes on the old Prestwick course. This was only 12 holes so had to be played three times. Par was 49, so Young Tom was only two strokes over. The lowest score ever returned in an open championship at Prestwick was by James Braid in 1908, then at his best, with a score of 291, two over the present par. Jim

Barnes in winning the title at Prestwick in 1925 had 300, 12 over, in 72 holes or six over in 36.

Young Tommy with the quaint, unwieldy weapons and sluggish projectiles of 40 years before, and the rough and unkempt condition of the course, was only two over. That he was a golfer of rare talent is unassailable even with the scant history that we have, as great in his time as any who came after him.

Not long after Young Tom won his fourth championship, thus equaling the record of Tom Sr., his young wife died, and six months later young Tom was laid by her side. Since there was no previous history of illness, the Scots have always said that he died of a broken heart.

In the old, old cemetery in the grounds of the great ruined cathedral at St. Andrews, over against a wall, old Tom who died in 1928 and young Tom lie buried and there is a bronze effigy of Young Tom about to play a shot in the game he began so brilliantly, played so well, and left so young.

30.
The Finest Round of Golf

The finest round of golf that Bobby Jones ever played was at the
Sunningdale Golf Club, in Surrey, not far from London, on June 16,
1926; his first round in qualifying for the British Open Championship at
the Royal Lytham and St. Anne's Golf Club course; 33-33-66, four under
the par 70 of the course, and six under 4s. There have been lower scoring
rounds, Bobby himself had scored better, but this card of 66 was played
with a precision and a freedom from error never attained before or after
by the greatest precisionist of them all; incomparable in steadiness of
execution. There was a single error in the round. At the thirteenth hole, a
one-shotter of 175 yards, Bobby's iron shot rolled into a shallow pot
bunker, from which he chipped and holed the putt. The mistake did not
cost him anything but it was a single flaw in a perfect round.

He had no assistance from luck and needed none. He played the
first nine in 33 and the last nine in 33. He had 33 putts and 33 other
shots. He had neither a 2 to bring his score down, nor a 5 to mar it.
The course is 6,472 yards around on the card, but it was a great deal
longer from some of the back tees used for this competition. It is especially lavish with long two-shot holes, the toughest pars. Bobby used
his mashie only twice and his mashie-niblick once, his second shots

continually requiring a full iron, and occasionally a brassie. He holed only one long putt of 25 feet, and to pay for it, he missed two putts of 5 feet, each for a birdie.

Bobby had picked up a beautifully modeled driver from Jack White at Sunningdale, and he seemed to have found a sudden inspiration in it. Old Jack had named the driver, Jeannie Deans. Anything in Scotland that is beloved or heroic, is Jeannie Deans, after the beloved heroine of that name. Bobby never played with any other driver in competition thereafter and he won ten major championships with Jeannie Deans.

The next day Bobby shot a 68—134 total, a new record for the British Open Championship. Ten under 4s for 36 holes; 66 and 68 at Sunningdale at fullest stretch, one 5 and one 2, all the rest 4s and 3s.

The British critics were buzzing with admiration. Bernard Darwin, the greatest of the British writers, said in the London *Times*: "After a reverential cheer at the final green, the crowd dispersed awestruck, realizing that they had witnessed something they had never seen before, and would never see again."

Charley MacFarlane of the *News* said: "It is probably the finest golf ever seen in Great Britain. The boy's game was perfect and chaste as Grecian statuary."

Sporting Life said: "It would seem that in this qualifying, the limit of individual effectiveness has been reached."

Bobby said: "I wish I could take this golf course home with me."

But Bobby and I were well worried about this amazing display of golf at Sunningdale. We knew he had reached the peak of his game and the championship six days away. That night at the little Wheatsheaf Hotel, on the edge of Windsor Park, he was still pretty well strung up and we went with Archie Compston for a walk in the park. It is nine miles around Windsor Lake and we went all the way around. The luminous twilight still displayed the calm of the huge rhododendrons; and the golden crescent of a new moon hung in the sapphire sky. What a night it was—in Windsor Park.

The betting at Lloyd's suddenly went down to the inconceivable odds of 3 to 1, for the championship, the shortest ever quoted on such an event.

St. Anne's was a kaleidoscopic championship, the lead changing with every round; but the dominant and persistent impression was the brilliant duel fought all through the last day by Bobby Jones and Al Watrous; the young amateur who won and the young professional who was so near to winning. A grim and exhausting struggle with each other, which, it seemed, inevitably must kill off both of them and leave Walter Hagen, starting an hour and a half behind them, one of his finest openings. The plot was complete; two great golfers in a death grip—and behind them the Old Haig, set to knock them both off, when they should have bled each other white, and drained the last resource of nerve and courage.

They started the final round in a situation as chastely simple as it was dramatic. The cruel sifting process was over now; the magnificent gesture of Taylor; the steady play of Von Elm and McLeod had not brought them close enough to threaten, barring a ghastly collapse by the three leaders. Watrous, due to his spectacular 69 of the morning round, led Jones by two strokes, and Hagen by four. He was the pacemaker, and Jones to win needed to catch and pass him—and all the while that implacable menace in the rear, the dark shadow of Walter Hagen. All day long, no more than two strokes separated these three men from each other. It was a killing triangle.

Both Bobby and Watrous were out in 36, Al holding his lead, but the youngsters had not left Hagen a very wide opening on the first nine. At the fourteenth tee, Bobby was still two down with five holes left to play. Here I truly think he played the finest golf of his career, and won as hard-fought a tournament. His magic putter had failed him in the pinch, and he needed to win without it, if he was to win. He played the last five holes 4-3-4-4-4, the toughest five finishing holes I have ever seen.

He beat Al by two strokes, and arm in arm, they went to the club-house to await the verdict, Hagen being the jury. Oh, those rumors! We knew Hagen had done the first six holes two under 4s. He was greatly in the chase. Another rumor came up. He was out in 34. He was tremendously in the hunt. Another rumor. It was 33. Another. It was 32. I could not stand the suspense. I went down to the press room. On the way a man told me Hagen was 2 under for thirteen holes. That meant he could win with a 71. In the press room a British reporter was wrangling over the telephone much as we do in America, but with a different accent. Finally he said Hagen was two over 4s at the fourteenth. I turned right around and went back to the smoking room and shook hands with Bobby Jones. Undeniably we had again witnessed the old Hagen challenge. Four years in the last five Walter had given battle and his share of third place at St. Anne's was the lowest position he had occupied. And it is due the bronzed soldier of fortune to explain that he had a simple par on the last hole for second place. Walter Hagen does not play for second place. As at Worcester last year, he gambled boldly—this time with utter abandon, for he was trying to sink a mashie pitch—for top position.

It seemed that every great figure in British golf was in that big room, coming over to clasp the hand of the young American amateur, and not infrequently slapping him on the back or hugging him in the most un-British manner.

"Bobby is the world's most lovable sportsman," they said. "This is the most popular golfing victory ever seen in Great Britain."

And there was John Morris of Hoylake, the oldest of the professionals, shaking Bobby's hand as word came that Hagen had to do two 3s to tie. And there were the members of Britain's great triumvirate of the last generation, Harry Vardon, James Braid, and J. H. Taylor, with 16 British championships among them. Ted Ray, George Duncan, the brilliant Scot, and Harold Hilton, the distinguished veteran of all the amateurs, who won the British Open in 1897, five years before Bobby was born. All crowded about the quiet boy to do him honor. Forty national championships must have been around that table.

I couldn't help feeling sorry for those British professionals, with seven players from the United States and one from South America in the first 10. They were taking such an unmitigated lacing! Sorry and sort of remorseful, for they gave us the game and now we seemed to trample on them.

In all the realm of sport, I never expect to see a more affecting sight than old John Henry Taylor, 56 years old, who had made a magnificent gesture for old England, with a 71 in the third round, making his little speech at the cup presentation; how he stood there, square and solid and bald of head, and with the tears running down his cheeks, congratulated the victors and said Bobby was the greatest golfer who ever lived.

And Bobby made the best speech of his career, which has contained rather more actions than words; he told them it was honor enough just to have his name on the old cup with all those great names.

And the happiest part of the trip was the 50-mile ride through a soft English twilight from St. Anne's to Liverpool where Bobby and I took the night train for London and Home! Home with the Golden Fleece. I think Bobby and I were not especially coherent on that ride. I suppose we sat up and grinned idiotically at each other frequently; and at times pounded one another on the back. And we talked a lot about what the folks at home were doing at that moment. That really was the best of all, thinking of the folks at home.

Bobby Jones at a ticker tape parade in his honor.

31.
Return Victorious

Home again! The sweetest words in the lexicon! After all, what are championships compared to being home again? But undeniably it was great to be coming home victorious. New York did its best to welcome Bobby Jones, the conquering hero, with a display of enthusiastic hospitality that had never been surpassed for princes or potentates or pugilists.

As the *Aquitania* came through the Narrows, she was met by the municipal boat, *Macom*, her decks filled with joyous Georgians, a hundred of them who had come to New York solely to greet Georgia's first citizen. As the *Aquitania* anchored, the *Macom* came alongside with rebel yells and shouts for "Bobby," the band playing "Glory, Glory to Old Georgia," and then shifting to "Dixie," as Bobby appeared. The first to greet him was his beautiful wife, Mary; his father and mother, Big Bob and Miss Clara; and much to the surprise of everybody, Robert Tyre Jones, his grandfather, for whom he was named, the old Roman protesting that he just happened to be in New York on business; Major John Cohen, publisher and editor of *The Atlanta Journal;* Senator Walter George, and dozens of others. Bobby and his party were taken aboard the *Macom,* and given the courtesy of the port, something rarely done except for visiting royalty or very distinguished guests.

The little steamer *Macom* blasted its way through the shipping to Pier A at the Battery, with the harbor rocking and reeling under the waves of sound from the whistles, and just behind came a fire boat spraying the sky with a dozen towering jets—a Brobdingnagian fountain. I had never seen Bobby look so happy as he did when he stepped out on the Battery to face all those movie cameras, and a storm of cheers from the massed thousands in the street. The marks of battle and strain still lingered in his young face, despite the voyage and the rest, but he was a happy boy under that hurricane greeting by his countrymen—a prince of golfers and a prince of sportsmen—on top of the world, the unspoiled pet of a nation.

Broadway was turned over to Bobby Jones and his friends, a triumphal march with a solid gallery on each side for three miles of earnest hiking; traffic stopped, the snappy police force clearing the way, ticker tape flying in white spirals from the skyscrapers, and a continuous roar echoing like thunder through the canyon of downtown New York. Three solemn figures in front, Joe Johnson, former Atlantan, later city commissioner of public works in Manhattan, and chairman of the reception committee, Major Cohen, and between them, a stocky young sunburned boy, his blond head uncovered, more serious than ever he had been when the eyes of the world were watching him battling over a golf course. And I think there must have been a million Americans to welcome him back to his native land, as he walked along Broadway back of the band, to greet Mayor Jimmy Walker at the city hall.

Other winners of foreign titles had returned bearing laurels, but never in the realm of sport had a returning champion been given such a welcome. And best of all, this young boy from Georgia, about whom all this immense ado was being made, had brought home with him not alone the silver cup emblematic of the British championship, and the big gold medal, he had brought something finer than medals and silver cups, and all the championships in the world—the love of the English people and the esteem of a whole nation.

In his graceful speech at the City Hall, Mayor Walker said: "I have just learned, Bobby, that you were born on the 17th of March. If that fact had been made public before you arrived, the safety of the City Hall would have been imperiled, because the crowd would have flocked to this building and would have carried it away."

It was like stepping off the *Aquitania* into one of the Arabian nights; one of the very biggest nights of all. O. Henry was right—calling it the Modern Baghdad. And still a bit dizzy, Bobby and Watts and I set out for Columbus, Ohio, and the 30th Open Championship of the United States. It takes something out of a man, that furious grind across the sea; something not accounted for by mere physical weariness or loss of weight. And those who know golf did not expect Bobby to win both of these tournaments, certainly not in so brief a time. Golf is not played so much by musculature and physique as deep in the mysterious convolutions of the brain. Bobby and Walter Hagen, and George Von Elm and Watts—all were frayed and stale mentally when they went to Columbus. Bobby looked fit to the casual eye. He had got back the dozen pounds he lost at St. Anne's, but the look in his eyes was jaded and dull. And as he started out in his first round, he said to me: "I wish it was over."

And still so great was his game and so exemplary his determination that he went out the first day and shot 70, two strokes back of the inevitable 68—this time by Wild Bill Mehlhorn—and after taking his shower, walking slowly back to his locker, all broken out with heat rash across his broad young shoulders, he came up to me and rested his weary, wet head on my shoulder whimsically, and said: "Why can't I play this darned game?"

I knew what he meant. That 70 looked good on the board but it had been a struggle every stroke and every inch of the way. Next day came the worst round that Bobby ever shot in a National Open Championship—a 79, including everything in the name of trouble, from two penalty shots, one self-imposed, to a ghastly 7 on the last hole. This put him six mortal strokes back of Mehlhorn and four back of Joe Turnesa. On the fifteenth green, Bobby grounded his putter in front of the ball, squaring it on the line, and when he moved the putter, the ball turned half over. Nobody else saw it, but Bobby said it moved. Clarence Wolff, playing with Bobby, said: "This action of Bobby Jones should be an example to every American boy and every American competitive athlete. Nothing finer has ever come under my observation."

Bobby had set his heart on winning the two big open championships, but fate and nature and human endurance all seemed to be against him. Turnesa had been moving along at a relentless clip, and at the end of the third round on the last day, Bobby was still three strokes back of the flying Italian. In the afternoon, Turnesa started 15 minutes ahead of Jones, and stroke for stroke they played the first eight holes, and then at the tricky ninth, which had cost Bobby a 4 every day he had played it, Joe went ahead another stroke with a par 3. Four strokes behind and nine holes to play. The young Georgian was on the verge of disaster. It was not only a question of golf now but of heroic courage. Bobby began closing the gap on Turnesa at the long twelfth and stroke by stroke he closed with an advance as immutable and as certain as fate itself. On that windswept last nine that had wrecked so many scores that week, he gained back those four strokes and one more—the winning stroke.

If ever I had a proper excuse for a panegyric, this was the time. Starting the year as U.S. Amateur Champion of 1925, Bobby added inside the space of three weeks—17 days to be exact—the British Open and the U.S. Open Championships, which never before had been won in the same season by any man. He occupied a throne on which no other golfer had ever sat. It was incredible. It was impossible. But it was true. But instead of boasting, instead of shouting, "1 told you so," and I had been telling them for five years, I was extravagantly quiet and thankful. A beautiful dream had come true, a dream we had held on to through so many grim vicissitudes and so many bitter disappointments.

I remembered so well back in 1921 at St. Louis when Bobby, apparently primed to win the championship, went down in defeat before Willie Hunter, and the boys in the press tent were shaking their heads. The idea was that he couldn't win. I remember how I stood up before them then and told them out of a full heart that was pretty close to breaking that one of these days they would be sitting before those same typewriters and writing the line for all the world to read, that Bobby Jones was the greatest golfer of them all. I would now let them do the panegyrics, and moderated and chastened by adversity, I would not argue with them this time.

In his last six open championships, five in the United States and one in Great Britain, Bobby Jones had won three times, tied once, and finished no worse than second in the other starts. There is no use looking for expletives to describe this showing in a game that is rarely consistent. He had played the last nine holes at Scioto under smashing pressure, through a driving, roistering wind in eight 4s and one 3. What words are left to add anything to the greatness and the glory of this achievement?

The last two days were the hardest possible tests of golf at Scioto. The western sirocco struck on Friday afternoon and Saturday the skies were gray with intermittent rains, the wind fairly whistling.

The rough was a pet development of George Sargent's, the pro and relative of the celebrated English landscape artist who assuredly never painted anything more utterly intriguing. Indeed, before the tournament started, stories began to crop up about the rough, in the practicing rounds. One was attributed to Jock Hutchison.

"I was in a little money match," said the Hutch, "and on the second fairway, I knocked my ball into the rough, which was the easiest thing you could do with it along that slope. The caddy and I went over into the tiger country to look for it. We couldn't find it. The other fellows got tired of waiting. They said drop another ball without penalty. I dropped a ball over my shoulder and lost that, and while I was looking for it, I lost the caddy."

The Fourth Estate was looked up to at this tournament. We were on the roof, perhaps the only cool spot about the scene of battle, overlooking the grandstand and the tenth tee and the eighteenth green. Perfect. On the evening of the first round, the sun was setting in a clear twilight over the golf course of the Scioto Country Club. Every competitor known to fame was in. Every typewriter was clattering like a machine gun. Clickety-click went the typewriters; and clickety-click went the concomitant telegraph implements. The leads were all in and everybody was happy. Substantially the leads recited, plus the decorative fancies of the various writers, that Wild Bill Mehlhorn was leading with a par-busting 68; that the inevitable Bobby Jones was second, with a brilliant 70; Joe Turnesa, third with 71.

Suddenly panic broke out. Here came a courier from the front, galloping up, buckety-buckety, with the startling report that on the last tee stood one John H. Junor of Portland, Oregon, and that the hitherto unheralded Mr. Junor needed a par 5 for a 70. There were howls of wrath and dismay and frantic queries as to who was this John H. Junor, and why. Especially why. Another 70 or 71 or even a 72 would utterly disrupt all the early leads and smear a hundred thousand miles of telegraph wire with corrections and explanations and revisions. But that is precisely what John H. Junor did. Something went wrong with his game and he shot a shocking 70, and all the stories had to be recalled and rewritten and refiled. And on the hapless and innocent head of the story wrecker were discharged ornate expletives and horrid ambitions for his future state that would have appalled a thoughtful person who had not already filed the front part of his story.

Not a correspondent at that tournament will ever forget John H. Junor, or the little lesson he imparted concerning the inadvisability of writing one's lead before all the returns are in from Oregon, or China, or anywhere. So Bobby came home in the highly technical position of wearing one crown on his blond head and one draped on either ear. Home to another magnificent reception, all the way from the Terminal Station to the new home of the Atlanta Athletic Club. The roar of the crowd, the packed streets. Such a welcome as only Atlanta can give, after all . . . seemed to be worth anything or everything in the world, just then. And Lord, how it made your eyes sting!

32.
The Battle of Baltusrol

Bobby Jones passed out of the picture of the United States Championship at Baltusrol for the first time in three years. He had won two championships in a row, at Merion and at Oakmont, and four matches in the third, but in the final round with George Von Elm he was not wearing the iron glove. Luck and the breaks of the game had drawn him in the same bracket with Chick Evans and Francis Ouimet, two of the greatest golfers who ever lived, and he had to shoot no worse than par for two long and stricken days to eliminate them. This undeniably took its toll, and the iron grip relaxed, and George Von Elm, a great golfer and a great sportsman, came to the crown he had sought so long.

Bobby had qualified with 143, one stroke above the record, set by Clark Corkran two years before at Merion. George had played so miserably he had to work desperately to qualify. In his first match, Ellsworth Augustus had him beaten at the eighteenth and again at the nineteenth, only to let him get away. George had been coming on his game and Bobby had reached the peak too soon.

Twice the Rose of the Rancho had traveled 7,000 miles back and forth to be beaten by Jones; in the final at Merion, 9–8; in the semifinals at Oakmont, 7–6; and now, the third time, George was on his toes, intent with the glowing fury of three years to win. In losing, Bobby showed the greatest fighting spirit in all his career. Of all his championships, I loved him best in that long and losing battle as he fought his way to the thirty-fifth green, again and again refusing to quit under the grimmest pressure he had yet encountered in the amateur championship.

At the seventeenth hole, with Bobby 2 down and 2 to play, Von Elm was out in front with two heroic shots, which was a feat in itself, and played his pitch a dozen feet above the pin. Bobby trying desperately to carry the match to the last green, played a shot that he never surpassed, seven feet from the cup, wrung out of a game that was wrong all day. It was his last punch and a good one, swung from the canvas. He had not sunk a long putt all day, and this one refused him in the crisis. He had shot one over 4s for 35 holes, but it was not good enough for the master golfer from the West Coast. The champion had passed from the picture and Von Elm had achieved his greatest ambition—Amateur Champion of the United States.

Von Elm had the reputation of a cold-blooded match player, a killer. When the handsome Uhlan went swaggering down the fairway, you could hear the sabers clink. He looked like a German uber-lieu-tenant. But at the seventeenth green of the morning round, there was a beautiful demonstration of something that is finer than golf itself—sportsmanship. Both were on this long par five hole. George putted first, 30 inches from the pin. Bobby went boldly for his birdie, overran, but sank coming back. The gallery applauded and started walking away. George was left with a puzzling putt for a half, easily missable. He hesi-tated and stepped back from his ball; he was nervous and the motion of the gallery had upset him. Bobby walked over and tapped the ball away, and said: "I'll give you that one, George."

That was a pretty and gracious thing to do and not to be outdone, at the next green, George gave Bobby one of about the same length. In a match of such intensity, the chivalry of these two reveals them as sports-men, neither killers nor cold-blooded match players. And Bobby said in his speech at the presentation: "You can't expect anyone to go on beating as fine a golfer as Von Elm."

Six years before Baltusrol, Bobby, then a lad of 18, after winning his last Southern Championship at Chattanooga, had gone on to Memphis to play in the Western Amateur Championship. After qualifying with 69–70, a new record for the tournament, he went on to meet Chick Evans, perennial champion of the Western Association, in the final round. Three down and seven to play, Bobby won back those three holes in dizzy succession, and Chick beat him with a birdie on the thirty-sixth green. They had never met again until Baltusrol. Bobby had despaired of getting revenge for Memphis until the draw brought them together for the second time. Bobby shot a 70 in the morning round and was only 2 up. He was 2 up at the twenty-seventh. He simply could not get away from the monarch of yesterday. He was a stroke under par for 34 holes on that awe-inspiring Baltusrol course, when the holes gave out, and a great veteran of a hundred campaigns slipped out of the picture. Great and sincere as my admiration for Chick Evans had been for the last dozen years or more, at Baltusrol it reached the peak.

Here is the brief story of the semifinal match between the Damon and Pythias of golf, Bobby and Francis Ouimet. Francis had spanked Bobby decisively in 1921, at the Engineer's club; Bobby, come to man's estate, had given Francis the most severe drubbing of his career at Merion. But that was a different Francis from the gaunt machine that stalked around Baltusrol. Francis was himself again and was shooting almost impeccable golf but Bobby picked off six pars and three birdies on the first nine holes, against par by Ouimet, was 3 up at the turn and the match ended 6–5.

Bobby's mother, Miss Clara, followed Bobby's match with Ouimet. She was either philosophical, or a grand actress, or else she had never seen her young son in difficulties. She was as calm and as placid as a morning in May, but at the time I saw her, Bobby was winning the ninth hole with a birdie 3, which gave him a 32 going out.

Bobby Jones.

33.
An Interview with Bobby

In response to a request from the general manager of the Associated Press, Kent Cooper, to John S. Cohen, then editor and publisher of the *Atlanta Journal*, I obtained the following "interview" from Bobby Jones in July 1926—his first and probably his last interview on how to play golf.

Bobby Jones, open golf champion of America and Great Britain, and amateur champion of America, all at the same time, is a difficult boy to interview. But that is not at all because he is the first official golfing champion of the world. It is because he is one of the most modest boys in the world. It required a deal of convincing to gain his first, and very likely his last, formal interview on golf. I told him the greatest of press associations believed that many people wanted to hear from him in his own words, how he played golf—the "Master Stylist"—and how he won championships. Bobby at last blushed and gave in.

"All right," he said. "Where do we start?"

"Where you started golf," I suggested. "How did you get your game?"

"Luck," he answered succinctly. "The biggest piece of golfing luck I ever had was when the Atlanta Athletic Club got Stewart Maiden for its professional. I was five years old then, and lived opposite the gate of the East Lake golf course. Next year Dad moved our family into a little cottage on the club property, alongside what is now the first fairway. I had taken up golf in a small way with a sawed-off cleek one of the East Lake players had given me. Stewart never gave me any lessons; I just followed him around the course and watched him. I wanted to play golf, and he was the best player about the club, and I imitated his style, like a monkey, I suppose. The luck was in the fact that Stewart had the finest and soundest style I have ever seen. Naturally, I did not know this at the time. But I grew up swinging like him. In the last 10 years I've changed a good deal in some ways. My build is not like Stewart's, you know."

"You're fatter," I suggested. Bobby's ears reddened.

"Never mind that. I'm not as fat as I was when I got off the *Aquitania* 10 days ago. I lost 12 pounds those three days at Scioto. And I'm not fat anyhow. As I was saying, I don't swing just like Stewart today. But that was the foundation, and I can go out on a golf course anytime and swing exactly like him. He has a sound and orthodox style."

I asked what he meant by orthodox.

"In golf I should say it was a style which would suit fundamentally any player unless he was anatomically freakish. There is nothing odd or unusual about Stewart's methods."

"And yours?"

"Well, at times my methods seem unusually hard to get along with. Maybe I haven't helped the original style by changing it. Anyway, I can't help believing that is the best way to acquire a sound game—imitation of a good player, in childhood. If you don't get started in childhood, take some lessons. A good professional can work out a style that will suit you, if you will do what he says."

The subject of style characteristics came up, Bobby now being universally regarded as the glass of fashion and the mold of form in golf. Bobby did not want to talk about this phase. I insisted.

"Well, judging by the pictures I see of myself," he admitted, "I keep my feet closer together in the full shots than almost anybody else in the world. And, keep my hands low and close to my knickers in addressing the ball. My arms do not seem to get far away from my body in the backswing, and I suppose this is what they mean in saying my style is compact. My stance is very slightly open for all shots except the putt; that is, the left foot is a bit farther back from the line of the shot than the right. I do not regard this as important. Sometimes I play shots with my toes level, and I know fine players who employ a very open stance, and others with a square stance—the toes level—and still others with a closed stance, the right foot being drawn back. The main point in my stance, as I understand it, is to play the ball opposite the left heel in all normal full wood shots, and in most normal full iron shots for distance. Two or three years ago I was getting into a lot of trouble, pulling and smothering, by carelessly letting the ball stray back toward the line of the right heel. I play many pitch shots and irons, when a low flight with much backspin is needed, from between my feet or even toward the line of the right heel. But to get a normal, well-behaved shot with a full swing, I have found that the place for the ball, for me, is opposite the left heel. Mind you, I don't say that is right for everybody, but it certainly is Stewart's method for practically all shots, and he even plays the ball as far ahead as opposite the left instep. I think the idea is to keep the weight well back of the stroke. When it gets in front, anything can happen, and usually does."

I asked about hands, arms, and grip.

"I never think about my hands. The regular overlapping or Vardon grip seems to take care of that phase pretty well. I think that grip is best, if your hands are reasonably big and strong. The little finger of the right hand overlaps the forefinger of the left, the left thumb of the hand being buried under the right palm; a very compact grip which tends to keep the hands from working against each other save in the proper way. The club is held strictly in the fingers, rather delicately. Don't squeeze it. I can spoil a shot any time by tightening my grip consciously. I use the same grip for every shot down to the putt, where I reverse it. For me, the putt is essentially a right hand stroke, and I put all the right hand on the shaft and overlap the right little finger with the left forefinger. I take the putter back with the left hand and stroke the ball with the right. It has worked very well at times, as at Merion and Oakmont, and not so well on this last trip. I putted like an old woman in that last round in the British Open. Thirty-nine putts—it was terrible!"

Bobby needs only 31 or 32 strokes in his average round of championship play, and in his first round at St. Anne's he used only 29. His card of 74 in the last round of the British Open, with 39 putts and only 35 other strokes in it, was a wonderful achievement.

"The left arm should be kept straight on the backswing and through every shot until the ball has been struck. Except the putt, of course. I mean, my left arm is kept straight; and I think any bending of that arm tends to make a chop instead of a swing. And here is a point I am just learning: the left hand should be regarded as the master in the swing. I'm not sure it really is the master. I know the right hand provides the punch, or most of it. But if I get to thinking about the right hand, or ignoring the left, the right seems to get in too soon and all kinds of trouble results. By regarding the left as in control, I can get a sort of 'feel' in the stroke; and the right, no matter how ignored, comes in at the proper juncture. At Sunningdale, when I had those rounds of 66 and 68, qualifying for the British Open, I felt as if I were literally making the shot with my left hand. It seemed I could not get off line. I felt as if I could spank that ball just anywhere I wanted to. I'm going to study this phase seriously in the next few months and try to improve my game, which certainly has not been consistent this year."

Bobby was at odds with most of the critics, but I passed that up for the oft-debated question as to how much thinking a player could do while a stroke was in progress, and what, if anything, he should think about.

"Do you ever think about more than one thing while making a shot?" I asked.

"If I do, I don't make the shot," he said emphatically. "I don't know if I think of even one thing. I never seem to remember. Maybe you recall that shot to the eighteenth green at Inwood, in the play-off with Bobby Cruickshank."

I recalled it—well. That was the shot which won for Bobby Jones his first major championship: a perfectly executed iron shot of 190 yards, finishing over water, six feet from the pin. A championship rode on that shot. And next day on the train, Bobby had asked me, somewhat shyly, if he took a long time over the shot, or played it promptly; and if he took a full swing or a three-quarter swing. He said he did not remember one single thing about the playing of that shot, after he decided to go for the distant green.

"What did you think about last Saturday when you stood on the last tee at Scioto, with a 480-yard hole on which to get a birdie four to go ahead of Joe Turnesa?" I asked. Bobby grinned reflectively. "I thought I'd sock this one," he replied. "But that was before I swung. I didn't think of anything consciously while I was swinging."

Well, he socked it 310 yards, with the wind against him. And he got home with a spared mashie iron second, and got the birdie four, and won the championship. This indicates it pays not to think—while swinging.

"There's another thing," said Bobby. "I try never to force a club anymore. Rather than hit hard with a mashie, I take a number four iron. It seems I can keep the 'feel' of that left hand better, that way."

About the nerve strain in tournament play: "There are two kinds of golf," said Bobby seriously. "There is golf—and tournament golf. And they are not at all alike, inside. I have found that out from experience, much of it bitter. I'm more nervous before medal competition than match. In a match you have a single human opponent, who may make some mistakes. In medal play you are up against Old Man Par, who never gets down in one putt and never takes three. The first round of an open championship always causes me the most suffering. It's worse than the last, oddly enough. You see, in starting, I don't know how I'm going to be hitting my shots the first few holes. The start at Scioto was torture, because I had played wretchedly in practice and was uncertain if I could hit the ball decently. I do not think nervousness hurts my game. The more nervous I am, the better I play, usually. I suppose it means being keyed up. Some of the sloppiest rounds I have played, I was not nervous at all. As to the strain, I don't seem to be conscious of it during a round. Afterward—well, I know something has been done to me. I sort of collapsed at Columbus after getting back to the hotel. I was all in."

This was after shooting the last 12 holes of the final round two strokes better than par. Apparently the killing strain did not affect his game detrimentally.

"I've another idea," said Bobby suddenly. "I think this habit of grim concentration straight through the entire round is a mistake—for me, anyway. If I walk along like an Indian, concentrating desperately on the next shot with an eighth of a mile to walk before reaching the ball, I feel sort of fagged in my head when I stand up to the shot. Lately, I have found out that a word or two with the man I am playing with, or the referee, or maybe some friend in the gallery relieves the tension. Then when I get to the ball I can snap on the concentration as hard as I need to."

"One thing more, Bobby. There is a lot of interest in those penalty strokes you have called on yourself. At St. Louis and Brookline and at Worcester—they say that one cost you the championship—and the one at Scioto, in that awful round of 79 when the ball moved on the green—"

Bobby held up a warning hand.

"That is absolutely nothing to talk about," he said, "and you are not to write about it. There is only one way to play this game."

Which is such an excellent finishing line that I am risking a violation of confidence to use it. Because there is so much of Bobby himself in that estimate: "There is only one way to play this game!"

*Bobby Jones in
the rough.*

34.
The Black Scot

Again the boys came back to Oakmont. And again the Big Course
whipped them. In the most dramatic finish the U.S. Open
Championship had seen, Tommy Armour, the Black Scot, and the
confident little English-born professional, Lighthorse Harry Cooper,
were tied at 301. In this all-British playoff, the Scot won 76 to 79.

To add to the already numerous hazards on this 6,900-yard-long,
truly championship course, the bunkers, or as we say in America "traps,"
were furrowed. Every morning the sand in every trap was gone over with
a curious sort of rake, which arranged the sand in grooves and ridges,
the grooves about as deep as the diameter of a golf ball. As far as possible the grooves were set crosswise with the line of play from any part of
the bunker. The fairways were side-guarded severely, and if off line, the

ball might take refuge in the most scientifically placed traps a golf architect could devise, perhaps 200 yards from the green. The boys did not take a No. 2 iron and attack that ball from a clear lie in the sand, with the idea of reaching the green and saving a stroke. No, they took their trusty niblicks and excavated, grimly intent on getting the ball back on the fairway. Nothing more. Oakmont's theory, of course, was that the player was not forced to shoot into a bunker, and when he did, "the punishment should fit the crime." To save strokes at Oakmont it was imperative to stay out of those furrowed bunkers.

Bobby Jones finished with the biggest score, 309, and lowest position, in a tie for eleventh place, of his eight open championships. He was never on his game, yet he was never sufficiently off to indicate scores of 76-77-79-77, never under 76. Six strokes back of the lead as the final day dawned, Bobby was feeling confident enough, and we decided that a couple of 72s would be good enough. After which he came in with 79 and 77. Yet, as he stood on the thirteenth tee in the third round, with all the trouble he had found in the furrowed bunkers and all the dismal golf he had played, he was in the best position in the field. He was just one stroke behind Cooper, who was leading, and looked set for no worse than 72. His shots were finally going well; he was hitting the ball beautifully. That was the only interval in the tournament when he was really going.

On the thirteenth, par 3, his drive was off line, winding up in a narrow ditch. He was in an ugly place and had little room to swing. He knocked the ball out into a big bunker, failed to get out on his first try, finally reaching the green on his fourth shot, eight feet from the flag.

"Then," said Bobby, "I carefully missed the putt."

How those par 3s punished him. On the four par 3s in this round he had 19 shots, and those seven extra strokes were the championship.

Starting eight strokes back in the fourth round, he did not work too hard, although he did not stop trying. He was not pleased with his game; neither was he grieving about it. He was just out of Emory

University where he finished his law studies and was admitted to the state and federal bars, as a junior partner in his father's law firm. He had had very little opportunity to practice, and Bobby, probably better than any man living, knew that no golfer could stay on top of his game all the time, or even a better part of the time. It was the first open championship in years without an amateur threat at the finish.

So the debonair Black Scot, who started playing golf at the age of six on his native heath at Edinburgh, who enlisted as a private in the British tank corps, came out a major, losing the sight in one eye, was tied at the finish with Lighthorse Harry Cooper, 22 years old.

As at the historic championship of 1920 at Inverness, three men came up to the last green with a putt to tie. Cooper's score was already on the board, 301. Gene Sarazen came first, needing a birdie to tie. He hit his 50-foot putt bravely, but failed and was a stroke outside. Armour came next. He had started the round one stroke back of Cooper. They had turned in 39 each. Armour started the last nine with a wretched six and it looked as if he were through. He picked up a birdie at the eleventh, but on the long twelfth, the "ghost hole," which had wrecked so many scores during the tournament, he took seven strokes. Now he surely was through. But the Black Scot was still fighting. He was now three strokes back of Cooper and something of the old Jacobite cavalier spirit must have come out in Tommy's heart as he started that final six holes. He went 3-4-4-3-4, and now he had a birdie at the eighteenth to tie Cooper.

I shall never forget that last hole. I sat at the edge of the green to see what the Black Scot would do. He was the best iron player that I had ever seen, as I have said more than once. On this 460-yard hole, his fine drive left him 180 yards from the green. This was the shot that would tell the story—a chance to get the putt down—or not. Low moans from the gallery marked the progress of his perfect iron shot. It was exactly on line. It stopped 10 feet, a long 10 feet short of the pin. A 10-foot putt for a tie! And his first open championship!

Tommy could not stand still. He walked back and forth out of range of his partner's vision. His face was gray, and his black eyebrows were startlingly dark. The silence had a tension that hurt. Suddenly I became conscious of a conversation behind me. Two men were talking, so low that their voices seemed to be inside my own head: "No man on earth could hole that putt under the pressure that's on him now," said the first voice.

"I would not say that," came the reply. "Do you know what he did in the World War?"

" 'No, what?"

"He got out of his tank and strangled a Prussian officer with his bare hands. D'ye think he will miss that putt?"

He sank it.

Hail, Black Scot!

In the playoff, the stern old course still resisted their assault. Both were out in 39. Tommy again lost a stroke at the tenth, and another at the eleventh, started his comeback on the thirteenth, and pulled up square with a 50-foot putt at the fifteenth. The treacherous sixteenth gave him a mortgage on the title when he went up two strokes, and the seventeenth foreclosed it. On the seventeenth Cooper had played a magnificent second shot, 18 inches from the pin. To shoot for the pin, Tommy had to pitch over a deep bunker that might cost any number of strokes, but he shot boldly for it, and was a few inches inside Harry. Tommy won less with his hands than he did with his heart. The extra stroke gained on the last hole was not needed.

That very complete failure at Oakmont accounted for Bobby Jones' trip to Britain in 1927. Disappointed at his showing at Oakmont, Bobby wired the U.S. Golf Association to see if it were too late to enter the British Open Championship. His entry was cabled and two weeks later, he sailed and arrived at St. Andrews with five days left for practice before the tournament began.

Bobby Jones being lifted up on the shoulders of the crowd.

35.
The Second British Open

The tumult and the shouting had died. The captains and the kings had departed. There was a brooding content in the soft, long twilight over the Firth, and the old turf of St. Andrews showed gray in the foreground. The British championship of 1927 was over, and Bobby Jones was champion again, the first time a golfer had repeated successively in 20 years. The "Unofficial King of Scotland," he was affectionately called.

If ever an athlete was set to win an event, it was Bobby at St. Andrews. Six strokes ahead of the field with a new record score of 285 for the British championship, one stroke better than the American record held by Chick Evans. He finished five strokes better than par and was never over par for a single round. In the good old Scriptural phrase, his face was set like a flint on the goal, and as the rounds went by the shadows deepened beneath his eyes; as the strain took its toll, more than one Englishman asked if the boy were physically well. It was simply unparalleled concentration on the work in hand. I have seen something like it on the face of a chess player, pondering over some deep and vital problem. Bobby was thousands of miles from the scrambling mob at St. Andrews. He was no nearer than China to his playing companions. Bobby was entirely absorbed in the shot he was playing at the moment.

I have never seen nor hope to see another such round as Bobby played on the first day of the tournament. His score of 68 was the first time he had ever broken 70 in an open championship in twelve starts, and was a record score for St. Andrews in competition, shot from the tournament tees. He was leading the chase from then on, a rare achievement for one man to set the pace at the beginning of a tournament and still be in front at the finish.

Coming off the last green, he looked at me with a vague wonder in his eyes, and said: "Did you ever in all your life see so absolutely crazy a round?"

To elaborate: when I went up to his room in the Grand Hotel, hard by the eighteenth green, Bobby was sitting in one corner, still somewhat dizzy; Big Bob sat in another, smiling solemnly; Jack MacIntyre, Bobby's caddy, occupied another corner, smiling contentedly; Stewart Maiden, Kiltie the King Maker, had the other corner, saying nothing eloquently, but I thought I could discern a wee twinkle in his eye. Bobby was talking: "It was the hardest decent score I ever shot. I have played harder rounds, scoring worse, but I have never scored so well in so hard a round. Kiltie was right. He said if I ever got to missing my big shots, I might sink some putts. I sank some today. It seems you can't play the other shots and putt all at once. At least, I can't."

The cumulative luck of a dozen years was upon him about the greens and the putts that had denied him in a score of championships went down that day. He could not have putted on any other golf course in the world as he did at St. Andrews for on no other course could he have been on the green and so far from the cup. He had 28 putts, six of them more than 100 feet, did not miss one under 12 feet, and on the fifth, sank one of 120 feet for an eagle. This is the double green of the fifth and thirteenth holes, where Watts Gunn made his famous putt of about the same length in the amateur championship of 1926. After this spectacular exhibition, Bobby was off on a run that needed only seven putts on six consecutive holes. He played the next nine holes in 30 strokes. He went around the famous Loop, eighth through the twelfth, par 3-4-4-3-4, in sixteen strokes, opening a gap between himself and the rest of the field that was never closed.

I asked him how it felt to be leading the field.

"Don't worry," he replied, "somebody will come in with a 67, maybe a 66."

Nobody did.

In his second round of 72, Bobby had 33 putts, four more putts, four more strokes; in the third, his best played golf of the tournament up to the greens, he had 73 with 36 putts; and in the final round, 72 with 34 putts; as regularly mathematical in scoring and execution as golf could possibly be.

Bobby started badly in the last round and I was sick with fear that the great strain would kill him off at last. Big Bob confessed that he could not follow him. I confessed that I had not intended to go all the way, only to see him well started, then go back and rely on his lead of four strokes and the fine golf he was shooting. But he had not started well. He was three over 4s at the long fifth, and a sort of morbid fascination had carried me along until he reached the Loop, which he had entered with a bad 4 on the eighth hole, missing a yard-long putt. There he arose in his might, took that Loop by the tail, and jolly well twisted it. He went 3-3-3-3, and the championship was settled as a champion should settle it.

Big Bob said he had heard that Bobby was three over 4s, which was discouraging; then he heard he was two under 4s and he knew that was impossible. As he stood around the eighteenth green, wondering what was happening and waiting for the army to charge, somebody jogged him in the ribs. It was Stewart Maiden.

"Let's go," said Stewart.

"Where and what for?" queried Big Bob.

"Let's go. It's all over," persisted Stewart.

"What's all over," said the puzzled father.

"The show. He's in," said Stewart curtly.

Whereupon Stewart and Big Bob set out for the hotel. Stewart had never been so confident of his famous pupil. The night before the tournament began he had told me in a burst of confidence that he was certain Bobby would win, that no man in the field could beat him when he was hitting his shots as he was that week. It was the only prediction that Stewart ever made in an important event, an average of 100 percent.

Bobby, carried off the eighteenth green on the shoulders of a roaring mob, was rescued by six stalwart Scottish policemen, who worked their way to the hotel. Twenty thousand men and women and children were cheering him. "Good boy, Bobby," they called as he passed, and vied for an opportunity to pat him affectionately on his stained old sweater he had worn throughout the tournament. "Good boy, Bobby," they shouted, swirling acres of fans about the home green, the first tee, the Royal and Ancient Golf Club, and the hotel. I have never witnessed such an ovation in any sporting event, and they say the British are not demonstrative.

At the door of the hotel, Big Bob was waiting, as he had waited so many times for a tired little boy in rompers to come in at dusk from a long afternoon on the old course at East Lake. I took off my glasses to wipe them about this time but the mist was not on the glasses. If for no other reason than that Big Bob had come all the way over there to see it, it would have been Bobby's greatest triumph.

Even old St. Andrews was benign for once. There was practically no wind all week, and the North Atlantic was as placid as a mill pond.

Rare behavior for this seaside battleground. Enormous crowds followed the players, and on the last day, Bobby played through a narrow, solid mass of humanity from tee to green.

When Bobby went down to receive the most prized trophy in Britain for the second year, before that vast throng, stretching down to the Swilcan Burn, he made his most graceful speech and becoming gesture: "I had rather win a championship at St. Andrews than anything else that could happen to me. You have done so many things for me that I am embarrassed to ask one more, but I will. I want this wonderful old club to accept the custody of the cup for the coming year."

Harold Hilton replied: "Bobby Jones has done a simply magnificent thing in coming back to defend his title. It was a sporting thing to do, and our people, who already loved him, now simply adore him. He has won British hearts as well as British championships."

Truly the Unofficial King of Scotland.

36.
The Silent Scot

Carnoustie is a dear little Scottish town, whose name is not unfamiliar in my home town, Atlanta, which has had upwards of a dozen golf professionals from this small, Caledonian village. One was Willie Mann, dear old "Wullie," who was the first professional that the Druid Hills Golf Club had. There was Alex Smith, Jimmie Maiden and his brother Stewart, Kiltie the King Maker, and Willie Ogg and Charley Gray; all from Carnoustie, a town of 6,000 inhabitants and five golf courses; where an inexorable law says you may not play golf on the Sabbath day; and where the inhabitants carry curious little walking sticks on Sunday, the top fashioned in the shape of a golfclub head, which they swing, meditatively, as they take their Sabbath evening walks.

Sunday was the Sabbath in most of Scotland. At St. Andrews, there was nae gowf on Sunday. It was suggested that there might be conceivably a bootleg sort o'gowf; a putting course, mind you, hid out in the low hills among the heather to which steal unobtrusively certain desperate addicts of the game, of a Sabbath afternoon; and jouk in amang the heather for a roond or twa on the wee links. But naething legal! They played gowf on Sunday at Gleneagles, which was an American and ungodly type of perfectly beautiful golfing resort. I was there twice and approved it thoroughly, especially the day Mr. Jones shot a 67.

Our visit to Carnoustie was a sort of pilgrimage, especially for Bobby, the home of his friend and mentor and the man who was responsible for his golf—Stewart Maiden. Bobby had just been crowned British Open Champion at St. Andrews for the second successive time, his name was ringing through the land and he was going over to play an exhibition round on his teacher's old home course at Carnoustie.

Stewart was along of course, and George Low, who arranged the event. In all my experience in golf, which has been certainly not brief and perhaps not inconsiderable, there is nothing that quite compares with that pilgrimage to Carnoustie across the Tay River from St. Andrews. Even Stewart, the taciturn Caledonian, loosened up. We crossed the Tay on a ferry boat, and Stewart, spying a Scottish piper in full regalia, sidled off from the rest of the party, and the next thing we knew, the piper was strutting up and down the deck, and no true piper can pipe unless he is strutting, blowing "Cock of the North," quite lustily. He made them skirl with a will. My ambition heretofore had been to play a trombone or sliphorn, but right there, I was a convert to the bagpipe. But it needs a lot of room. It is strictly outdoor music.

At Dundee, the far side of the Tay, a thousand citizens, mysteriously apprised, were waiting to salute Bobby Jones, the unofficial King of Scotland. The way those people loved golf and Bobby is beyond words. It was ten minutes before his car could get started for Carnoustie. And there the mayor, or provost, awaited him with the key to the city and after luncheon, Bobby went out to play golf. About 6,000 of the population—which is estimated at 6,000—went along with him. I took a few pictures, then I found Stewart, and we turned back toward his old home.

I wished the boys from East Lake might have been along on this pilgrimage to visit the town and the golf course and Stewart's old home. We went along a substantial sort of street, all the houses of Scottish stone on both sides; low, solid, built for centuries. And we came to the home of Stewart Maiden. . . .

Stewart's mother was out in the little garden in the rear of the house and we spent an hour there. The dearest lady I have seen was Stewart's mother and I took a picture of her and Stewart on a bench in the garden. They thought a deal of Stewart, his mother and sister. And Stewart loved them no less.

It was a wonderful thing to see the way Stewart's fellow townsmen greeted him, as we were walking about the golf course, or walking through the town.

Up came a big Caledonian who had not seen Stewart in 20 years.

"Aye, Stewart," said he, as if it had been 20 minutes.

"Aye, Wullie," said Stewart in the same unexcited tone.

And they talked, Wullie doing most of the talking until another Scot strolled up.

"Aye, Stewart," said the newcomer.

"Aye, Sandy," said Stewart and Sandy joined in the conversation.

Another with flaming red hair walked up.

"Aye, Stewart," said he.

"Aye, Red," said Stewart, and they all were talking, although I would say Wullie kept up his end rather thoroughly.

In five minutes six of Stewart's old cronies strolled up, unconcernedly. I gathered they had heard most completely the story of Stewart's success in America; and certainly they knew accurately the triumphs of his famous pupil. But there was a curious lack of demonstration.

"Aye, Stewart," they saluted him in his home town. And "Aye, Sandy," was the Silent Scot's rejoinder.

*Bobby Jones in front of the
East Lake Golf Club.*

37.
The Cup Runneth Over

Bobby had gone, had seen, and had conquered Great Britain. At
Minikahda, he won his third national championship by defeating
Charles Evans Jr., 8–7. The long, long trail was turning. I was curiously
relaxed and happy. I would never have to argue again in any press
room. I would never have to make any more impassioned speeches
about this young man, who was now beyond all cavil or question the
greatest living golfer. The other fellows were all agreed at last with
what I had been telling them for seven long years. At Oakmont, the
more casuistic critics had said that Bobby was slipping when he failed
to win the Open Championship, indeed shot the worst golf of his
career. Ten weeks later at Minikahda, they were all saying that the
greatest golfer of all time had reached the pinnacle.

Bobby was fortunate enough to know the lash of misfortune in many years of defeat. It is in the fire of failure that great souls are made, not along the rose-red path of victory. Jones, beaten year after year, acquired the needed seasoning under the black shadow of depressing fortune. It was there he discovered the jewel in the toad's head of defeat. In this tournament he was like steel that had gone through the furnace.

Chick and Bobby, traditional rivals who had each won the amateur championship twice, were now in quest of the third. Here at Minikahda in 1916, Chick had won the U.S. Open Championship with a record score of 286, which stood for many years. He had gone on to win the Amateur Championship the same year, the first amateur to achieve this honor. He had not reached the final round since 1922 when he was defeated by Jess Sweetser, and after the reversals of several years, fortune had smiled and given him another opportunity. His return to first rank competition had been welcomed by all true golfing fans.

It is true the dauntless Chick had been defeated hither and yon during the past few years, but nobody had ever gone quite so fast against him as Bobby started at Minikahda. From the first hole where he took a birdie, Chick felt the cold iron grip upon his neck and the hand of a master heavy in his collar. He won only four holes during the match. Bobby had five birdies and an eagle for the 26 holes that were played, a string of seven 3s in the first 11 holes, was 5 up at the end of the morning round.

On the ninth hole, Bobby played the finest shot I have ever seen him make, irrespective of importance. The hole was a gigantic dog-leg, 512 yards long, with a finish up a steep slope to a small elevated green, two enormous shots to get home. Harry Vardon, the old master, said the most difficult shot in golf was the pitched approach to the green, meaning of course, the shot that carried to the green with power to hold it. Bobby played a spoon second with an eighth of a mile carry, or more, that stopped two feet short of the cup, toward which it trickled straight as a ruled line, and wanted only a grasshopper's kick added to the silken swing of Bobby Jones to have rolled in for a deuce. The only eagle ever made on that hole. That was the finishing touch.

Cold rain was pelting down as the gallery shivered around the twenty-sixth green. Chick putted first about four feet past the hole, and Bobby laid his putt up safely. As Chick stood addressing his ball, knowing that a half would only prolong the inevitable, he accidentally moved the ball with his putter. Smiling, he picked it up and held out his hand to Bobby. He had called the stroke on himself, and for a moment the gallery did not realize what had happened. Then they sent up a resounding cheer for Bobby's superb golf, and a tribute to the man who had fought so bravely when there was no chance to win.

After Bobby had gone, the gallery gathered around Chick to shake his hand. Chick, always willing to give a victor his laurels, said: "It was worth a good drubbing to see such a marvelous exhibition of golf."

In the first round of qualifying, Bobby had shot a very poor 75, and was worried. He decided the thing to do next day was to shoot for the medal, in other words, shoot the works. He reached the turn in 31, came home in 36, and was medalist with a card of 142, a tie for the record that was only lowered twice before the adoption of regional qualifying. In match play he had only one close call. In the first 18-hole match against Maurice McCarthy, he won only 2 up. He reached the top of his game in the 36-hole matches and trounced Harrison Johnston, Ouimet, and Evans decisively. More even than at Merion, he held them in an iron hand, and the best of the amateurs were as children before him.

I will never forget the face of Big Bob Jones as he walked slowly into the friendly little lounge upstairs in the club after Bobby had shot a 67 in the morning round and was 5 up. I had seen Big Bob's face set like a mask under the punishment of seeing Bobby go down to defeat, fighting; and again I had seen him at St. Andrews when his son was coming in with a championship and a record. But I had never seen quite the same look on the face of the gallant old Roman—as when he walked into the lounge at Minikahda. Others came along presently, and there was harmony, in considerable volume. Big Bob was singing bass and everything he sang sounded for all the world like "Glory, Glory, Hallelujah," or "The Battle Hymn of the Republic," or maybe "The Marseillaise."

My own heart wasn't so empty with all the boys coming around, shaking hands and congratulating me, as we said good-bye for another year until we would meet again at the championships in 1928.

And though I never mentioned it to Bobby, or he to me, this 1927 championship at Minikahda went into the book as one more consecutive year in which Bobby was a champion of the United States in the string he was trying to stretch to six.

Minikahda made it five in a row.

☐

All innovations are met by opposition hither and yon. The new standard ball adopted by the United States Golf Association in 1927 met furious opposition from the duffers, who imagined with no very good reason that it would curtail their range on the infrequent occasions when they managed to get the club head and the ball in approximately correct contact.

The Royal and Ancient and other golf arbiters decided something should be done about the golf ball—steps should be taken, resolutions adopted, or something. It turned out to be measures—weights and measures, you might say. And now we have the wretched ball in our power at least in one direction. We have it standardized, that is, it must not weigh more than a certain weight (1.62 ounces) and it must not be smaller than a certain diameter, which I believe is about 1.68 inches.

The golf ball was not always thus, a lively and expensive globule of rubber core and rubber strands. Before Mr. Haskell, a man with a vision probably by no means commensurate with what he actually accomplished for and to humanity, devised the rubber-cored ball, the sedate old "gutty" held sway. And before that was the "feathery." I suppose prior to the "feathery" the hardy Caledonian shepherds used round pebbles and drove, approached and putted with their shepherd's crooks, which looked as much like golf clubs as some of the putters now in alleged use.

The rubber-cored ball which made its appearance about 1920 was opposed bitterly until old Alec Herd espoused it and won his first and only British Open Championship with it, and thus established himself among the immortals.

The gutta-percha was opposed when it was first presented in the crude, hand-marked form in the days when Allan Robertson was king of the professional ranks in Britain. Allan was born in 1824, and died at the age of 34, the greatest golfer of his day. He set two records with the old "feathery." He was the first recorded golfer to break 80 for 18 holes, which he did with a 79 in 1857; and he was never beaten in a set match.

The Haskell, or lively rubber ball, proved to be the most radical and revolutionary innovation the game has known. It was directly responsible for the prodigious growth of the game, which with the old gutty was restricted in interest mainly to persons who were willing to study and work with it until they were at least decently proficient.

The fascination of the new ballistics was by no means restricted to players of golf. The manufacturers, after catching their breath, started out on an orgy of experimental production. They put practically everything inside the rubber strands from soft soap to some sort of acid that ruined the eyes of inquisitive children who cut into the missiles or bit them open. They made the balls smaller and smaller and wound the strands tighter and tighter, and Ted Ray and Abe Mitchell hit them farther and farther until finally the legislative powers took hold of the situation to prevent the standardized golf courses from being scrapped and made over on the Great Plains of the middle west or the Desert of Sahara; and for other purposes as the conventional legislative bills recite.

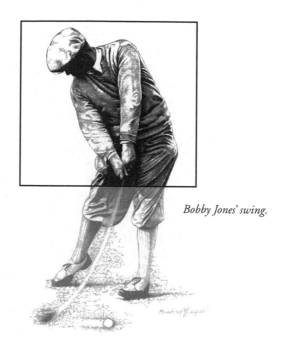

Bobby Jones' swing.

38.
Olympia Fields

For the third time in five years, Bobby Jones was tied at the end of the Open Championship of 1928, and again he lost in the playoff by one stroke. This time he was beaten by handsome Johnny Farrell in the most dramatic finish ever seen in an open championship. To finish with two birdies is so hectic an achievement that the fact that one man won and the other lost fades into comparative insignificance as we salute the greatest finish in all golfing history. Not one man alone made two birdies. They both made them. Farrell finished 3–4, and Bobby finished 3–4. The style in which they played those last two holes must have caused the gods of Olympus, if they were paying proper attention to their earthly Fields, to kick over the nectar pot and go thundering down the slopes to get a wee nip of a certain Georgia product.

One stroke behind as they drove from the eighteenth tee, it looked as if Bobby might catch his opponent when his second shot was nicely in front of the green, and Johnny was in the rough, 60 yards away. He pitched on 10 feet from the pin, and Bobby chipped dead for a birdie 4. The fighting spirit of the Irish was in a grim humor, and there was a curious steely glint in Johnny's dark blue eyes as he stood up to this long putt with his face set like a cameo. Just as he started his backswing, a movie camera began to whir, a sound beside which, to a tense golfer, the buzz of a rattlesnake is bland innocence itself. Johnny checked the stroke, stepped back from the ball, and smiled. Then despite all the strain, he struck the ball as smoothly and crisply as the beat of a Curtiss engine. It rolled along a curving line, beautifully predestined on the slanting green, drawn to the cup as if by a magnet, and dropped in for the championship.

What a roar went up. It was as if some giant finger had touched off a giant gun. Johnny smiled in his fine, boyish way, and I knew why he was called the "beautiful Irishman." A sort of flare of the spirit had Johnny. I had seen Lou Tellegen in his blazing younger days when he was leading man for Sarah Bernhardt, and was rated the handsomest man in the world, but I think he was never handsomer than Johnny was on this memorable occasion, when he won his first and only open championship.

All honor to Johnny. And all honor to Bobby. He was superb in defeat. There was no sting. Nothing but glory in the finish.

On the thirty-fifth green, Bobby had a putt four times the length of Johnny's winning one to keep him in the hunt, and this too had clicked into the cup with the certainty of a natural phenomenon. True, he did not catch the handsome Irishman, but it took a birdie to win against a birdie. I am sure that no golfer who ever lived, not even the mighty battler, Hagen, could have squeezed from a slipping and uncertain game, the four rounds that Bobby fashioned in his own miraculous manner at Olympia Fields, to tie, and then to carry the playoff to the home green.

Bobby started the tournament with a fair round of 73, went into the lead at the half with 144, and was two strokes ahead as he started the last round. His driver had betrayed him and he had been struggling all the way with difficult and sometimes impossible second shots with remarkable recoveries, and was putting better than anybody in the field on the bent greens. Olympia Fields was a course which required above all else accurate tee shots.

In that final round, Bobby, with the championship in his hands, kicked it away. He picked up two birdies at the first and fifth holes, and there, as far as human reckoning applied, he had the title in hand. He was past the toughest part of the course and had a lead of at least five strokes. And this happened. It is a sort of confession. Bobby was worn out fighting the course. He was tired of struggling, and had a big lead. I think, after that fifth hole, he looked more a certain winner than he had looked at the same stage in any other open tournament, even at St. Andrews. And he made the fatal mistake of telling himself that he would just coast in from there, the most dangerous mood a competitive golfer ever encounters.

Beginning with the sixth hole, par is 3-4-3-4-4. Bobby's card for those holes was 5-6-4-5-5. Seven strokes lost to par in five successive holes. That is what coasting can do even to a Bobby Jones. The jolt came at the sixth where he pulled his drive into a ditch and did well to get a 5. The rest of the debacle came naturally, trying too hard. After he had coasted out of a great lead, he began playing golf once more and scrambled in with a card of 77. Hagen and MacDonald Smith had not taken advantage of the opportunity he had presented them in the last round, but Johnny Farrell with a fine round of 72 had picked up five strokes on him and they were tied.

In the playoff, Bobby picked up his usual birdie at the first hole and was never in the lead again until the thirteenth hole. Johnny played steadily and beautifully. Bobby would present him with a couple of strokes at a time, work like a beaver to get them back in the next four or five holes, and then present him with a couple more. Johnny had a remarkable score of 70 in the morning round and led by three strokes. In the afternoon, Johnny started 5-5-5 and with 4-4-4, Bobby went into the lead for the first time since the first hole in the morning. Johnny squared with a deuce at the short sixteenth, his third deuce of the match.

Johnny's score was 143 and Bobby's 144, in this first scheduled 36-hole playoff in the Open Championship.

Olympia Fields had much drama in this tournament. In the second round, Walter Hagen had 40 strokes on the first nine, under lowering skies but no rain, and then in a torrential downpour came back in 32. This 72 kept him very much in the chase.

But it was Roland Hancock, a young professional, who had both Bobby and Farrell beaten as he stood on the seventeenth tee of the last round after a wonderful burst of golf, scoring 33 going out. Par 4 and 5 on the last two holes would have given him a card of 69 and the championship by two strokes. A grim, bitter tragedy of golf for this kid. Glory and fame lay ahead. A simple 4 and 5 were all that was in the way. The great Bobby had collapsed. The great Hagen was back of Bobby. Farrell was tied. Everything rested on Roland's broad shoulders and the brightest coronet of sport was an inch above his brow. But the strain, aided by a wildly enthusiastic gallery, was too great. He finished 6-6. The kid had learned very young what the murderous strain of a final round in an open championship could be.

And Bobby Jones was left with a set of harrowing memories of golden opportunities tossed away, more than in any championship in which he had ever played.

Bobby Jones with the Calamity Jane putter in the background.

39.

After Brae Burn—A Look at the Records

In his triumph over Thomas Philip Perkins, the British Amateur Champion, in the first real international championship ever played, Bobby closed out one of his greatest years at the Brae Burn Country Club, in the U.S. Amateur. He tied the old record of Jerome Travers in winning four amateur championships, and in all future battles, Bobby would have to travel alone in uncharted territory. No golfer in the three hundred years of the game had achieved the conquests of the boy from Georgia. Since June 1923, his blond head had never been without a national golfing crown. In addition to the four U.S. Amateurs that had fallen to his irons, he had twice won the U.S. Open Championship, and twice the British.

Although Bobby was still suffering from wildness off the tee in his final match, it was not as acute as earlier in the week, and in most instances, he was able to pull a club from his bag that would nullify any mistakes his driver had cost. He had 71 in the morning round, and after the first six holes, Perkins did not have a chance until the seventeenth where Bobby went over par for one of the only two over par holes of the day. In the afternoon, he was out in 35, and could have beaten any golfer in the field easily. His short game was more perfect than I had ever seen it. Calamity Jane, his favorite and famed putter, had been restored to favor, after having been in disuse for some time, and he gave Phil a putting lesson he likely would never forget. The golfing brigade was put on notice that they had nothing to look forward to but years of Jones.

Vanished were Perkins' great shots of the earlier rounds, and the Lancashire lad was never close to par. He said wistfully after the match was over:

"When one plays against Mr. Jones, he has only the pleasure of being defeated by the greatest of all golfers and the finest of all sportsmen."

Bobby was over the peak when he reached Brae Burn after playing in the Walker Cup matches at the Chicago Golf Club, where he had led the Americans to their greatest victory. A long string of sub-par rounds, a dozen in all, seemed to have used up all the golf he had for the time being. He qualified safely but not brilliantly, and got by his first 18-hole match on "Red Wednesday," as George Trevor of the New York Sun had called those calamitous 18-hole matches. In the second match, he met Ray Gorton, who held the course record, and this turned out to be the crucial match of the championship.

Against Gorton, Bobby went incredibly off his game, taking 42 strokes on the first nine holes, and still was square, for Gorton was equally wild. Then came the fireworks. The tenth hole was 491 yards long. Gorton smacked a brassie second 12 feet from the flag, and sank an eagle 3, while Bobby was happy with his birdie 4. The eleventh hole was 463 yards, par 4. Gorton was nicely on with his second, 20 feet from the pin. Bobby's drive was sliced into the deep rough with a small tree almost in his line and a group of tall trees directly between his ball and the green, 200 yards away. He had to get elevation on the shot promptly, a niblick or spade shot, for the ball was in deep grass. It looked as if he would go 2 down here. Bobby took out a No. 4 iron, swung as hard as he could, tearing up a big strip of turf and long grass, and the fascinated gallery saw the ball soar over the trees and land 15 feet from the flag. Bobby has always said this was the finest iron shot he ever played, not excepting the one at Inwood.

After which, Gorton, not in the least perturbed, holed his putt for a birdie, and Bobby promptly holed his for a half. Up and down they went to the seventeenth hole, match square. This was a tricky par 3, 255 yards, with a drive from a hilltop tee to a small green in the valley. Neither hit the green but Gorton chipped up close for his par. Bobby was bunkered and his blast left him a putt of seven feet on the most deceptive green on the course. Watching from the hillside above, I thought Bobby's ball would never get as far as the cup, so slowly it traveled, and when it finally dropped out of sight I surprisingly found myself sitting on the ground. I had dropped too.

The eighteenth at Brae Burn required a tremendous carry of 220 yards over a large mound and a brook. Bobby was over but sliced behind a similar mound farther on. He was on with his third, 20 feet from the flag and it looked as if the match was over when Gorton's drive sliced into the woods, and he had played out safely, reaching the green in 4, five yards past the pin, but from this elevation, he sank for a half. Again on the nineteenth hole, he was in the woods, and again he almost sank a terrific putt for a half. This match was the tournament for Bobby. Nobody was ever close to him again.

Former champions fell like leaves on this Red Wednesday: George Von Elm, Jess Sweetser, Max Marston, and Francis Ouimet.

At the close of 1928, Bobby had been national champion six years in a row. His ambition of 1925 had been realized. I think perhaps we both at that time had the hope that the string might be longer—but we did not say so—lest we break the charm.

Preparing for the International Walker Cup Matches at the Chicago Golf Club, Mr. Jones, being captain of the American team that won, worked with more faithfulness than he ever displayed in getting ready for an individual competition. He felt his responsibility as team captain. He went up to Asheville for four practice rounds, in which he scored 69-71-69-68. In Chicago, at Old Elm, a beautiful course, which he had never seen before, he set a new record with 68. Then he moved over to the Chicago Golf Club and broke the record of that great course with 68. Next day he broke it again with a 67. Then another 68. This seemed too good to last, and when he started raggedly at Flossmoor in the Warren K. Wood Memorial tournament, everybody thought the natural reaction had set in. He was 2 over par for seven holes. He then shot seven 3s in a row, and one more, three 4s, and the long last nine in 30 for a 67 and another broken record, 3-3-3-3-3-3-3-4-3-4-4.

Everybody was predicting a letdown in the Walker Cup matches. Mr. Jones touched off a 70 under the hapless Philip Perkins in the singles. He then went over to Boston, and played a benefit match with Johnny Farrell, against Hagen and Sarazen, shooting 69-67 at Woodland. Including the very excellent 70, and counting the rehearsal affairs, we have one dozen rounds as follows: 69-71-69-68-68-68-67-68-67-70-69-67.

A simple mathematical calculation reveals that this is an average of 68 2/3 strokes per round on five different courses, or 40 strokes under 4s for 12 rounds.

After Bobby's defeat by Johnny Farrell, one stroke in 108 holes, in the National Open at Olympia Fields, there were those who said it was too bad Bobby was slipping.

Ah, yes, too bad.

The 1928 international golf matches played at the Chicago Golf Club produced the most complete drubbing for the visitors in the history of the event, 11 points to 1; a clean sweep in the foursomes, and 7 out of 8 singles. It also produced one of the greatest lines ever spoken on a golf course or anywhere else in the realm of sport.

Tony Torrance, a tall, handsome Scot, playing in No. 6 position against Chick Evans on the American side, had a fine battle through the morning round; and then with Evans, suddenly slipping, at the turn in the afternoon, Tony was 5 up. By this time it was certain that this was the only match the British could win, but the match was not at all certain. With a flash of courage and a return to his normal form, Chick took back hole after hole until he cut Torrance's lead to 1 up with two holes to play. A hard par 4 on the seventeenth and Tony was dormie 1. Evans made a great fight to the finish, planting his second shot well on the final green, while Torrance was many yards away, and his pitch left him a tough putt of nearly two yards for a half.

One lone match for Britain of all the list —and the tall Scot from the Royal and Ancient Golf Club must sink that putt. He sank it, rapping the ball straight to the back of the cup. As he walked off the green, a reporter asked him how far the ball had been from the hole.

"I didn't see the hole," said Tony, and there was a tremor in his voice. "All I could see was the Royal and Ancient clubhouse in the background!"

Bobby Jones at Winged Foot in 1929.

40.
The Greatest Thrill

After being mixed up with golf for somewhat more than a quarter of a century, it still was easy for me to select the greatest thrill I experienced in competitive sport—as an observer, of course. The funny thing is that the great thrill producer was a 12-foot putt, which I did not see although I was entirely surrounded by several thousand gasping maniacs who were looking right at it, and within an arm's length was a tall stepladder on which was balanced precariously a press photographer, making a picture of the performance. I have this photograph on my study wall. But I personally did not see the putt.

The time was an hour before sunset on Saturday, June 29, 1929. The place was the home green, West Course, of the Winged Foot Golf Club at Mamaroneck, New York. The occasion was the 33rd playing of the United States Open Championship in 1929, the fourth and final round in progress.

When Bobby Jones walked off the twelfth green on that final round he had a clear lead of six strokes over Al Espinosa, who had blown himself to an eight on that hole. Now see what can happen when the pressure comes off. Espinosa, convinced that his doom was cemented, played the last six holes with an incredibly brilliant run of four 4s and two 3s for a round of 75 and a total score of 294, and was on the board, leading the field.

And now the pressure was on Jones. He lost a stroke at the thir-teenth, and then picked up a devastating 7 after a sliced drive at the fif-teenth. His lead was gone. He needed 4-4-4 to win by a single stroke and the sixteenth was a par 5.

Pressure? After a great drive and iron, he was on the sixteenth, 20 feet from the flag. His first putt was five feet short and he missed the second.

Now it was 4–4 to tie.

He got the first 4 easily. His drive on the eighteenth was good enough. His steep pitch was nearly good enough. A yard, half a yard, more and the ball would have been neatly on the undulating, puzzling putting surface. Instead the shot just failed to carry the rim of a deep bunker at the edge of the green, and rolled down, stopping short of the sand in the long grass, leaving a tricky little pitch for Bobby.

And he had to get down in two from there.

As suggested earlier, the last I saw of the Jones' play on this hole was the result of that tiny, tricky pitch, leaving the ball a dozen feet from the flag, with a borrow of about a foot on the left; a curving, rainbow putt on a green as fast as ice. . . . A putt of a dozen feet for a par 4 and a tie with Espinosa.

It was that or nothing. If he missed, it would be the first time he had scored as high as 80 in the Open Championship. He would have blown a lead of six strokes, and one more, in the last six holes. I knew in a sort of bewildering flash that if that putt stayed out, it would remain a spreading and fatal blot, never to be wiped from his record.

I just didn't try to watch it. Someway it seemed that the ball could not sink if I were watching it. Bobby stood up to putt and the gallery subsided into a strange, breathing silence pressing into the ears; somewhere a long way off, I could hear a bell ringing slowly. I heard the faint thin click of the stroke, and the beginning of a sort of sigh in the gallery. The ball was on its way!

Only a dozen feet to go! How long it took! The sigh grew in volume, changed to a gasp—

Missed?

No!

The gasp changed to an exultant roar—the crash of a thunderbolt. The ball had rolled slowly and more slowly across the sloping green, fast as ice, to the rim of the cup—hesitated—stopped—then dropped in!

I will always believe that the remainder of Bobby's career hung on that putt and that from this, stemmed the Grand Slam of 1930.

After a few drinks, I had recovered sufficiently to ask Al Watrous, who had been Bobby's playing companion for the day, to describe this putt to me, the same Al Watrous who had played with Bobby in the final round of the British Open Championship at St. Anne's. Al said the putt was twelve feet past the cup and the range was so nicely gauged, if the hole had been a four-and-a-quarter-inch circle on the green, the ball would have stopped in the middle of it. Bobby was not accessible. The crowd had him.

Next day—the rebound. Al Espinosa, one of the finest professionals, had gone as far as he could at Winged Foot. Jones played nothing but par against him until he was hopelessly beaten. A par 72 in the morning, and a 69 in the afternoon, stood out as the finishing touch of 65 medal rounds in the U.S. Open Championship, in which he had never been above 80. He had won his fourth tie in the last seven open championships; the first at Inwood, he won against Cruickshank; the second at Worcester, he lost to Willie Macfarlane; and to Johnny Farrell the year before at Olympia Fields.

Bobby established another record at Winged Foot. After spotting his inveterate friend and enemy, Old Man Par, a matter of four strokes on the first three holes of the opening round of the championship he smacked the ancient and honorable duffer for seven blows the rest of the way, finishing 3 up on the old gentleman and leading the Big Parade for the first time in his 10 seasons of play. I mean, he did a 69 for the round. I mean he broke 70 for the first time in a national championship on this side of the Atlantic. I mean he equaled the lowest nine holes ever shot in the open championship, by Willie Macfarlane at Worcester. Bobby had played only 10 rounds of golf in the last six months before coming to Winged Foot, not enough practice for a national open, and that accounted for his collapse in the fourth round.

The old story of Walter Kennon came to the front. After all, it's an invitation tournament, to see if anyone can beat Bobby.

And it all hung on that 12-foot putt!

*O. B. Keeler and
Bobby Jones with
his Grand Slam
trophies.*

41.
An Unexpected Record

Golf championships are a good deal like omelets. You cannot have an
omelet without breaking eggs, and you cannot have a golf championship
without wrecking hopes. Let us consider Pebble Beach where the 33rd
Amateur Championship of the United States Golf Association was
played. Bobby Jones, National Open Champion, went out to Pebble
Beach with four records in prospect, if he could win. There was the
record of Chick Evans, who won the Open and the Amateur the same
year in 1916. There was the record held jointly by Jerome Travers and
Bobby, four amateur championships. And there was the record also held
jointly by Bobby and the very distinguished Englishman, John Ball, of
nine major championships. Mr. Ball won the British Amateur eight

times and the British Open, once. There was a chance for Bobby to take the United States Amateur title three years in a row.

And what did Bobby do at Pebble Beach?

He came away with one other record, which of course had been thought upon by a few of us, but seemed to have been utterly unconsidered by the Four Million of Golf. For the first time in his career, Bobby was defeated in the first round of a national championship. One lone record remained. Bobby never failed to qualify in any tournament he ever entered. At Pebble Beach he was tied with Gene Homans for medalist with cards of 145.

His defeat by Johnny Goodman of Omaha obviously was a shock to the gallery and to the golf fans of the nation. But not so much to Bobby nor to me. Bobby had, in a way of speaking, become a tradition in golf. In our sudden American way, he had become a tradition too soon. I, who had followed his career from the beginning, found something quite exasperating in the general idea that he was invincible, the bland and childlike conviction that he could win a major tournament whenever he chose. Golf is not that sort of game, which possibly is why golf is the greatest of all games. No man ever has had golf under his thumb. No man ever will have golf under his thumb. The game is greater than the man. Golf is like the game of life. No man ever will be its master. Up to this time, I do not believe there were a half dozen persons in the world who realized that Bobby Jones could be beaten at any time in an 18-hole match. Bobby was one. I was another.

Bobby had engaged in exactly 19 18-hole bouts in the last five years in British and American amateur championships. He had lost two and won seventeen. He had close calls, as close as the home green or beyond, half a dozen times. In 1926 in the sixth round of the British Amateur, young Andrew Jamieson beat him 4–3. And now Johnny Goodman, equally young but considerably more capable, had beaten him.

Seventeen victories out of nineteen starts would hardly indicate that the incomparable Bobby was a pushover, even at the shortest dashes. Also in the last five years, Bobby had played ten 36-hole matches in national amateur championships, winning nine and losing one, which proved that it was possible for him to lose at the longer route, also.

The defeat of Bobby and George Von Elm in the first round was by no means a bad thing for the game. For the first time in six years, the tournament became an open affair, a fine old-fashioned fight, now that George and Bobby were on the sidelines. The galleries were disappointed but they saw a real golf tournament. The accepted method of playing a championship called on a man to play medal golf for two rounds in qualifying; short-route golf in two 18-hole matches; long-route in the 36-hole matches. A champion must be able to excel at all three, and Harrison Johnson, affectionately known as Jimmie, did just this at Pebble Beach and a more worthy champion had never been acclaimed. Jimmie, 33 years old, was treated roughly in World War I. He was gassed severely and had suffered from long periods of poor health, which often kept him out of golf. He looked more rugged at this tournament than I had ever seen him, and in winning this, the sixth championship in which he had played, he seemed very happy and a little puzzled. This quiet, modest young man behaved just as a champion should.

Dr. Oscar F. Willing, of Portland, Oregon, the runner-up, also behaved with great credit; so well indeed both after and during the match, that many of us felt somewhat ashamed of the rather harsh criticisms we had handed him during the previous matches. His tactics were as deliberate as ever, it is true, but he omitted his habit of walking over to watch an opponent in trouble or playing from a tough situation. Dr. Willing had done yeoman service for his flag and for his country in the international matches, was well esteemed as a foe, and a formidable golfer, but he was incredibly slow, especially around the greens. That in itself gets a player in wrong with the gallery, which wants action. That may have been the gallery's fault and not Dr. Willing's, but it was a cold fact nevertheless. The gallery, as I know from long experience, this curious cloud of witnesses, will think and do and say pretty much what it pleases. When Johnston had Dr. Willing down and was sure to win, I found myself feeling extremely sorry for the 40-year-old dentist, who in all probability would never reach the final of a national championship again.

Carrying the terrific burden of popular fancy, Bobby started badly against Johnny Goodman, the villain in the plot. He was very nervous before the match, but this was not unusual. He always was nervous before an important match, and the more nervous he was, the more brilliantly he played. This time it worked in reverse. He missed every shot on the first three holes and was 3 down. Under this jolt, the slackness went out of his shots and he promptly won back two of his losses. The seventh hole, I believed to be the turning point. This was a beautiful hole, 110 yards long to a small green, surrounded by white sand traps and a background of the blue Pacific. Both balls were on, Goodman inside. Bobby, 1 down, was ready to press his fortune, went for the deuce and missed coming back. Instead of square, he was 2 down. Bobby thought the fatal holes were the thirteenth and fourteenth. He got a half at the thirteenth by lofting a stymie in a manner that sent the huge gallery into the seventh heaven, but he should have had a simple win after his great drive and Johnny's excursion into a trap at the back of the green. Still they were square on the fourteenth tee and Johnny was trying hard to explode. Jones' drive was perfect down the center of the angling fairway. Johnny was in the rough, was still in the rough with his second, and had to play safely into the fairway. And this is where Bobby made his fatal error in judgment. Still trying for a birdie, he cut the trap guarding the green in front too closely, rolled back in, and Johnnie with one putt, went 1 up and stayed 1 up to the dramatic finish, where Bobby's putt on the eighteenth curled up six inches from the cup, and Goodman had two putts for victory.

Goodman was a fine golfer. Out of more than a thousand entries in the sectional qualifying for the Open that year, he led the qualifiers with a card of 140 at Omaha, on a rather simple course. The story went that he rode the rods to Kansas City that year to win the Trans-Mississippi championship, and that he went to the Open on a cattle train. He was a determined and cocky young man, and proudly joined the exclusive ranks of those who had defeated the great Bobby Jones.

Bobby went out the day after his defeat to referee the match between Francis Ouimet and Lawson Little, the Pacific coast youngster, who had disposed of the Omahan in the afternoon after he had defeated Jones. On every green of the long match, and it went 39 holes, when Jones walked onto the green to judge which player was away, the gallery gave him a delighted hand. Bobby's ears got very red and he tried very hard to be inconspicuous, but at every green, the same thing happened. It was the prettiest tribute I have ever seen from an assembly trying to show a popular idol that, though he had met defeat, they loved and admired him just the same.

I think Bobby played the best golf of his career in his practice rounds on the wonderful courses at Los Angeles and Del Monte. And every round was an exhibition match where everybody was absurdly curious and determined to see him. With a gallery of several thousand people, a golfer cannot help trying his best to give them a show, and it is quite possible that he had lost a measure of the essential keenness by the time he had worked through the qualifying rounds to tie at 145 with Eugene Homans for the low medal.

Bobby set course records all over the place, the most memorable being Pebble Beach where he clocked a drama of golf that the Pacific Coast golfers had never dreamed of—and the stoutest supporters of the hitherto invincible Pebble Beach course were the first to applaud as he reeled off birdies and pars in the greatest round of golf ever compiled in California. His miraculous score of 67, and especially the 32 on the incoming nine will stand as long as Pebble Beach is played in the same tournament form.

At Cypress Point, the most dramatic golf course in the world, so beautifully did he play, missing tying the record by one putt, that I almost forgot to look at the course, which would have been a most deplorable oversight.

At the risk of shock beyond repair, in all fairness, I have to record that the Californians, in one single instance, were guilty of underestimation—their incomparable golf courses. The climate is not nearly as perfect as advertised; and the countryside, except where the hand of man has wielded the watering pot and the horticulturist's hoe, is as dismal as Oklahoma or Arizona; but the golf courses are so much better and so much more beautiful than those we know in the dear old South that any comparison would be absurd, and even the effete east may doff its hat to the Golden State. The turf on the fairways holds the ball up consistently and Bobby said he did not remember a really tight lie during his visit.

Even in defeat, the scenic surroundings at Pebble Beach were absolutely dazzling, the dream of an artist who had been drinking gin and sobering up on absinthe. It is too extravagantly decorated not to be a painting. Snow-white sand in the numerous bunkers, vividly green turf. The Bay of Naples is no more lovely and not as blue as the inlet, Carmel Bay, along which the course is built. At Cypress Point is found the Monterey cypress, said to grow only in this vicinity, a descendent of the Biblical Cedars of Lebanon, a flat-foliaged cedar that you cannot believe. A sea as blue as if stained with cobalt sweeps the fringes of the course with fleecy rollers, and the sky is as blue as the sapphire country of North Carolina.

Bobby thought the two courses equally tough though Cypress Point is shorter, 6,814 yards to 7,000. The penalties are heavier at Pebble Beach, but the shots are more exacting at Cypress Point. Each course he thought about three strokes easier than Winged Foot as played in the open that year.

When we drew near Atlanta, after traveling over nine thousand miles, it was raining and for once, the rain looked good to us. The only rain we had seen on this trip was at the Grand Canyon, where the Hopi Indians put on a rain dance, and so help me, Jupiter Pluvius, before those Hopis had quit hopping, the rain was coming down!

42.

A Charming Guest

A very charming lady came to see us in Atlanta, Miss Joyce Wethered, of England, four times Amateur Champion of Great Britain, but now retired. She and Charley Yates, of Atlanta, played an exhibition match at East Lake against Bobby Jones and Dorothy Kirby, Atlanta's foremost feminine golfer.

For a fortnight, I had been telling the golfing public what a great golfer Miss Wethered was. I knew perfectly well, for I heard it on all sides, that the golfing public, particularly the male golfers, were skeptical. And when I came to watch the match, her game was much greater than I had written.

Miss Wethered played well, but that is no way to say it. Miss Wethered played magnificently. The gallery was charmed beyond expression to see the two greatest golfers of this generation playing all they knew at every shot in gallant and generous complement to one another. There was in their brilliant play something beyond the urge of championships and the spur of competition to inspire them. Straight through to the final five-yard putt at the home green, to save a half for his side, Bobby played with all the verve and debonair abandon of the brave days when he was the youthful D'Artagnan of golf, out to take the world. He went for everything in the old confident way, and got down an astonishing number of long putts, including the one at the last green, a climax that no Hollywood director could hope to improve.

In sheer power, Miss Wethered's game was bewildering. She picked up a birdie 4 at the 565-yard fifth, and another at the 506-yard ninth. She drove level with Bobby up the long hill across the lake on the tenth hole.

At the fourteenth tee, a sudden gale came up to blow full against their drives, and Miss Wethered played a low, raking shot that landed beyond the beautifully struck tee shots of both Jones and Yates. She was hole high on this 405-yard hole with a brassie, the ball curving into a shallow bunker beside the green. This contretemps resulted in the most whimsical shot of the afternoon. Miss Wethered was of course as innocent concerning the peculiarities of our local bunkers as of our local Bermuda greens. The ball was lying well and she essayed a half-blast with the niblick. But the suppositious sand was not there. The blade ricocheted from the hard packed surface, clipped the ball cleanly, and sent it flying 50 yards over the green to the amazement of the spectators, as well as the players.

At the seventeenth tee with a cross wind off the left from the lake she swung without a trace of extra effort, while her partner hit one with such enthusiasm that he confessed afterward, he had never hit a better drive in his life. It caught the down slope just right but when he got to it, Miss Wethered's ball was a mere dozen yards behind.

"I still don't believe it," said Charley. "No girl can hit a ball that far. First time I ever played 14 holes as a lady's partner before I figured once in the match; or four holes for that matter. Reckon I should have been pretty embarrassed but I was sort of hypnotized watching her play."

In her amazing score of 74, Miss Wethered made two mistakes from the tee, shoving out her drives at the seventh and fifteenth, just enough to find trees and trouble. Two strokes went there. She missed a short putt on the unfamiliar Bermuda surface on the first green, and needed three putts on the seventeenth and that was the difference between her first round and a 69 at East Lake. At the finish, Bobby had beaten her 2–1 and she was one up on Charley.

When I congratulated Miss Wethered on her marvelous display of golf she smiled and said: "I wanted so much to play well here. This match meant a great deal to me. I simply could not let Bobby down. I had to play well at East Lake, his home course. This round will help me the rest of my tour, and afterwards. Somehow watching Bobby play smooths out the little wrinkles in my game."

Joyce Wethered is the only woman golfer I ever saw who played golf just like the masculine experts. It was the opinion of the British critics, when they were speaking candidly and not for publication, that if ladies had been included on the British Walker Cup team (which was not being done, you know), Miss Wethered would have been playing No. 3, or no worse than No. 4.

Perhaps the greatest match ever played by women was the final round of the 1929 British Ladies' Championship between Miss Wethered and Glenna Collett. Glenna had already won four of the United States titles out of the seven she eventually acquired, but she had never won the British title; nor had any other woman golfer from outside the tight little island. This was her third attempt. Miss Wethered had defeated her at Troon in 1925. Miss Wethered had come out of four years' retirement, because she loved to play at St. Andrews and had never won a championship there.

With all to win and nothing to lose, starting the morning round, Glenna shot golf at her opponent that would have blown any other woman golfer into the North Sea off the gray coast of St. Andrews. Out in 34 and 5 up; back in 38 on the toughest golf course in the world. Up 2 at noon. Except for one deuce, her card going out showed nothing but 4s. Golf that would have annihilated any other living opponent.

But, alas, in the afternoon round, the scene changed. The weather in the morning had been gray, but there was no wind; in the afternoon, the wind rose, the skies were threatening, and it was cold. The year before a violent storm at Hunstanton had no doubt contributed to her defeat, so it was no wonder that Glenna complained that the weather in Britain conspired against her.

Miss Wethered took the lead at the first hole in the afternoon with a birdie, getting down a 6-foot putt. She was out in front for the first time at the twenty-second hole. She duplicated Glenna's 34 for the first nine and was 4 up. Glenna, with grim determination, cut this to 2 up at the thirty-third hole, but after a half at the thirty-fourth lost to Miss Wethered's par at the thirty-fifth, 3–1.

Heroines both. Both showed more than great golf. Miss Wethered showed that she could face a deficit of 5 down and go on hitting her shots, which is the next hardest thing to do in golf. Miss Collett showed that she could see a great lead converted into a deficit and go on hitting her shots, which is the hardest thing to do in golf. Glenna played like a champion and lost like a champion, fighting to the last, but it was against an invincible foe.

Bobby Jones shooting a rifle.

43.
The Big Year Opens

It is to be hoped that the uninterrupted rush of incident and action in this narrative will not engender in the reader's mind the idea that Bobby Jones did little or nothing except play golf. That impression would be greatly in error. His tournament season, which he observed so closely in these later years, really was a brief affair. In the last eight years of his competitive career, including three ventures to Britain, Bobby averaged just three months of the twelve for the period that comprised his play in the major championships and his journeying to and from. And except for the three years in which he went to Great Britain, most of the tournament season was spent quietly at home, with no more time at golf than is devoted regularly by a businessman who likes an afternoon round with his habitual foursome whenever it is convenient. Bobby without any doubt played less formal or competitive golf in the eight years of his championships than any other first-rank golfer, amateur or professional, in the world.

The year 1930 offered a substantial program for Bobby. He was again captain of the Walker Cup team for the biennial match, to be played this time at Sandwich, England; and this meant that he would play in the British Amateur and the British Open. Of course, he intended to play in the U.S. Open and Amateur; it would be the third time in his career he had competed in all four major championships in the same season.

Whether Bobby had any idea, at the beginning of the 1930 season, that it was to be his last in competitive golf, I do not know. I do know that the recurrent strain of major competition was increasingly unwelcome. His uninterrupted succession of national championships with his various British successes had established him as the leading golfer of the world, and for years he had been ranked the favorite of every competition in which he engaged. A considerable proportion of the sporting public seemed naïvely to expect him to win every time he started—a tribute which lost much of its force from a lack of understanding of the uncertainties of the game and the eccentricities of fortune that afflict even its best and most consistent player.

Bobby was now 28; his family included two children; he was seriously engaged in the business of law; and even two major championship tournaments a year seemed to be taking up a good deal of time and requiring a good deal of travel. Major championships were also taking out of Bobby more than time and travel. He had always played golf in a manner to take a lot out of himself and it was obvious that the time was coming to call it quits.

Whether or not Bobby felt this way about it at the early beginning of the 1930 season, he prepared for the British expedition with more than usual care, and for the first time in three years, he entered a winter tournament. Indeed he entered two, the Savannah Open and the Southeastern Open at Augusta, to brush up his game in competition with many of the best professionals in America.

At Savannah, late in February, Horton Smith, after a brilliant season on the winter circuit, beat him out by a single stroke in an erratic and spectacular tournament, in which Bobby set a new course record of 67 in the first round. Horton brought it down to 66 in the second; Bobby placed it at 65 in the third, after which they were tied. Horton outfinished him 71 to 72 in the fourth round, and the rest of the field were half a dozen strokes behind.

And that was the last formal competition Bobby Jones lost to the end of his career. He won every start from then on.

Bobby's four rounds at Augusta on two good stiff courses were 72-72-69-71 respectively, including a careless lapse at the last three holes of the final round, when he was 18 strokes ahead of the field. He finished 2 strokes better than par and 13 strokes ahead of Horton, who was second.

It was while Bobby was playing his fourth round that Bobby Cruickshank, who had finished earlier, asked me if I knew what was going to happen in the coming season. I said I'd like to know.

"Well," said he, "Bobby is just too good. He's going to Britain and he's going to win the British Amateur and the British Open and then he's coming back here and win the U.S. Open and the U.S. Amateur. They will never stop him this year."

I did not tell Bobby this. As for believing it myself—I couldn't even regard it seriously. That was the Impregnable Quadrilateral that Bobby Cruickshank was talking about. No man ever had taken more than half of it in any one season before.

We sailed on the *Mauritania* late in April, with the American Walker Cup team. Mary went with Bobby this time, along with quite a party of Atlanta people. A comfortable sailing list—not crowded and by no means loose enough to shake around in the lazy intervals. Sir Harry Lauder was along and Douglas Fairbanks, Sir Joseph Duveen, and Maurice Chevalier. Mr. Fairbanks had an extremely definite object in his trip to Europe.

"I'm going to Sandwich," said Mr. Fairbanks, with great particularity, "to watch the Walker Cup matches, then I am coming home. Just between you and me I have a remarkable desire to watch Bobby Jones play golf when he is really keyed up. I want to see the greatest artist of them all when he is putting out. I may come back again for the British Open."

So Mr. Fairbanks thought shockingly little of two trips—round trips—across the Atlantic just to watch a couple of golf events. Certainly he was terribly keen on golf since he had played with Bobby and Chick Evans; and recently reduced his handicap to 4.

The Royal St. George's Golf Course at Sandwich offered the Americans typical American weather.

Bobby said, "Do you know I really wish it would blow. These boys over here think Americans cannot play in the wind."

His wish went ungratified. Bobby won his singles match against Roger Wethered, former British Amateur Champion, and with Dr. Willing, the doubles, the team winning 10 points to 2. Again as at the Chicago Golf Club two years ago, Tony Torrance won the only singles match for the Britons, this time defeating Francis Ouimet.

The American Walker Cup team always had a junior, or "baby" member, which differed from the more conservative British, which inclined strongly to seasoned veterans of golf. The international team at Sandwich presented Donald K. Moe, of Oregon, a brilliant youngster who was yet to vote; but who as the individual hero of the outfit upheld nobly the gallantry of the traditions established before him by Jess Sweetser, Roland McKenzie, Watts Gunn, and Bobby Jones when they were in the romper role.

I told the British golf writers about Don Moe, and they were very polite, but they did raise their eyebrows. The inference was that Don was not as good as I said he was, and furthermore, he could not be as good as I said he was; nor could anybody else. I just said no more about it, and when at noon, Bill Stout was 4 up on Don in their singles match, I continued to say nothing more about it. But a number of the working pressmen made a point of saying something to me about it.

And what did Mr. Stout do after lunch but start 3-3-3 on the first three holes. Of course I did not want to see any more of that so I strolled disconsolately over to watch some of the other matches. Word came by the grapevine that Don had turned on the fireworks and I set out at a brisk trot, arriving at the ninth green in time to see him sink a six-foot putt for a birdie and a card of 33. Seven down and fifteen to play, Don, beginning at the fourth hole, had shot the works—five 3s in six holes.

The gallery was completely overwhelmed.

"Are you never going to let up on us?" a young Englishman asked me. "What use to murder Bobby Jones when you always have another prodigy coming on?"

Stout was playing fine golf, not giving away a thing. One of his friends approached him and was heard to exclaim:

"My word, Stout, this is not golf. It's a visitation from God!"

As they stood on the thirty-sixth tee, Don had par for 35, and the match was square. On this 441-yard hole, his drive was over 250 yards, the ball stopping on a down slope, a wretched, hanging lie. Don squared around, hooded the club, turned fast on the stroke, and smacked it almost into the cup for a birdie 3, the work of a master.

His card of 67 was an official record for match play in the Walker Cup matches, and had he sunk the conceded putt, he would have broken the medal play record that had withstood all attacks for 19 years. It was the greatest match in the history of the series, and when Bobby Jones is asked which is the greatest match he ever saw, always he includes this Stout-Moe extravaganza.

When I went into the press tent, I said:"Well, boys, what do you think of L'enfant now?"

I will say for the British golf scribes; they know how to take it. Their eyebrows remained in place this time, but their hats came off.

Bobby Jones and Cyril Tolley.

44.
Men Call It Fate

This was written the Sunday morning after the conclusion of the 1930 British Amateur Championship at St. Andrews with a happy sort of night journey in between—those British had a luxurious special train at the St. Andrews station waiting for those in a hurry to get to London, and with a large party of Americans aboard, it was not unlike a football train home after your side has won.

Bobby Jones had won the British Amateur Championship at long last. I think he was happier over this victory than any other since he broke through with a major triumph in the U.S. Open Championship in Inwood in 1923. I talked with him after he had been rescued by a squad of big Scottish policemen from about fifteen thousand admirers at the twelfth green, who apparently had determined to take the new champion apart to see what made him tick, and brought back to the hotel. There was a band at the home green to play him in but the band got involved in the crowd and never sounded a note.

Bobby said, "There has been nothing in golf I wanted so much. I can't believe it really happened."

But when word came that they were ready to present the cup, Bobby, apparently convinced that he was not dreaming, brushed his tousled hair hastily and went out to face the huge gallery for the last time—out to the same small veranda where he stood in 1927 to receive the Open Championship trophy.

The story of the 1930 British Championship seems to me to confirm, or at any rate, strongly to support a sort of hypothesis that had been forming in the back of my head for years—that golf tournaments are matters of destiny, and that the result is all in the book before a shot is hit. Looking back over Bobby's eight matches, you may see crisis after crisis in those furious encounters with Tolley, Johnson, and Voigt where the least slip in nerve or skill or plain fortune would have brought defeat to Bobby's dearest ambition. Yet at every crisis he stood up to the shot with something I can define only as inevitability and performed what was needed with all the certainty of a natural phenomenon.

"The stars are with Bobby in this tournament," said a man with whom I was walking. "His luck is as fixed as the orbit of a planet. He cannot be beaten here."

It sounds absurd to say this but it is the gospel that at the very moment my companion made this remark Bobby in the semifinal round was 1 down to George Voigt, in the last of the 18-hole matches, and had just blown a four-foot putt at the fifteenth green which would have squared the match. From the sixteenth tee, George's drive went into the bunker, known as the "Principal's Nose," and the match was squared. On the most treacherous hole on the course, the famous Road Hole, George's ball was stone dead for a birdie 4, and Bobby with an iron second none too good had a putt of four yards for a half. All I could think of was that it was the same length and with much the same borrow as the historic 12-foot putt he had holed at Winged Foot the year before to tie for the U.S. Open. The stroke and the result were also a fair replica; the ball rolled easily to the front of the cup and fell in.

Bobby had something rather curious to say about that putt too.

"When I stood up to it, I had the feeling that something had been taking care of me through two matches that I very well might have lost, and that it was still taking care of me. I knew that however I struck that putt, it was going down."

There was another putt earlier in the week that meant an incalculable saving to Bobby. On Thursday afternoon, he came to the home green with the U.S. Amateur Champion, Harrison "Jimmie" Johnston, 1 up on the heels of the most spectacular rally of the tournament. Bobby, going along in his accustomed mode, gradually had put the gallant Jimmie under, and as they left the thirteenth green, Bobby was 4 up with 5 to play. The gallery began to drift away in search of more excitement. The few thousand who remained got the excitement.

Jimmie took back the long fourteenth with a birdie 4, smacking a long iron dead. Bobby threw away the fifteenth, finally missing a four-foot putt for a half. He got a half at the sixteenth and was dormie 2. Jones very properly played the Road Hole for a par, leaving the burden for Jimmie, who shouldered it handsomely by producing a magnificent birdie and a win. At this stage I recalled very vividly a match Jimmie had played in the Western Amateur Championship in which he was 5 down and 6 to play and had won the next six holes and the match. One glance at Johnston showed he was in precisely such a humor now. Another slip by Jones, another birdie by Jimmie, and the U.S. Open Championship would be out in the sixth round. If Johnston squared the match on the home green, it was certain he would win the extra holes.

The strain was working on both the players. Jimmie's pitch to the eighteenth ran and ran to the upper left-hand corner of the green, a good 30 yards from the flag. Here was a great chance for Bobby, who needed only a half, but he needed it about as much as he had ever needed anything in his life. But he too was wavering and his pitch was almost a duplicate of Johnston's, going to the same distant corner, perhaps two yards nearer the pin. Now it was up to the putting.

Jimmie putted first, a good one, 30 inches from the cup. Bobby's estimate of range and grade for once was faulty, or his deadly touch for once was gone. The ball, apparently on a good line, died eight feet from the pin. There remained a downhill, sidehill putt, but with the same inflexible certainty that marked the other crises of the week, the putt went down. Bobby said it was the longest eight-foot putt he had ever seen, and Jimmie's the most remarkable rally.

"I gave him one hole," he said, "but remember he took the others."

No more fitting combat was ever arranged than that in the fourth round between Jones and Cyril Tolley; the British Amateur Champion defending his title and the U.S. Open Champion, attacking with all his skill and courage and determination. What an utterly amazing battle it was—these two fine sportsmen probably were the greatest exemplars the game has ever seen of the casual demeanor in competition. Neither Jones nor Tolley condescended to reveal by the slightest trace or symptom of eagerness his intense desire and his concentrated will to win. In this attitude I should say that Tolley was even more casual than Jones for Bobby could not by any trick or superior power of the will keep his face from growing gray under the furious strain nor his eyes from sinking deeper into his head. But not in one gesture or in one pose or in one hurried or willfully delayed shot did he betray the terrific strain under which he played and finished and pulled out a match that was squared six times. Never more than a single hole separated the combatants, so that at times one might have guessed them not to be contestants in a desperate, living, and undecided sporting event, but rather actors going through well-rehearsed roles in some tremendous drama.

Only once did Bobby take more than his usual swift deliberation on a shot—his second on the diabolical Road Hole, where they were square for the sixth time, and Tolley slightly ahead on his drive, left Bobby to guess first on the ominous problem of the shot to the long, narrow green with the horrid road along the other side. A bold shot for the pin ran a risk of catching the deep pot bunker in line with the pin, or going over the green into the road. Bobby stood there for a long half minute pondering. Then he motioned the stewards to move the gallery back from the rear of the green, well to the left of the bunker. I was standing with Dr. Alistair McKenzie, the famous golf architect. He shook his head.

"It's a very bold conception," he said. "It will take some clever playing."

The gallery at this time numbered around 12,000, and the stewards could not get them very far back of the green. There may have been a shade of destiny in this. Bobby hit a truly great iron shot, aimed to pitch deep in the swale and run up to the back of the green. The ball hit just where he intended it to hit, but it went up on the big bound into the gallery; Jones had asked it to be moved back. It might have been down below the eighteenth tee; it might even have been in the road. "Men call it Fate." Anyway, and uncompromisingly, it was a break in luck. The pressure on Tolley was vastly increased and when the big fellow's iron was short of that wicked bunker, I could see nothing but a win for Jones. I felt that no man living could execute so deft a pitch as would clear the bunker and stop anywhere near the hole, cut in that absurdly narrow plateau green.

See how a golfing situation can change. Jones' simple little approach was eight feet short. Tolley, pitching with the most exquisite delicacy, stopped his ball within two feet of the flag—the finest shot he ever made, he assured me afterwards. One minute, Jones had the hole and inferentially the match in his hand; in another minute he was putting for his life, a perilous eight-foot putt with his adversary comfortably and convincingly established for a half. Here was another crisis but again the putt went down.

Two drives close to 340 yards on the eighteenth, two chips, neither too good, and a half in par. Close play by the U.S. Champion at the nineteenth; loose play by the British Champion, whose pitch was far outside and whose approach left him open for the stymie which ensued; and the great bout was ended.

But these three hard-earned victories were not the only close calls that Bobby had during the week. The trouble with the British Amateur Championship is there are so many golfers in it whose names are not in the stud book. In his first match with Sidney Roper, an ex-coal miner, Bobby started 3-4-3-2-4 against Roper's par of 4-4-4-4-5, and was 3 up, and that is the way the match ended 3-2. Bobby was never able to increase this margin by a single hole. I have seen Bobby hot before but I had never seen anybody stand the blast and show no signs of folding up as Roper did. Bobby said he had been told that Roper would shoot steady 5s at him. He shot 15 4s and one 5.

Sid Roper learned his golf on the public course at Bulwell Forest a few miles from Nottingham, where Robin Hood used to operate on opulent travelers and remove purses from them. I told Bobby this.

"He darned near removed me from this tournament," was the rejoinder.

The biggest first round gallery I ever saw witnessed the shot the U.S. champion confessed was the best he ever produced—the 120-yard pitch from a bunker into the hole for a deuce at the 427-yard fourth hole. Bobby's drive went into the Cottage Bunker, around 300 yards from the tee, never laid down to catch drives. I was standing at the back of the green as he waded down into the bunker. The ball lay perfectly clear on the windblown sand. Up came a feather of sand instead of a divot. The ball, obviously struck as if from turf, came on in rather a steep pitch, hit in front of the big green; the spin took hold promptly and the ball rolled slower and slower and dropped in softly without touching the flag stick.

"They ought to burn him at the stake. He's a witch," said one man in the gallery.

Another said, "I came 8,500 miles to see this tournament, and that shot is worth the trip."

That shot will stand up like Washington's monument at St. Andrews, where Scotsmen know and love golf. Generations unborn will hear about it with Caledonian unction. Despite Bobby's success in working through seven 18-hole matches, he still did not like the short-route. It was curious to see with what a different attitude he attacked the longer problem. Where he had mixed superbly brilliant golf with decidedly blue splotches in these short-route engagements, he set about the 36-hole final round, with Roger Wethered, in the workmanlike manner that characterized his best medal play performances.

He went the 30 holes of the match two under 4s. Roger played bravely but was not able to endure the pressure exerted by the great medalist over the long route.

After observing Mr. Jones in 25 national championships, never had I seen him steal a show so spectacularly. Every day he in some way managed to produce the Big Feature of the day. He was a long time winning the British Amateur, but when he did, he extracted every sensation, every emotion the great drama had to offer.

45.
The Double

At the British Open Championship at Hoylake in 1930, it was my good fortune to be the first person to broadcast a sporting event across the Atlantic Ocean, from the studio of the British Broadcasting Company in Liverpool, over the network of the National Broadcasting Company of America.

After the final round at Hoylake, I said: "It is possible that I will be forgiven if this brief broadcast of the conclusion of the British Open Championship is a trifle confused, or even incoherent. It is not every day or every year, in the history of sports that an American homebred amateur can add the British Open title to the British Amateur title on the same campaign. And with Bobby Jones on top of his 11th major championship, and the first four competitors all from the United States of America, I feel sure you will be patient with a very tired and bewildered war correspondent, who for two of the longest hours that ever crawled across a clock this afternoon, wondered what was happening."

Bobby Jones won his third British golf championship in three starts with a score of 291 at the Hoylake course of the Royal Liverpool Golf Club, 10 strokes better than the former record of Walter Hagen in 1924. Leo Diegel, American homebred professional and Macdonald

Smith, a transplanted and naturalized Scot from Carnoustie, were tied for second place with 293. Horton Smith, youngest and most brilliant of the Yankee professionals, and a homebred from Missouri, was tied with Fred Robson, the British veteran professional, who had been rejuvenated by steel shafts in his clubs, and led for his country at 296. Jim Barnes, originally a Cornishman, now an American citizen, former Open Champion of the United States and of Great Britain, was next in line, tied with Archie Compston, the gigantic British professional, whose 68 in the third round had sent him into the lead.

Four men fought it out to the finish, right up to the wire. This immortal quartet was composed of Bobby Jones, Leo Diegel, Macdonald Smith and Archie Compston. Of the four, it was Archie Compston, whose astounding performance first dazzled the world, and then like the final finish of a rocket's flight, dissolved in sparks and darkness, buried deep in the limbo of lost hopes.

At the beginning of the last day's play, 61 golfers took the field with Bobby leading by a single stroke at 142, two strokes better than par for the great Hoylake course at full stretch; Robson next with 143; Horton Smith, 145; Compston, Mac Smith, and Diegel, 145. As it always does, the third round produced battle, murder, and sudden death and devastation. Bobby started this crucial round in as ghastly a fashion as ever a budding champion opened a final day. Par on the first three holes was 4-4-5, and Mr. Jones might reasonably have been expected to work out 4-4-4 with the prevailing wind, which would have done no gross injustice to his method or his luck. Instead of which he lost no fewer than eight strokes, and spotted the great field a hideous assortment of shots which he had to take up by the most desperate golf of his career, from the third hole on. After a frightful struggle, he got his game working, and from the fourth to the fourteenth holes, he was four under 4s. You can believe it or not, the aggregate yardage of the last five holes at Hoylake was 2,288 yards, or an average of 457 yards to the hole, the toughest finishing holes I have ever seen, including the old course at St.

Andrews. Only two par 5s and it requires extraordinary golf to make par without figuring the wind, which invariably blows at Hoylake. It is the sort of finish that competitors lie awake and brood over, knowing full well that even 4s would have won the title.

Archie Compston, coming from next to nowhere and playing like a frenzied giant, gained five strokes in the first four holes and had caught Jones. Compston was out in 34 with a six in it, to Jones' 37, but Bobby was still leading by one stroke at the turn. But when Compston began that blistering rush homeward 3-3-3-2, Bobby stepped with him only two holes and Archie had caught him again. They were playing about five holes apart and Jones of course could hear the explosive roar of the Compston gallery, as he was battling for his fives at the long holes toward the end. Much as they loved and admired Bobby in Britain, they still wanted a native to win. You could trace the blond giant's progress about the links by the blasts of cheering that swept like a hurricane across the dunes and burst like a bombshell over the clubhouse. Compston, with only one slight lapse, finished with 68, smashing the course record to bits—unquestionably one of the most dramatic episodes in the history of British golf. Bobby finished with 74, and they stood 215 to 216.

And so into the fourth round with a blackening sky and a sprinkle of rain in the heavy air, a fine setting for a murder—or a vast upset in the golf championship. It was impossible, as you can understand, for one reporter to be in four places at once, but I think I can tell you where Compston lost his lead; where Diegel went down; where Jones won. The winning hole for Bobby, if any hole can properly be called that, was the second of the afternoon round. From the tee, on a long drive and pitch affair, he wheeled out a drive that went far enough to the right to land on the convenient head of a steward, rebounding 40 yards into a bunker on the farther side of the fourteenth green, at least 30 yards off line. From the sand he played a splendid pitch to the green, and sank a 20-foot putt for a birdie, where he might logically have been expected to get out with a difficult 5.

This break was a stimulant for the Open Champion and he went so well to the eighth hole that any decent score there would have closed the door and barred it. This was a very fine hole of 482 yards, which he had been reaching regularly with a drive and a spoon. He hit a good drive and a good second, curling a bit and breaking to the left, down a slight slope but practically green-high, in no sort of trouble. And this is how Bobby Jones, not only could, but did take a 7 on a hole in the last round of the British championship without being in a bunker or any other trouble. Bobby looked over the situation, and not at all perturbed, elected to play a simple run-up shot. He missed the shot. That is the only explanation. The ball hopped feebly up the slope, stopped and sat down well short of the green. Bobby changed his club for a chip. It still looked like a 5. His pitch was 10 feet short and his ears were getting red. He naturally went for the 5, slipped 12 inches past. Then he walked up and hit it without looking at the line, and there was a 7.

"It was the most inexcusable hole I ever played. An old man with a croquet mallet could have got down in two. I will play that hole over a thousand times in my dreams, " Bobby said.

I had had nightmares before watching Bobby play in major tournaments. I sat by a certain bunker at Winged Foot the year before and watched him play from a bunker across the green into another, then back into the original bunker, then almost fail to reach the green with his next shot for a horrid 7. But those were bunkers and here at the eighth hole at Hoylake there was no bunker, no hazard. A simple forthright hole where he was pin high in two and took a 7. Right then I began to agree with Miss Joyce Wethered that competitive golf was a game not worth the candle.

With that 7 on his card, Bobby was out in 38, and he played the last nine under the savage spur of adversity in 37. That last five holes in one over 4s was the winning streak, especially the 4-4-4 on the last three. With a total of 291 on the board, Bobby went up to the club-house and suffered for two long hours, while waiting for the jury to come in, the jury being Diegel and Macdonald Smith.

As a matter of record Bobby and Diegel were tied at the seventieth hole, and Bobby salvaged at this hole the tournament he had won by his birdie 3 at the second. The sixteenth is the longest hole on the course, 582 yards. Bobby knew he needed a 4 there. He went for it and was bunkered short of the green. The ball was lying well enough on the sand, if a ball can ever be said to lie well in a bunker. Bobby had a nib-lick Horton Smith had given him in the spring at the Savannah Open, an odd club with a concave face and a flange sole, weighing 25 ounces or nearly twice as much as an ordinary club. All it required was to take a slow backswing and hit the ball. Bobby did this and the ball was within four inches of holing out, rolling around the cup as if trying to get in and missing by the proverbial whisker.

Leo Diegel, two strokes back at the last turn, picked these up at the two par 3 holes, and as he stood on the seventieth tee, he was tied. Tied after 69 holes. Gallant Leo Diegel. He went for that long hole with all the strength in his somewhat frail body, knowing that it would take three 4s to finish in a tie. He was in the same bunker that Bobby's sec-ond had found, but he failed to get out and finished with a wretched 6. Then he needed a 3 and a 3 to tie, and they were not making 3s on those last two holes at Hoylake that day.

Compston set out in the final round apparently full of confidence. Photographed and congratulated at the first tee, he was good-humored and laughing. But there is no way to escape the tension that comes from leading the pack as the last round comes on, especially when you have set a new course record to break away.

I shall always believe that if Compston had holed the 30-inch putt for a par at the first hole, he might have settled his vast stride into a championship round. He looked at the ball like a man dazed when it stayed out, knowing that the American champion had wiped out his lead, and knowing, I am sure, of Bobby's miracle birdie 3 at the second. He was out in 43, four strokes back and was done. Big Archie paid plenty for that miracle round with the terrible 5s that bled him white in the afternoon.

Mac Smith, past 40 years of age, cold, calm, and a mechanical robot of golf, with the most perfectly grooved swing in golf, came in with the finest round of the day, 71. So, 36–35, a stroke under par on a dark and rainy afternoon with the wind steadily increasing, was by all odds the big show of the last round. Mac started six strokes back of Bobby and that is a lot of strokes to spot Mr. Jones in the fourth round. It was too much to ask of the valiant veteran. He clipped one stroke off par in that last spin of five holes but he could not close the gap.

Bobby had now won 11 major championships in the space of seven years. He had passed the record of Mr. John Ball, the only amateur who had won as many as nine. He had equaled Mr. Ball's feat of winning both the Open and Amateur of Great Britain in the same year, a record that had stood for 40 years. And I beg you to believe that there was a lot besides the eccentricities of an uncertain game in those four rounds at Hoylake. There was the experience of 14 years of major competitive golf; experience gained from 7 lean years when he played in 11 national championships without winning one; experience and stolid patience and tempered philosophy, gained from years of defeat and seasons of disappointment over every kind of championship course and against every type of field the game affords.

It is as far as possible from depreciating the great field at Hoylake to say that Bobby Jones won with his game far from its top. His game was as good, the course considered, as any he had ever shot; and a score as good as his best game was entitled to wring from this great course. The score is what goes on the board. But if experience and patience and philosophy and grim determination were enough to produce that score from his game at Hoylake, I will say that he never played a greater tournament, perhaps never one so great.

Then: "This is O. B. Keeler, finishing off the summary of the last day's play in the 1930 British Open Championship, speaking from the studio of the British Broadcasting Company in Liverpool, over the network of the National Broadcasting Company of America. And this eventually and very happily and sincerely is 'goodnight.'"

46.
The D'Artagnan of Golf

So Bobby Jones sailed for home on the *Europa* with his flag firmly planted on two sides of the Impregnable Quadrilateral. On the boat train from London to Southampton, Cyril Tolley, who was coming over to play in the United States Open, said to Bobby: "How long have you been over here?"

Bobby said about six weeks.

"Well," said Cyril, "Do you think you ever played quite so badly for so long a period before?"

Bobby, going home with both major championships, said "No" before he had time to think it over. After thinking it over, he still said no. And it wasn't in the least a matter of conceit. It was the admission of fearfully hard work, and breaks that had favored him—and a vague conviction that we both had shared for several years, that if it is in the book, you are going to win. Still he was carrying two championships home with him, and that was a remarkable illustration that winning a major golf competition requires something more than hitting the ball correctly—even in the competition itself.

Once again there was a thrilling welcome, fairly dazzling New York with its fervor, when a hundred of the home folks, including

Bobby's father and mother, came up to meet us; and once again the *Macom* came out to take the conquering hero off at quarantine, and we steamed in with the fire boats spraying the sky, and rode up Broadway with the ticker tape flying. Nothing could have come at a more timely juncture to a very tired young man, after that furious campaign in Britain, than this joyous assurance of Atlanta's love and admiration.

Bobby went directly from New York to Minneapolis to play in the United States Open Championship at the Interlachen Golf Club. There he was delightfully surprised to find that his game was working well, much better than in either of the British tournaments. He played well in practice and started the show with a very creditable 71, on the hottest day that we had ever seen, a sort of Turkish-bath heat that rose from the pretty little lakes set artistically about the countryside. Water is very pretty and quite useful at times but it unquestionably contributes to what is popularly or unpopularly known as humidity. The thermometer on the shady side of the clubhouse registered 101. Bobby did the first nine in 34, and the last nine in an hour and a half with only one instinct and desire, to get it over with and get under a cool shower.

He finished in the hottest part of the day and came into the locker room so drenched with perspiration he could not unknot his tie and I had to cut it off, and it was promptly snatched up for a souvenir. Yet with the somewhat shabby 37 coming in, his 71 stood up until late in the afternoon when the thermometer had gone down to a cool 96. When the shades of night were falling and a few fleets of well-gorged mosquitoes had settled around Mirror Lake, two veteran Scots, Tommy Armour and the inevitable Macdonald Smith, came in with brilliant cards of 70 to take the lead.

Bobby had bunched about him the toughest cluster of challengers he had ever encountered as he started the second round. Besides the two leaders, there were Sir Walter Hagen, Horton Smith, Wiffy Cox, Lighthorse Harry Cooper, Long John Rodgers, Joe Turnesa, Craig Wood, Charley Lacey; all these and several others, the greatest aggregation of scoring machines that had ever entered the Open Championship. It is tough when upwards of a dozen have a man hemmed in. One opponent, or even several may skid a bit, but when it is a pack, one of them is going to maintain the pace.

It was in this round that the famous "lily pad" shot came to his rescue. Bobby had reached the ninth tee with a par left for 35. This hole was a dog-leg to the right, the second shot a big one across one of those pretty little lakes to a small, well-guarded green. Bobby had been getting home regularly in practice and had a birdie there in his first round. His drive was cut slightly and was in a tight lie near the bank of the lake. He half-topped the spoon shot and it started away at a nearly flat trajectory, certain not to reach the farther bank. A ball in the water would leave him another shot from the same place, plus a penalty stroke, so the best he could hope for, barring miracles, was a 6.

The ball, struck fairly low with little or no spin on it, hit the water 20 yards short of the bank, skipped like a flat stone once—and again— and hopped out on the smooth turf, 30 yards short of the green. It was proclaimed far and wide that the ball had hit a lily pad and jumped out, due credit being given to the beautiful lily. Much as I dislike to destroy so romantic a story, in truth the ball hit only the water, skimming across as hundreds of little boys have skidded stones.

With time and need to recover a modicum of his equilibrium in walking around the lake, Bobby stuck a wee pitch up one yard from the pin and holed his birdie 4. That's the way it goes in championships. If your name is up, the ball will walk on the water for you. He won the championship by two strokes. Nobody can say surely that these were the strokes—or that they were not.

At the halfway mark, Bobby with a card of 73 in the second round, total 144, was in a triple tie for second place with Cooper and Lacey. Horton Smith had taken the lead with 142, Mac Smith had 145. There were at least ten others strung out behind with a chance to win. The gang had him on the spot and I had a cold premonition that one of these grim musketeers would go mad and dash to the front. The gang had Bobby out for a ride.

Bobby was fortunate in having an early starting time on the last day. It so happened that he was very much on his game, and the reports of his scoring trickling back along the grapevine did not help the other fellows. He was out in 33, turning just as Horton Smith started, and in the face of that jolt, Horton produced one of the finest exhibitions of sheer courage ever displayed in the Open Championship, to reach the turn in 36, even par. Still Bobby had picked up three strokes on him and managed to maintain this pace for the first seven holes coming in. I fancy the blasts of cheering that must have reached Horton had their effect for he slipped to 40 coming in.

At the seventeenth, Bobby needed a par 3 and a par 4 to finish with a 66, which would have been the lowest round ever shot in a U.S. Open Championship. But the strain and heat were taking their toll, and he went one over on each of these holes, finishing with a 68. This was still a course record and the best round he had ever played in this tournament. It could not have arrived in a better place. With a score of 212, he had a commanding lead of five strokes as they entered the final round, Cooper next with 217; Horton Smith, 218; Mac Smith, 219.

It was all over but the hanging on, and he found that singularly hard to do, and Mac Smith certainly did his best to make it impossible. Just as at Hoylake a few weeks before, he chased him almost to the wire, starting seven strokes behind him and an hour later. Bobby started by losing three strokes to par in the first three holes and four to Mac, who started 4-4-2. Here was a fine chance for a fatal break. One more bad hole and Bobby might very well have been caught and passed. But the fourth hole at Interlachen had been good to him all week, a par five of 506 yards. In each of the previous rounds, he had a birdie, and this time in his great need, it did not betray him. Bobby was out in 38, Mac Smith in 34, playing like a man in a trance, now only three strokes behind. Bobby regained a stroke at the long eleventh, Mac took it back at the twelfth, and then picked up two more at the short thirteenth where Bobby once again had a catastrophic five on a par 3 hole. At this point, an hour later Mac Smith was only one stroke back. He had gained six strokes in 13 holes.

It was the D'Artagnan in Bobby who finished that round. He rammed down a long putt for a birdie 3 at the thirteenth, picked up another birdie 3 at the sixteenth, and at the seventeenth, 272 yards, the longest par-3 hole in the world, he took another 5. This hole was his bête noire of the week. In the four rounds, he lost four strokes to par here, and picked them all up on the friendly fourth, which I suppose proves in a vague way that the breaks will even up in the long run, if the rule is long enough. The 72 holes at Interlachen proved long enough, and the ride had been too fast for the gang. At the eighteenth, where Bobby had finished more than an hour before, with a 40-foot putt for his third birdie 3 on the last nine, Mac was faced with an eagle 2 to tie. It was the long putt that had barred the door, the last stroke of the championship. Mac finished with a par 4 for a 70. He had cut away five of a seven-stroke lead, and once again in the same season he had finished second by two strokes. Once again a wholly admirable and exemplary figure in the world of sport had come so near only to be defeated.

Golf is indubitably the most uncertain of games, and yet in the face of this singularly accurate reproduction in two great championships in the space of 24 days on courses four thousand miles apart, it would be stupid to say there is no such thing as playing form. Three great golfers, counting Horton Smith, finished these two tournaments in precisely the same positions, all three being four strokes better at Interlachen than at Hoylake, which is probably about the difference in the two courses.

With tears in my eyes and drenching perspiration on the rest of my anatomy, I welcomed the end of this tournament and the moment when we could head south for Dixie and comparative coolness. It was beautiful at Interlachen among the lakes but you would have to stay in one of the lakes to keep from sizzling, and it would be somewhat inconvenient to carry a lake around the golf course with you. The heat was too much for some of the contestants. Charley Hall, the hard-hitting professional from Birmingham, Alabama, where it occasionally gets pretty warm, gave up.

"This tournament," said Charley, "will go to the man with the thickest skull."

After he had won, I told this to Bobby. He grinned and said: "Maybe it did at that."

Fancy if you please, Mr. Cyril Hastings Tolley, former British Amateur Champion, under such climatic conditions. Where does dignity go when it melts? One lady spectator sitting beneath a large tree thus portrayed Mr. Tolley, climbing slowly and damply up a slope: "Mr. Tolley," she said, "looks just like an iceman who has carried one hundred pounds of ice up five flights of stairs and found that the lady of the house was not at home."

Mr. Tolley lost nine pounds in one three-hour round.

It was in an upper room at the Interlachen Club, while waiting for Mac Smith to come in, that Bobby made his momentous decision. In the secretary's room at Hoylake, while he waited for this same Mac Smith and Leo Diegel to come in, he had begun to think that this might be his last year in competitive golf. Nothing in the world, Bobby said, would be worth the agony of those last three days at Hoylake. So here at Interlachen, he decided that he had had enough. No matter what happened at Merion, he was through with competitive golf. The third trick of the Impregnable Quadrilateral had been accomplished. There was one more major championship to play in and then—finis.

Next stop: Merion.

Bobby Jones with his Grand Slam trophies.

47.

The Impregnable Quadrilateral

As Bobby Jones walked onto the fourth green in the afternoon round in his final match against Eugene Homans, after a beautiful little pitch across the brook, at the Merion Cricket Club, Big Bob Jones, his daddy, asked another spectator how he stood. The answer was that Bobby at the moment was 8 up and was winning that hole, which would be 9 up.

Big Bob meditated a moment. Then he said, not to the gallery but all to himself: "Nine up and 14 to go."

And then, it might seem more inconsequentially, he began to sing, very softly, quite to himself: "There's a long, long trail a-winding into the land of my dreams."

I think with all the magnificent talk about the pinnacle of golf and the crest of sporting records–I think, after all, that song of Big Bob's told more of the story of Bobby's greatest victory than all the reams of adjectives that had blazed across the newspaper firmament in the 2 million words that flashed away from Ardmore about this championship in which the greatest of all sporting champions achieved his heart's greatest desire.

It was more than a mere Amateur Golf Championship of the United States, great and coveted honor that this title is. Bobby had won four others, but none like this one. This victory, the fourth major title in the same season and in the space of four months, had now and for all time entrenched Bobby Jones safely within the "Impregnable Quadrilateral of Golf," that granite fortress that he alone could take by escalade, and that others may attack in vain, forever.

The Grand Slam of Golf, many are calling it, and while I invented the term to describe what I believed to be an absolutely impossible achievement, I fear it is too casual and futile for this supreme feat of the sporting world. It was in the book now. Nothing could change it. But winning this championship was, as I had suspected, the toughest and most grueling of Bobby's campaign. He had said to me: "It is the first tournament in which I have ever played that I could not sleep at night. There is something on my mind that I cannot shake off. I go to sleep all right from fatigue, but about midnight or later, I wake up and have to get up. I have always been able to sleep. There was only one night, no, two, when I remember I did not sleep. One was at Worcester in 1923, the night before the playoff, but the heat contributed to that. The other was at the British Amateur Championship at Muirfield in 1926. I sat in the window and marveled that I could see cattle in the distant fields at 11:30 in the long Scottish twilight. There is something bearing down on me in this tournament that was never there before."

I knew perfectly well what it was—the specter of the fourth championship. Mickey Cochrane, the clever catcher of the Philadelphia Athletics, was walking with me. He, too, understood. After seeing Bobby miss a few shots, Mickey said: "I know just how he feels. He is going after his fourth championship of the season, and it is just like a baseball club trying to win its fourth consecutive world's championship. He feels fine but inwardly his nerves are seething, and when he gets ready to make a shot he cannot get the proper grip. It's the old championship strain bearing down and every ballplayer knows what that means."

As the huge gallery left the first tee in the morning round, Francis Powers of the *Chicago News*, paraphrasing Grantland Rice's story on the Notre Dame team, said: "There goes another race by the Four Horsemen of the Apocalypse over the fairways of Merion, and this time their names are Jones, Jones, Jones, and Jones." Queerly enough he was right. There was Jones, Amateur Champion of Great Britain; there was Jones, Open Champion of Great Britain; there was Jones, Open Champion of the United States; and there was Jones, fighting for the fourth side of the quadrilateral, the Amateur Championship of the United States. The premier golfing firm of all the world, Jones, Jones, Jones, and Jones. Succeeding ages may match it if they can.

The mathematical details of the last day's play are interesting mainly as illustrating the effect on Bobby's concentration by the greatest opportunity he had had to reach the top of the golfing world. All through the tournament he was incomparably brilliant and incredibly sloppy by turns. Between rounds, standing 7 up on Homans, with a card of 72 that was saved by a gorgeous spin of 33 on the last nine, he showed nothing of elation. He was puzzled and unhappy over his putting.

"I can't understand it," he said. "The greens are practically perfect. For a few holes I putt decently, and then like an old woman. Somebody asked me if the greens were too fast. I told him I simply could not say with my touch as it is. The greens are fine. There is something the matter with me."

Yes, there was something the matter with Bobby. The same thing that rode his sleep at night and scattered his calmest dreams, and set him walking about the room before daylight. There was something that touched his arm in the big swing, and diverted his short putts off line as he worked about the course that I think he loves best of all in this country. And I knew what it was. Bobby may have been puzzled, but what rode with him at Merion was the Fourth Horseman of the Apocalypse of Championship.

Had this been just another amateur championship? If Bobby had not won the other three, it would have been a breeze in the field in which he found himself after his first match with Ross Somerville. But just behind him every step of the way there was riding a horseman he could not see: the white horseman of the fourth championship. And I am very sure that the thunder of his pursuit would have broken any other golfer in the world.

The significance of Jones' victory furnished more interest and excitement than the final match. That he would win was accepted as a foregone conclusion from the beginning. He won the qualifying medal with a record-equaling 142, and he was never down to his five opponents in match play. Homans in the final round, through his courageous finish, extended the match farther than it seemed possible after Bobby was 7 up at noon. Bobby's golf was not always Jones' golf in the machine-like perfection it is usually considered, but it was much too good for his opponents to match. Like Alexander the Great, Bobby had no more worlds to conquer. And he was only 28 years old.

Bobby and Jess Sweetser had played in a dozen championships but had met only once, so the match at Merion was a sort of return bout. Bobby with a card of 72 was 4 up on Jess at noon, and in the afternoon he was fully as innocuous as Hamdryas or King Cobra, the match ending on the tenth green. Jess said: "I did want to take the match to the eleventh green, and let it end 8–7. Then I could have said we were still square. That was where our match ended at Brookline, you remember."

Bobby blushed, or might have blushed had it not been for several layers of sunburn.

"I felt sort of mean at that tenth green, the way that pitch stuck up there," he said, "like a stab in the back or a shot in the dark."

"It was no shot in the dark," said Sweetser.

On a September day eight years before in the semifinal round of another national amateur championship, it was Jess who spanked a pitch of 90 yards into a hole for an eagle, and went on to give Bobby the greatest defeat he ever absorbed in a tournament, 8-7. History has a curious way of repeating itself, sometimes in reverse.

Among the telegrams Bobby received as the great test got under way was a brief one, in Greek, from Johnny Boutsies, proprietor of a restaurant in Atlanta. It must have been a struggle to get the telegram transmitted, Greek words in English letters, but it came through. It read: "E TON E EPITAS."

You remember what the Spartan mothers of old said to their Spartan sons, as they buckled on their shields, setting out for battle. The English equivalent is rather difficult but the meaning is clear, about the shield and the warrior's return: "With it, or on it."

Bobby came back with it.

The match of the tournament was the ferocious battle of 28 holes between George Von Elm and Maurice McCarthy, the black Irishman and the blond Prussian, that set a record for stubborn bouts in the U.S. Amateur Championship. Von Elm, playing by his own declaration in his last amateur championship, was not shooting as good golf as McCarthy, but Maurice was giving the holes to him by taking three putts. He did this four times when he had the Uhlan in his grasp. So it came to the home hole all square. A half there and they were off on the most amazing struggle in all the annals of golf. At the end of nine holes, they were still square, the last six holes being halved in pars. Then came the break. At the 10th extra hole. After good drives, Von Elm was on a dozen feet from the pin, safe for a par. McCarthy's pitch ran closer—it ran still closer. It touched the cup, rolled around and stopped a few inches away. That was the winning stroke, the coup-de-grace, a birdie 3 at the 10th extra hole. McCarthy had also set another record by scoring an ace in the qualifying round, the only ace ever shot in qualifying for the amateur championship.

So it was good-bye at Merion, as, long ago, it had been good morning there. It was at Merion in 1916 that Bobby had played in his first national championship; it was there in 1924, he had won his first amateur championship; and there he finished. The chunky schoolboy had grown into the calm and poised young man, whom the world called the master of golf—and who was not less truly master of himself.

"There is a destiny that shapes our ends."

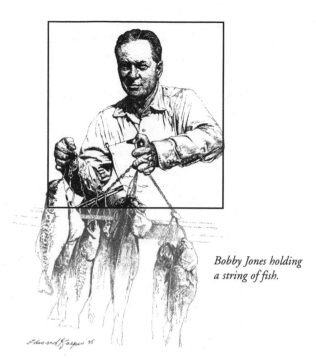

*Bobby Jones holding
a string of fish.*

48.
The End of the Trail

In the middle of November 1930, Bobby Jones announced his retirement from all golfing competition. The greatest golfer the world had ever known had played in his last championship, the king of golf had laid down his scepter. So it was good-bye to golf for Bobby and, incidentally, for this correspondent. Bobby's retirement from competitive golf was the end of the trail that had carried us together more than 120,000 miles, three times to Europe and across the fields of 27 major championships. When Bobby told me of his decision, I could not say anything. I just held out my hand. I was happy, in a way. And I was— well, you don't come to the end of 15 years with the grandest sporting competitor, and the greatest boy you have ever known, without something that hurts.

It was the thing to do, eminently. As Bobby said whatever he might do, continuing in competitive golf would be anti-climax. He had finished off the seven fat years with 13 major championships. In the closing year 1930, he had accomplished the impossible—winning all four major titles.

But in the long memories there will be recollections of the seven lean years, the long pull against fate and fortune and the best golfers when the greatest golfer of them all played in 11 major championships and never won a single victory. In some ways, those are the dearest of the green memories. Those were the days before we traveled in drawing rooms and private cars, when we were lucky to have lowers; when in 1921, on the way to the Amateur Championship in St. Louis, he said to me: "I wonder if I'll ever win a championship."

And I said: "Son, when the day comes that you can get out on the first tee with any man in golf, and know in your heart that you are better than he is, then you'll win a big tournament. Because you are better, if you only knew it."

Bobby laughed.

But eventually he developed an ambition. After he had won the U.S. Open at Inwood in 1923, and followed with the U.S. Amateur in 1924 and 1925, he said to me: "There is one thing I would like to do. I'd like to be national champion, either open or amateur, of the United States for six years in succession. Then I would be ready to hang up the old clubs and let them all take a shot at that. But of course it can't be done."

And we both laughed. Of course, it could not be done.

And now the fantasy had become cold reality. He had been a national champion eight years in succession; Open Champion, 1923; Amateur Champion, 1924 and 1925; Open Champion, 1926; Amateur Champion, 1927 and 1928; Open Champion, 1929; both Open and Amateur, 1930. Added to which he had been Open Champion of Great Britain in 1926, 1927 and 1930; and Amateur Champion, 1930.

There were no more records to shoot for. Bobby was the first competitor to win five U.S. Amateur Championships. He equaled the British and American records of winning both the Amateur and the Open the same year. He was the only competitor who had won both the British and U. S. Amateur Championships in the same year and he had done this twice. And no other golfer, amateur or professional, had won 13 major championships. He played in the first international Walker Cup matches in 1922, and in four more, being captain of the U.S. team in 1928 and 1930, never losing a match at singles, and only one in the foursomes. He stood astride the sporting world like the Colossus of Rhodes, and I am sure that this record will stand forever.

"Was it after you won the fourth major title at Merion that you decided to retire?" I asked Bobby.

Bobby grinned reflectively. "Before," he replied. "It was when I won the open at Interlachen."

I recalled an incident in an upstairs room at the Interlachen Club that hot afternoon when Bobby had finished and it had just been established that Mac Smith would not catch him. I went up to the room to tell him, and he was looking pretty well all in. I put my hand on his shoulder and asked him: "Bobby, when are you going to quit this darned game?"

Maybe I did not say darned. It had been an unusually tough finish. Bobby looked a shade more serious.

"I don't know," he said, "but pretty soon, I think. I am awfully tired."

And I remember he had said the same thing in an upstairs room in the old clubhouse at Hoylake while waiting to know whether he had won the British Open Championship or not.

Bobby was only 28 and no other champion in any sport had ever decided to leave the competitive field at so youthful an age, and at the top of the sporting world.

"I don't enjoy competition anymore," Bobby said in explanation. "When I was younger, it was different. Nothing much was expected of me and I had a lot of fun battling with the boys. If I didn't win, or if I didn't show well, it made no difference. Golf was just a game and I loved it and met many good fellows and every tournament was a big show for me.

"But along in 1925, golf became a serious business. I was expected to win or to finish well up. It got worse and worse and the pressure became heavier and heavier, and at long last came the Big Year and I decided I had had enough. I'll never give up golf. I love it too well, and it has meant too much in my life. But it will be an easier and more gracious trail from now on."

I often wonder, and old timers should have a license to do a lot of wondering, if the Grand Slam, marvelous as it was, was Bobby's greatest feat. Personally I do not think it was, and there is another phase in Bobby's tremendous stretch of winning years, of which he might be just a bit more proud.

In the last nine years of his career, from 1922 to 1930, Bobby played in twelve national open championships, nine in America and three in Britain. He finished first or second 11 times in those 12 starts. That could easily be a greater achievement than the more startling Grand Slam. This constitutes, I think, his finest record.

The most important campaign of my life, which had been pretty much wrapped up in sports, found its climax at Merion. The end of the trail meant for me the realization of the only real ambition I ever had in the world of sports. Ever since, I had seen a stocky, ruddy youngster with tousled hair, a kid of 13, battling veterans in the Southern Amateur Championship at East Lake in 1915. I had wanted more and more to see him ranked where he now stands and will stand forever.

I was with him in his blackest depression, as after Willie Hunter beat him at St. Louis and when Sweetser defeated him at Brookline. I was with him when he failed by a single stroke to catch Sarazen at

Skokie; and when he lost by a single stroke to Johnny Farrell at Olympia Fields. I saw him lose through seven lean years, which the public tends to forget in the radiance of the years that followed.

I watched Bobby from the bottom to the top of the golfing world, when he brought home to his beloved East Lake all five major trophies, including the Walker Cup. Never had these five trophies reposed in the same club and it is a million to one bet that they ever will again.

And now it was good-bye to golf. And I could still say what I had said to people all over the world, they could see for themselves if he was a golfer, but I could tell them that he was a much finer young man than he was a golfer. His great personality was paralleled only by his inimitable swing. Wholly lacking in affectation, modest to the degree of shyness, generous and thoughtful of his opponents, it is not likely that his equal will come again.

It would be immeasurably more pleasant to write of Bobby Jones himself, than of his exploits— if that could be done surely. But you cannot pick out the details of a winsome personality or properly hold up for inspection the graces of modesty and the strong heart. Besides, good-natured as Bobby Jones is, he would be furious if any chronicler who knew him should attempt a thing like that.

So the greatest competitive athlete of history closed the book, the bright lexicon of championships, with every honor in the world to grace its final chapter.

The New York Times fittingly commented: "With dignity he quit the memorable scene on which he nothing common did, or mean."

It was the end of the trail for both of us. And the end was good.

Afterword

On a bright fall Sunday several years ago a woman named Clare McDonough approached me after church with a book under her arm. "I found this in the closet," she said, "and I immediately thought you might like to have it." She handed me a first edition of this volume, *The Bobby Jones Story.* I was quite touched at her thoughtfulness and my mind went back to when I first discovered this delightful book.

I was 16 years old, had taken up golf a few years prior, and was absolutely hooked on the game. My grandfather had died two years earlier, and I missed him very much. The funny thing was that I knew Bobby, but yet I felt as though I didn't know him. At least, I felt as though I didn't know that much about his life.

You see, Bob was very reluctant to reminisce—with me or most anybody else. He lived his life very much in the present, and to look back on former glories was, to him, a waste of time. This was probably a helpful trait in dealing with his illness in that it kept him from dwelling on thoughts about "what if" or "why me." But it wasn't a good thing in dealing with a grandson who wanted to know all about his grandfather. How was I to learn about my grandfather's exploits and life? Who could possibly be my teacher?

That summer of my 16th year, I was stuck at home on a rainy day with thunderstorms keeping me off the golf course. I was rummaging through the den of our home in Nashville when I happened on a book covered in red leather. It was by O. B. Keeler, and of course I knew who O.B. was. It was called *The Bobby Jones Story*. I took it down from the shelf and opened it with idle curiosity. I didn't expect to be swept away into generations gone by, but swept away I was—into the world of my grandfather.

Very few people could tell a story like Oscar Bane Keeler. When he wrote, his subjects came to life—not in the faded black and white of old photographs, but in vibrant, almost digital, clarity and color. O.B. made my grandfather come alive, not as the sweet man in the wheel-chair, but as the bright, impetuous boy who was excited to be in the "big show," the U.S. Amateur in 1916.

When I was a teenager, Perry Adair was well into his seventies and had not played golf for years. But when I looked through the lens of this wonderful book, Perry was one of the "Dixie Whiz Kids," and was, in fact, the one from whom great things were expected in golf. When I was 19, I had the privilege to meet Alexa Stirling Fraser, the great lady amateur who was a contemporary of my grandfather. The occasion of our meeting was the opening of the Jones Room at the Atlanta Athletic Club. Mrs. Fraser was kind and gracious. However, although I was polite and thrilled to meet her, I was shocked. To me, Alexa Stirling was the beautiful young lady who strolled the fairways of East Lake with my grandfather. I had trouble picturing her as the grandmother who stood before me. That's how well O.B. wrote.

O.B.'s relationship with my grandfather was special. He was a sportswriter for *The Atlanta Journal*, and he covered just about every shot of my grandfather's career. But he was more than a writer. People forget how young my grandfather was when he began playing in championships. As a teenager in those days, it would be unthinkable for my grandfather to travel unaccompanied. O.B. often filled the bill of chaperone, as well as companion. They had an almost intuitive closeness, and O.B. was able to exert an influence on the young man that few others could. When my grandfather would become despondent over his early failures, O.B. always knew what to say to put him on track. In many ways, O.B. served the same function for my grandfather that sports psychologists serve today.

His relationship with and obvious love for my grandfather make for an interesting reading. From the story of "Little Bob" to "The End of the Trail," O.B. gives insight into Bobby that few other writers could bring. However, my personal favorite chapter in this book details my grandparents' wedding. O.B. paints an impressionistic word picture of the event that was so important in my grandfather's life. You can hear the love in O.B.'s words as he describes the event.

I hope that you enjoy this word picture of my grandfather. But I also hope that you will take the time to further appreciate the genius of the man that wrote it. Oscar Bane Keeler had that rare gift of word-smithery. It's a gift that has been forgotten in our video age. But 50 years after its first publication, O.B.'s book returns to remind us once again of the gift.

God bless you, too, O.B.!

—Dr. Bobby Jones IV

Chronology

1911
At the age of nine won the East Lake Junior Championship

1916
Won first Georgia State Amateur Championship
Qualified in first National Amateur Championship

1917
Won Southern Amateur Championship

1919
Runner-up to Jim Barnes, Southern Open Championship
Runner-up to J. Douglas Edgar, Canadian Open Championship
Runner-up to S. Davidson Herron, National Amateur Championship

1920
Won Southern Amateur Championship
First National Open, finished in tie for eighth place
Medalist, National Amateur Championship

1922

Won Southern Amateur Championship

Tied for second place in National Open Championship

1923

Won National Open Championship after playoff
    with Bobby Cruickshank

Medalist after playoff with Chick Evans,
        National Amateur Championship

1924

Second in National Open Championship

Won National Amateur Championship

1925

Second in National Open Championship after playoff
    with Willie MacFarlane

Won National Amateur Championship

1926

Won British Open Championship

Won United States Open Championship

Medalist, United States Amateur Championship, and
    Runner-up to George Von Elm

1927

Won British Open with a new record score, 285

Medalist and winner, United States Amateur Championship

1928

Second in United States Open Championship after playoff
   with Johnny Farrell
Won National Amateur Championship

1929

Won National Open Championship in playoff with Al Espinosa
Comedalist with Gene Homans, National Amateur Championship

1930

Won British Amateur Championship
Won British Open Championship
Won United States Amateur Championship
Won United States Open Championship

Major Championships

United States Amateur Championships: **1924, 1925, 1927, 1928, 1930**
United States Open Championships: **1923, 1926, 1929, 1930**
British Open Championships: **1926, 1927, 1930**
British Amateur Championship: **1930**

Index

Page numbers in *italics* refer to drawings.

Adair, George, 5–6, 54–56
Adair, Perry, xxiv, *4*
  at American Red Cross War Relief
    match, 15
  Bobby Jones IV on, 248
  at Bobby Jones' wedding, 87
  business career of, 67–68
  at Canadian Open (1919), 19
  early years with, 5–6, 96–97
  at East Lake Country Club
    celebration, 91
  in Montgomery (AL) invitation
    tournament, 7–8
  at Southern Championship
    tournament (1923), 55–56
  at U.S. Amateur Championship
    (1916), 11
Adair Realty Company, 67
Alexander, Skip, xii
American Red Cross War Relief match,
  15, 97
Aquitania, 123–25, 150–52
Armour, Tommy, xxviii, xxix
  at British Amateur Championship
    (1920), 37
  at Canadian Open (1919), 19
  at U.S. Open (1927), 167, 169–70
  at U.S. Open (1930), 230
Associated Press, xxiv
Atlanta, 94–95, 99, 111
Atlanta Athletic Club, 77, 156, 161
Atlanta Georgian, xxii–xxiv
Atlanta Journal, xxiv, xxx
Augusta Chronicle, xxx
Augusta National Golf Club
  Eisenhower's presentation of
    portrait at, xxx
  founding of, xxix
  Southeastern Open at, 211
Augustus, Ellsworth, 157

Ball, Errie, *90*
Ball, John, 198–99, 227
Baltusrol, 157–59
Baptist Minister's Alliance, xxiii
Barnes, Long Jim, xxviii, xxix
  at British Open (1930), 223
  at Canadian Open (1919), 19
  at Prestwick (1908), 143–44
  at Southern Amateur tournament
    (1919), 18
  at U.S. Open (1921), 45–46, 48
  at U.S. Open (1922), 58
  at U.S. Open (1923), 70
Belmont Springs, 97
Bendelow, Tom, 6
Big Course. *See* Oakmont Country Club
Birmingham (AL), 14–15, 55–56
Black, John, 57, 58
Blue Hen's Little Baby, 56
Boston, benefit match at, 192
Boutsies, Johnny, 239
Bradford, Vincent, 108

Bradshaw, Tess, 88
Brae Burn Country Club, 189–93
Braid, James, 143, 148
British Amateur Championship, xxviii, 37
  1920, 37–40, 38–39
  1921, 41–42
  1926, 128–33, 143
  1930, 215–21
British criticism of American
  competitiveness, 37
British golf courses, 41–42
British Ladies' Championship (1929),
  207–8
British Open, xxviii, xxix
  1921, 41–44
  1926, ix, 145–49, 163
  1927, 170–75
  1930, xxiv, 222–28
broadcasting of golf matches, 222–28
Broadmoor, Amateur Championship
  (1959), xv–xvi
Brookhaven Country Club (Atlanta), 8
Brookline golf course, 60–64, 66, 108–9,
  166, 180
Brookwood Station, 77, 94
Broughton, Len G., xxiii
Brownlow, W. H., 129
Bulwell Forest golf course, 220
Burke, Jack, 30, 104
Byers, Eben, 11

Calamity Jane putter, *189*, 190
Callaway, Cason, 123
Camp, Edwin, xxiii
Canadian Open (1919), 17, 19–20
Carnoustie, 176–77
Carruthers, Frank, 132–33
"Challenge Belt," 143
Chattanooga, 25
Cherry Valley, 99
Chevalier, Maurice, 212
Chicago Golf Club, 190, 192–93
Cochrane, Mickey, 236–37
Cohen, John, xxiv, 151, 160
Collett, Glenna, 97, 99, 207–8
Columbia Country Club (Washington),
  45–48
Columbus, Ohio, ix–x, xxix, 152–56,
  164–66
Compston, Archie, 146, 223–24, 226–27
Coolidge, Calvin, 46
Cooper, Kent, 160
Cooper, Light Horse Harry, xxviii,
  167–70, 230–32
Corkran, Clark, 91, 157
Cottage Bunker, 220
Country Club of Virginia, xiii–xiv
Cox, Wiffy, 230
Crooks, Stanley, x
Cruickshank, Bobby, xxviii, 69–76, 164, 211
Cypress Point golf course, 203–4
Cyril Tolley, *215*

Deans, Jeannie, 146
Demaret, Jimmy, xii

Diegel, Leo
  at British Open (1930), 222–24, 226
  at U.S. Open (1920), 26, 28, 30–31,
    33–34, 104
  at U.S. Open (1930), 234
  on Walter Hagen, 119
Druid Hills Golf Club, 56, 176
Duncan, George, 48, 58, 148
Dundee, 177
Durham, Reverend Plato, 72, 87
Duveen, Joseph, 212
Dyer, Frank, 11

East Lake (GA), 1–3, 54–55
East Lake Country Club, 1–3, *17, 60,
106*, 179
  celebration at, 91, 95
  course record, 65
  early experiences at, 5, 161
  exhibition match at, 205–8
  Junior Championship of the, 6–7
  U.S. Open (1923) awards banquet
    at, 77
Eden and the Jubilee (New Course), 135.
  See also St. Andrews
Edgar, J. Douglas, 19–20, 20–21
Eisenhower, Dwight D., xxx
Eisenhower Trophy march (1960), xiii
Engineer's Country Club, 36
Espinosa, Al, 195
Europa, 229
Evans, Chick, xxviii
  at British Amateur Championship
    (1920), 39–40
  on bunkers at Merion Golf Club, 90
  defeat by Jess Sweetser, 62
  and Douglas Fairbanks, 212
  record, 171, 198
  at U.S. Amateur Championship
    (1919), 22–24
  at U.S. Amateur Championship
    (1921), 52
  at U.S. Amateur Championship
    (1922), 64, 66
  at U.S. Amateur Championship
    (1923), 78, 79
  at U.S. Amateur Championship
    (1926), 157, 159
  at U.S. Amateur Championship
    (1927), 179–81
  at U.S. Open (1916), 57
  at U.S. Open (1920), 26, 33–34
  at U.S. Open (1921), 48
  at U.S. Open (1922), 58
  and U.S. Open trophy, 68
  at Walker Cup matches (1928), 193
  at Western Amateur Championship
    (1920), 25–26

Fairbanks, Douglas, 212
Farrell, Henry, 133
Farrell, Johnny, xxviii, xxix, 185–88, 192
Flossmoor Country Club, 64, 78–82, 192
Flowers, Buck, 56
Fownes, W. C. Jr., 125

Fraser, Alexa Stirling. *See* Stirling, Alexa
Fraser, W. G., 98

Gardner, Bob, xiii–xiv, 26, 52, 138
Gardner, Robert A., 12, 132
"The Gate to Golf," 20–21
George W. Adair Trophy, 54–56
George Walter, 151
Georgia School of Technology, 54
Georgia State Championship, 8, 96
Georgia Tech, 25, 56, 67, 86
Gillen, S., 129
Glass, Dudley, xxiii, xxiv
Gleneagles, 176–77
Godchaux, Frank, 55
golf balls, 182–84
golf clubs, 140–41, 226
golf courses, 41–42, 203
Golf House, x
Goodman, Johnny, 199, 201–2
Gorton, Ray, 190–91
Grand Slam (1930), xiii, 196, 236, 237, 244
Gray, Charley, 176
Greenwood, George, 132–33
Grout, Jack, xi, xv
Guilford, Jess
    defeat by Jess Sweetser, 62, 64
    at U.S. Amateur Championship (1921), 52–53
    at U.S. Amateur Championship (1923), 78
    at U.S. Open (1922), 58
    on Walker Cup team (1926), 123
Gunn, Watts
    clubs of, 141
    at U.S. Amateur Championship (1925), 23, 106–13
    at U.S. Amateur Championship (1926), 173
    at U.S. Open (1926), 152
    at Walker Cup matches (1926), 122–23, 135–37
Gunn, Will, 108

Hagen, Walter, xxviii, xxix
    at benefit match in Boston, 192
    match against Bobby Jones, 115–21
    record, 222
    at St. Anne's (1926), 147–48
    at U.S. Open (1920), 26, 35
    at U.S. Open (1921), 48
    at U.S. Open (1922), 57, 58
    at U.S. Open (1923), 70
    at U.S. Open (1924), 85
    at U.S. Open (1926), 152
    at U.S. Open (1928), 187–88
    at U.S. Open (1930), 230
Hall, Charley, 234
Hamilton, Ontario, 17, 19–20
Hamlet, Mr., 42
Hancock, Roland, 188
Harding, Warren, 46
Harlow, Bob, 98, 133
Harper, Chandler, xii
Harris, Robert, 131, 143
Harvard University, 54, 65–67

Haskell, Mr., 183
Havemeyer cup, 95
Heard, Bryan, 7
Herd, Alec, 183
Herron, S. Davidson, 23, 79
Hezlett, Major, 135
Hilton, Harold, 148, 175
Hogan, Ben, xi–xii
Holderness, Sir Ernest, 130
Holylake golf course, xxiv, 41–42, 142, 222–28
Homans, Gene, 199, 202, 235, 237–38
Honorable Company of Edinburgh Golfers, 132–33
Horn, Marian Burns, 99
Hudson, Scott, 113
Hunter, Willie, 42
    defeat by Jess Sweetser, 62
    at U.S. Amateur Championship (1921), 49–52, 154
    at U.S. Amateur Championship (1923), 78, 79
    at U.S. Open (1922), 58
Hurd, Dorothy Campbell, 98
Hutchison, Jock, xxviii
    at British Open (1921), 43–44
    on rough at Scioto, 155
    at U.S. Open (1920), 26, 28, 30–31, 35
    at U.S. Open (1921), 46, 48
    at U.S. Open (1922), 58

Interlachen Golf Club, xxix, 230–34, 243
International Jaycees Junior Championship (1957), xiv
Inverness Club (Toledo), 24–35, 104, 169
Inwood Country Club, xxix, 68–77, 164

Jacoby, Louis, 14–15
James River course (Country Club of Virginia), xiii–xiv
Jamieson, Andrew, 131, 132, 135–36, 199
Jeannie Deans (drivers), 146
Johnson, Joe, 151
Johnston, Harrison "Jimmie," 181, 200, 201, 217–18
Jones, Bobby, *4, 36, 96, 122, 160, 209, 241*
    on becoming a good golfer, xv
    at British Open (1927), *171*
    with Calamity Jane putter, *189*
    on club selection, 165
    on competitive golf, 113–14, 191–92, 242, 244
    with daughter Clara, *100*
    defeats, 12, 244–45
    at East Lake Golf Club, *90,* 179
    with father, *73*
    first championship won by, 6
    with Grand Slam trophies, *198,* 235
    with Grantland Rice, *xxvii*
    grip on club, *9, 83,* 163
    interview with, 160–66
    as lawyer, *67*

marriage, 86–89
modesty of, 91
operation, 54
putting, 163, 190
records, xxix, 153–54, 198–200, 202, 243
retirement, 210, 241–45
    in the rough, *167*
swing, *13, 30, 49, 115, 128, 134, 140,* 161–64, *185*
temper, 11, 15–16, 47
at a ticker tape parade, *150*
on tournament play, 165
at U.S. Open (1920), *25*
with wife, *86*
at Winged Foot (1929), *194*
as youth, xxvii–xxviii, *1,* 1–3, 96–97, 161
Jones, Bobby IV (grandson), 247–49
Jones, Clara (daughter), *100*
Jones, Clara (mother), 151, 159
Jones, Dick, 108–9
Jones, Mary Malone, 77, *86,* 86–89, 95, 151
Jones, R. T. Jr., xxviii
Jones, Robert P. (father), 2, 73
    on Bobby's defeat by Chick Evans, 26
    on Bobby's driving, 22
    at British Open (1927), 172–74
    on Junior Championship of East Lake Country Club, 6–7
    at U.S. Amateur Championship (1927), 181–82
    at U.S. Amateur Championship (1930), 235–36
    on U.S. Open victory (1923), 77
    at welcome home celebration, 151
Jones, Robert T. III (son), xv–xvi
Jones, Robert Tyre (grandfather), 151
Junor, John H., 155–56

Keeler, O. B., *198*
    Bobby Jones IV on, 247–49
    relationship with Bobby Jones, vii–viii, xxviii, xxix–xxx, 248–49
Kennon, Walter, 104, 197
Kenworthy, H. E., 62
Kid Wonders of Dixie, 7–9
King, Frank, 133
Kirby, Dorothy, 205
Kirkaldy, Andra, 136
Kirkwood, Joe, 48, 64
Knepper, Rudy, 66, 91

Lacey, Charley, 230–31
Lake Geneva (WI), xx–xxi
Lake Geneva Country Club, 142
Lakewood Country Club (St. Petersburg, FL), xii
Lauder, Harry, 212
Lewis, Reginald, 39–40
Lido Country Club (Long Island), 102
"lily pad" shot, 231
links, 41
Little, Lawson, 202
London *Daily Mail,* 125

London, strikes in, 122, 125–27
Long Island, xxix, 36, 68–77, 102, 164
Low, George, 176–77
Lytham & Anne's, ix

MacFarlane, Charley, 146
MacFarlane, Willie, xxviii, xxix, 100–104, 197
MacIntyre, 139, 172
Macom, 150–51, 230
Maiden, Jimmy, 3, 176
Maiden, Stewart, xv
  on Alexa Stirling, 97
  on Bobby Jones' driving, 23
  at Bobby Jones' wedding, 87
  at British Open (1927), 172–73
  at Canadian Open (1919), 19
  at Carnoustie, 176–78
  first meeting with, 3
  influence on Bobby Jones, 4–5, 161–62
  at U.S. Amateur Championship (1919), 22
  at U.S. Open (1922), 56, 57
  on U.S. Open playoff (1923), 76–77
Malone, Mary. *See* Jones, Mary Malone
Mamaroneck (NY), 194–97
Mangrum, Lloyd, xii
Mann, Willie, 176, 178
Marston, Max, 78–82, 190
The Masters Tournament, xvi–xvii, xxviii
  1948, xxix–xxx
  1964, xvii
  inauguration, xxix
  Jack Nicklaus at, xiv
Mauritania, 211–12
Mayfield Country Club (Cleveland), 97–98
McCarthy, Maurice, 181, 239–40
McDermott, Jack, 83
McDonald, Bob, 26
McDonald, Charles Blair, 91, 95
McDonough, Clare, 247
McGeehan, Bill, 133
McKenzie, Alistair, 219
McKenzie, Roland, 92–94, 107, 122
McLeod, Freddie, 48, 147
McNutt, Patterson, 104–5
Meador, Frank, 96–97
Medder, Frank, *4*
Mehlhorn, Wild Bill, xxviii, 57, 152–53, 155
Memphis, 25
Merion Cricket Club
  putting at, 163
  U.S. Amateur Championship at (1916), 9–14
  U.S. Amateur Championship at (1924), 90–95
  U.S. Amateur Championship at (1930), 235–40, 244
  U.S. Open at (1950), xii
Metzger, Sol, 74
Middlecoff, Cary, xii
Minikahda, vii–viii, 179–82
Minneapolis, 230–34, 243

Mitchell, Abe, 47, 184
Moe, Donald K., 212–14
Montgomery (AL), 7–8
Morris, John "Jack," 142–43, 148
Morris, Tom, 142
Morris, Tom Jr., 143–44
Muirfield course, 128–33, 143

National Broadcasting Company, xxiv
New Orleans Country Club, 18–19
New York, 150–51, 229–30
New York Times, 245
Nicklaus, Jack, ix–xvii

Oakland Hills, xxix, 83–85
Oakmont Country Club
  putting at, 163
  U.S. Amateur Championship at (1919), 17, 22–24
  U.S. Amateur Championship at (1925), 106–13
  U.S. Open at (1927), 167–70
Ogg, Willie, 19, 176
Ohio State University course, xiv
Old Course, 42–44, 135, 137–38. *See also* St. Andrews
Old Elm golf course, 192
Olympia Fields, xxix, 185–88, 192
Ouimet, Francis, xxviii, 61
  Bobby Jones' record against, 26
  at British Amateur Championship (1920), 38–39
  at British Amateur Championship (1926), 129
  clubs of, 141
  in tied match (1913), 72
  at U.S. Amateur Championship (1914), 22, 52
  at U.S. Amateur Championship (1919), 23–24
  at U.S. Amateur Championship (1921), 49
  at U.S. Amateur Championship (1923), 78, 80–81
  at U.S. Amateur Championship (1924), 92
  at U.S. Amateur Championship (1926), 157, 159
  at U.S. Amateur Championship (1927), 181
  at U.S. Amateur Championship (1928), 190
  at U.S. Amateur Championship (1929), 202
  at U.S. Amateur Championships, 91
  at U.S. Open (1923), 71, 73–74
  and U.S. Open trophy, 68
  at Walker Cup (1930), 212
  on Walker Cup team (1926), 122

Paine, Tom, 94
Palmer, Arnold, xvi
Park, Willie, 118
Pasadena (CA), 115–21
Pebble Beach, 198–204
Perkins, Thomas Philip, 189–90, 192
P.G.A., xii, xxix

Platt, Woody, 24
Powers, Francis, 74, 237
Prestwick golf course, 143–44
"Principal's Nose," 216

Ray, Edward
  and golf balls, 184
  at St. Anne's (1926), 148
  in tied match (1913), 72
  at U.S. Open (1920), 26, 30–32, 34–35, 104
Red Wednesday, 190–91
Rice, Grantland, *xxvii*, 237
Road Hole, 216–19
Robertson, Allan, 183
Robson, Fred, 223
Rodgers, Long John, 230
Roebuck Country Club, 14–15, 55–56
Roman, Frank "Wop," 86
Roper, Sidney, 220
Rosenthal, Elaine, 15, 97
Ross, Luke, 139
Royal and Ancient Golf Club of St. Andrews, 37, 125, 135, 182, 193
Royal Liverpool Golf Club, xxiv, 41, 222–28
Royal Lytham and St. Anne's Golf Club, 145
Royal St. George's Golf Course, xxiv, 210–12
runner-up year, 17–21
Russell, Randy, xxx
Ryder Cup (1931), xi

St. Andrews
  British Amateur Championship at (1930), 215–21
  British Ladies' Championship at (1929), 207–8
  British Open at (1921), 41–44
  British Open at (1927), 170–75
  Walker Cup matches at (1926), 122, 130, 134–39, 141–42
St. Andrews match (1926), 130, 132
St. Anne's, 139, 147–48, 163
St. Louis Country Club, 49–53, 98–99, 154, 166
St. Petersburg (FL), xii
Sands, C. E., 91
Sandwich, England, xxiv, 210–14
Sarasota (FL), 115–21
Sarazen, Gene, xxviii, xxix
  at benefit match in Boston, 192
  at U.S. Open (1922), 56–59
  at U.S. Open (1927), 169
Sargent, George, *90*, 154
Savannah Open, 211
Scioto Country Club, ix–xii, xvii, xxix, 152–56, 164–66
seven lean years, 13–16, 242
Shawnee-on-Delaware, 97
Simpson, Alexander, 128
Skene, Don, 133
Skokie Country Club, xxix, 56–59
Smith, Alex, 48, 176
Smith, Horton, xxviii
  at British Open (1930), 223

club from, 226
at Savannah Open, 211
at U.S. Open (1930), 230–33
Smith, Macdonald, xxviii
at British Open (1930), 222–23, 226–27
at U.S. Open (1928), 187
at U.S. Open (1930), 230–34
Snead, Sam, xii
Somerville, Ross, 238
Southeastern Open (Augusta), 211
Southern Amateur tournament (1919), 17–18
Southern Amateur tournament (1920), 25
Southern Championship tournament (1917), 14–15
Southern Championship tournament (1922), 54–55
Southern Championship tournament (1923), 55–56
Southern Championship tournament (1951), 7
Southern Open (1919), 17–18
Stewart, Tom, 141–42
Stirling, Alexa, xxiv, 96, 96–99
at American Red Cross War Relief match, 15
Bobby Jones IV on, 248
early years, 5
at East Lake Country Club celebration, 91
Stirling, Alexander W., 96
Stout, Bill, 213–14
Sunningdale Golf Club, ix, 145–49, 163
Sweetser, Jess
at British Amateur Championship (1926), 128–31
at U.S. Amateur Championship (1922), 60–64, 66, 108–9, 180
at U.S. Amateur Championship (1923), 78, 79, 81–82
at U.S. Amateur Championship (1925), 108–10
at U.S. Amateur Championship (1928), 190
at U.S. Amateur Championship (1930), 238–39
on Walker Cup team (1926), 123

T. Stewart factory, 140–41
Taft, William Howard, xxiv
Taylor, John Henry, 137, 147, 148
Thompson, W. J., 91
Toledo, 24–35, 104, 169
Tolley, Cyril, 215
at British Amateur Championship (1920), 37
at British Amateur Championship (1930), 218–19
on quality of Bobby Jones' play, 229
at U.S. Open (1930), 234
at Walker Cup matches (1926), 135–37
Torrance, Tony, 193, 212
tournaments, qualification for, 7
Trans-Mississippi championship, 202

Travers, Jerry, 61
at Detroit in 1915, 79
double victory of, 111
at East Lake Country Club celebration, 95
record, 189, 198
and U.S. Open trophy, 68
Travis, Walter J., 14, 128
Trevor, Greg, 190
Turnesa, Joe, ix, x
at U.S. Open (1926), 153, 155, 164
at U.S. Open (1930), 230

United States Golf Association
experiment at Oakmont, 107
on golf balls, 182
headquarters, x
and London strikes, 125
on U.S. Open (1925), 103
U.S. Amateur Championship, xxviii
1914, 22, 52
1916, 9–14
1919, 17, 22–24
1920, 36
1921, 49–53, 154, 166
1922, 60–64, 66, 108–9, 166, 180
1923, 78–82
1924, 90–95
1925, 92–94, 106–13
1926, 157–59, 173
1927, vii–viii, 179–82
1928, 189–93
1929, 198–204
1930, xiii, 235–40, 244
1955, xiii
1959 (Broadmoor), xv–xvi
U.S. Open, xxviii, xxix
1916, 57
1920, 24–35, 104, 169
1921, 45–48
1922, xxix, 56–59
1923, xxix, 68–77, 164
1924, xxix, 83–85
1925, xxix, 100–105, 166, 197
1926, xiv, xxix, 152–56, 164–66
1927, 167–70
1928, xxix, 185–88, 192
1929, xxix, 194–97, 225
1930, xxix, 230–34, 243
1950, xii
1962, xvi

Vanderbeck, Mrs. Clarence, 97–98
Vardon, Harry
on difficult shots, 180
at St. Anne's (1926), 148
in tied match (1913), 72
at U.S. Open (1920), 25, 26–28, 30–35, 104
Voigt, George, 216–17
Von Elm, George, xxviii, 91
clubs of, 141
at St. Anne's (1926), 147
at U.S. Amateur Championship (1924), 92

at U.S. Amateur Championship (1925) 92–94, 107, 110
at U.S. Amateur Championship (1926), 157–59
at U.S. Amateur Championship (1928), 190
at U.S. Amateur Championship (1929), 200
at U.S. Amateur Championship (1930), 239
at U.S. Amateur Championships, 91
at U.S. Open (1926), 152
at Walker Cup matches (1926), 122, 135

Wales, Prince of, xxiv
Walker, Cyril, xxix, 83–85
Walker Cup matches, 41
1926, 122–23, 130, 134–39, 141–42
1928, 190, 192–93
1930, xxiv, 210–14
1961, xiii
Walker Cup team, British, 207
Walker, Jimmy, 151–52
Walworth Country Club, xxi, 142
Warren K. Wood Memorial tournament, 192
Washington, D.C., 45–48
Watrous, Al, 147, 196
Westchester-Biltmore, 98
Western Amateur Championship (1920), 25–26, 217
Western Association, 25
Wethered, Joyce, 205–8, 225
Wethered, Roger, 37, 44, 212, 220
White, Jack, 146
Whitfield Estates Golf Club, 115–21
Whiting, Percy, xxiii
Whitney, Nelson, 17
Williams, Henry Jr., xii
Willing, Oscar F., 200–201, 212
Wind, Herbert Warren, ix–xvii
Windsor Park, 146
Winged Foot Golf Club, xxix, 194–97, 204, 225
Wolff, Clarence, 153
Wood, Craig, xxviii, 230
Woodland (golf course), 192
Worcester Country Club, xxix, 100–105, 166, 197
Wright and Ditson Company, 15
Wright, Freddie, 37–38

Yale University, 61
Yates, Charley, 90, 205–7